1001 REASONS TO STOP DRINKING

1001 Reasons to Stop Drinking

A whole book full of sobering thoughts to help you seriously cut down or quit.

by J.J. Kentucky

1001 Reasons to Stop Drinking
Copyright © 2025 J.J. Kentucky

(ALL RIGHTS RESERVED)

ISBN: 9798305578980
Printed in the United States of America

DISCLAIMER

All efforts have been made to ensure the accuracy of the information contained in this book as of the date published. However, as medical information can change rapidly it is strongly recommended that you discuss all health matters and concerns with your physician before embarking on any new diagnostic, treatment or health strategy. The author and the publisher expressly disclaim responsibility for any adverse effects arising from the use or application of the information herein.

COPYRIGHT

For purposes of copyright and obtaining permissions, the testimonial style contents in this book have been substantially edited/rewritten to be significantly altered from their original form/content and have been combined with other relevant materials and information for the purposes of originality and to provide additional information, interest and clarity on a specific subject. The stories herein contain facts and observations from real-life events but are presented in a reinterpreted and essentially rewritten format. Where permissions have been obtained for partial content or subject matter, the authors have requested that they remain anonymous.

ALL RIGHTS RESERVED

This book or parts thereof may not be reproduced in any form, stored in any retrieval system, or transmitted in any form by any means, electronic, mechanical, photocopy, recording, or otherwise, without prior written permission of the publisher, except as provided by United States of America copyright law.

For permission requests contact: 1001reasonsdrinkingbook@gmail.com

"No one's ever said, 'My life was going bad until I started getting drunk every day and then that just sorted everything out.'"

– Ricky Gervais

… continued 1 0 0 1   R E A S O N S   T O   S T O P   D R I N K I N G

CONTENTS

Why I put this book together..9

What's in this book...11

PART 1
Real-life examples of the sad, ridiculous, embarrassing
and catastrophic outcomes of excessive drinking..........................17

Real-life examples of the distressing, shocking and
unforeseen health problems caused by excessive drinking..................53

Real-life examples of the life improving benefits of not drinking..........101

PART 2
How, what and why people drink -Snapshots from Britain,
Ireland, Romania, Moldova, Russia, Finland, Germany, South
Africa, Kenya, India, South Korea, Japan, China, The Cook Islands,
Australia and Greenland..131

PART 3
How self-destructive levels of drinking hurt the whole family:
recollections from adult children of alcoholic parents....................175

PART 4
Dealing with the alcohol addicted: anecdotes and observations
from emergency workers, hospitality and retail staff and service
providers..191

PART 5
Dealing with the fallout from alcohol abuse: anecdotes and
observations from nurses, doctors and other healthcare professionals......201

PART 6
Real-life anecdotes and observations from people who have
experienced the consequences of heavy drinking............................229

PART 7
Medical conditions associated with uncontrolled drinking..................241

PART 8
More hellish experiences: withdrawals, delirium tremens,
alcohol poisoning and tolerance..247

PART 9
A closer look at the liver: what it is, what it likes, what it doesn't
and what to do when it's damaged..261

PART 10
Real life recovery stories..283

PART 11
The practicalities of quitting alcohol: battling the "fuck-its"................297

PART 12
Things people have done, some by choice and some by accident,
to stay off the booze...309

PART 13
Books and other resources that have helped people eliminate
or drastically reduce their alcohol consumption................................327

PART 14
Some thought-provoking one-liners..335

Why I put this book together

As a copywriter and ex-heavy drinker with a 17-year track record of embarrassment, probable liver damage and a shameful alcohol-related weekend in jail, I assembled this compendium of real-life "stop drinking" anecdotes because I kept paying the price for my lack of awareness of what this substance is really about.

You probably are, or were like me: one of a huge number of problem drinkers, who stands somewhere in the middle between regular social and compulsive binge drinker.

You aren't completely addicted but it's hard for you to go more than a day or two without a glass or can of something. After that you're a runaway train and can't stop. You don't class yourself as an alcoholic but suspect you are harming your health and don't like the way things are going.

Maybe your blood pressure is too high, you've put on weight or have been told you have a fatty liver. Perhaps you've lost your job, wrecked another relationship or been arrested for some booze-associated debacle. The more years of binge drinking you rack up the more likely these outcomes are. Correction, not likely. Inevitable.

For the deeply entrenched "crippled alcoholic" whose drinking is a daily necessity to reach baseline functioning level never mind a buzz, hopefully these pages will act like an information bomb to blast home the message that quitting is the best thing you can do for yourself and anyone or anything else that depends on you for their wellbeing, including kids, dogs, cats, fish and houseplants.

Whatever stage you're at, it's never too late to address the root cause of your problems, stop your slide into addiction and re-connect with the world.

I spent thousands of hours of sifting through books, listening to podcasts, watching documentary videos and scrolling through online forums and news comments sections collecting nuggets of information to educate /brainwash myself out of my slowly worsening drinking habit.

As a result, after multiple failed attempts and countless "day ones," I managed to leave my party of one and see my dependency for what it is: a shortcut to shame, disaster and premature death.

Here are the 1001 reasons that changed my mind about drinking.

J.J. Kentucky

P.S. Every word in this book is written by me, an actual flesh and blood human being. I did not get an AI writing generator to reassemble all the stuff you've read before. It has taken me around three years to put together the information you are about to read because drinking and its underlying causes is a very complex subject.

Plus, I also discovered a lot of interesting reasons why people in other countries drink that I didn't know before, so I went down a few rabbit holes I hadn't planned on investigating.

I've tried to write in the most undiluted, impactful way I could, avoiding wishy-washy ramblings and unnecessary words. One reason for this is that most people who drink have low boredom thresholds. The other reason is that there are enough books out there that go into micro details about one person's thoughts and experiences. I am not knocking them, it's just that there are enough of them.

Finally, the quotes in bold at the start of each section are genuine cries for help and I hope whoever posted them gets to read this book.

What's in this book

Section 1

"All of the dumbest, most destructive things I've done in my life have been under the influence of alcohol and I've done every drug there is. Please tell me your worst drunk story so I don't feel so bad."

In answer to the above, this book starts off with a compilation of some of the funny, tragic and bizarre situations people have found themselves in as a result of excessive alcohol consumption.

These are the kind of stories that are repeated years later with, "Oh my god do you remember when…" Some of these mostly former drinkers are lucky they're alive and not a contender for a Darwin Award.

Section 2

"Please list reasons to quit and even scare me if you can. I need a scare. No matter how much my stomach hurts and my mental health declines I can't stop. I can feel that alcohol is claiming me slowly and taking my personality and health away.

PLEASE Scare me straight!"

This is an overview of the physical and mental toll alcohol takes on the body as described by the sufferers themselves. The purpose of this section is to saturate your subconscious with shocking "make you think twice" information that's powerful enough to penetrate the deepest regions of your brain that drive your urge to drink.

These real-life anecdotes also provide effective ammunition against "the fading affect bias" where the brain fades out painful memories and suggests things weren't so bad.

Such delusions are especially frequent during the first three months of quitting. But even after that, former drinkers who have been coasting for years are susceptible to this unwelcome phenomenon which is why this section is worth a re-read every so often.

Section 3

"Please tell me all the ways your life got better after you quit. Isn't it boring? How do you have fun? I have to stop drinking but my brain doesn't want me to."

This question will resonate with everyone seeking ways to psychologically armor themselves against attacks from their inner booze-hound. After reviewing literally thousands of "I quit drinking and this happened" type reports, it is clear that the life-enhancing benefits of quitting alcohol are pretty universal. Which means there's a virtual certainty that you will experience them too.

In addition to the obvious things like no more hangovers and better sleep, some heartwarming and unexpected highlights are included.

This section provides solid, living proof that bypassing alcohol doesn't mean the party's over. For the vast majority it's a second chance at life and a level of contentment they had forgotten existed.

Everything else

I've added my recovery experience plus a whole lot more information to assist you in your quest to quit, including anecdotes and observations on drinking cultures around the world, opinions from medical professionals, information about the liver, ex-drinker recommended resources and some quotes that have helped people drastically reign in or abandon their excessive boozing.

If you would like your drinking-related observations or anecdotes to be included the next edition of this series, suggest resources or correct anything that's wrong in this one, please email me at:

1001reasonsdrinkingbook@gmail.com

"All of the dumbest, most destructive things I've done in my life have been under the influence of alcohol and I've done every drug there is. Please tell me your worst drunk story so I don't feel so bad."

From a 23-year-old drinker who is sick of waking up and saying, "WTF!"

Real-life examples of the sad, ridiculous, embarrassing and catastrophic outcomes of excessive drinking

1. Contacting your ex who you have a protective order against and telling them you miss them.

2. Puking through your nose while giving a blowjob.

3. Covering yourself in lighter fuel and igniting it.

4. Accidentally going into your neighbor's house, taking a dump in their sink, dropping a wine glass in their toilet and projectile vomiting over their Chihuahua.

5. Chasing after a beer can rolling across a freeway and getting hit by a car.

6. Being cited for felony vandalism and misdemeanor for drinking from the outlet pipe of a tractor trailer pulling a tank of wine.

7. Going from being a therapist graduating at the top of your class to losing your marriage of 17 years, being arrested for prostitution and getting four DUIs including a hit and run.

8. Riding a motorcycle through a stop sign and waking up on the road with your synthetic jacket melted to your arm and third degree burns from trying to lift your bike by the exhaust.

9. Vomiting red wine and pasta mush over the side of the bed and skidding in it the next day.

10. Waking up in hospital with your parents pleading with you to get help after being in a car wreck while driving drunk.

11. There's broken glass all over the kitchen, your girlfriend is gone and there's a business card from the sheriff with "CALL ME!" written on it stuck to your broken front door.

12. Waking up with a plastic bag stuck to your face after getting into a fight and eating the frozen peas you were given to put on your black eye.

13. Peeing through the seat of a patio chair because it's too far to walk inside to the bathroom.

14. Going to an ivy league law school, putting yourself hundreds of thousands of dollars in debt, passing the exam then being rejected from the bar for being committed to a psychiatric hospital after getting psychotically wasted.

15. Gaining a ton of weight because you eat everything in sight when you're trashed.

16. Being best man at a wedding then waking up the next day with your face stuck to the floor with dried blood, having taken a chunk out your chin while cutting your bow tie off with a razor blade.

17. Being removed from the cockpit of a plane and getting arrested for having a blood-alcohol level over four times the federal limit for a pilot.

18. Buying your third bottle of gin in a week and picking up a gift bag on the way to the counter so the cashier doesn't think it's for you.

19. Peeing on the way into the bathroom, slipping in it and crashing into the shower door.

20. Being removed from the stage in front of an audience and having your show canceled because you're too drunk to perform.

21. Rarely brushing your teeth or showering because you don't have anyone to impress except your friends who are all drunks too.

22. Living out your "Sons of Anarchy" fantasy and hooking up with a motorcycle gang member, losing custody of your kids to your ex-husband, getting kicked out of your rental and ending up homeless.

23. Jumping out of your chair to dance, falling over and being taken to urgent care with a torn ACL and fractured skull.

24. Waking up in someone's bed in a room you don't recognize in an apartment you've never seen before after being found passed out in a stairwell with no idea how you got there.

25. Being arrested for attacking a flight attendant, climbing over the seats and breaking a piece off the bathroom door.

26. Waking up thinking "Holy shit" then deleting your Facebook account after posting multiple over complimentary and provocative comments.

27. Slow roasting your arm and scorching your hand until your fingers resemble split open hotdogs after falling asleep on the edge of a bonfire.

28. Realizing that when you add up your total weekend alcohol expenditure over a three-year period you could have bought a 3-bed 2-bath, 2,200 sq ft townhome.

29. Breaking your hand in a restaurant after using it to smash open a crab claw.

30. Waking up in hospital with your arms and legs in restraints and an IV in the back of your hand after you threatened to kill your neighbor, assaulted a police officer and smashed your head into the wall of your jail cell.

31. Borrowing and stealing money and donating plasma to buy alcohol because you can't be sober for one minute because that's when you reflect on the hole you've dug for yourself.

32. Waking up with flashlights pointed at you and the sound of yelling, then being charged with criminal trespass for climbing onto the roof of a police building.

33. Waking up on the bathroom floor at your friend's house with your head in a bucket and your pants down.

34. Texting your wife to say you no longer want to be married with kids during a week-long bender in Vegas.

35. Waking up with bloody, lacerated legs after trying to shave them at 2:00 a.m.

36. Starting the evening happy, having drinks then doing shots with your partner and finishing the night single.

37. Accidentally sending a picture of a naked man covered in feces to your carpet cleaning client list and ending up working in a warehouse selling plastic.

38. Reaching over to your bedside table in the early hours and drinking a glass of water with your contact lenses in it.

39. Being wheeled out of the back of a five-star hotel on a luggage cart.

40. Waking up in the back of a pickup truck near your apartment without your pants or wallet which are brought to you by a police officer the next day in a bag marked "Evidence."

41. Falling down the stairs, throwing up and passing out at your parents' house and being told to clean the vomit off the stairs only to find it has already gone thanks to the dog.

42. Spending 18 days in a foreign jail before being sent to a mental hospital where nobody speaks English for a week of psychiatric evaluation for getting into a fight at the airport before your flight back to the USA.

43. Sleeping naked in the shower with the water running with your butt in the air and face near the drain ready for when you puke.

44. Dreaming you bought a car then waking up to find a BMW key in your pocket and the vehicle you had delivered from a town 70 miles away in your garage.

45. Waking up somewhere in Costa Rica, buying a donkey from a lady in a nearby village and riding around for an hour trying to find the way back to your hotel.

46. Getting arrested at gunpoint for threatening someone with an airsoft rifle while wearing a chicken costume.

47. Being arrested for DUI then calling your drinking buddy to drive you home.

48. Vomiting with such force you shit your pants.

49. Being woken up by fire alarms and firemen breaking down your door after leaving a pizza in the oven all night.

50. Falling asleep with a blanket over your head, refusing to fasten your seatbelt and being escorted back to the airport terminal by police officers.

51. Being removed from a sports stadium in a wheelchair by police officers and charged with drunken disorderly conduct on the way to the emergency room after throwing up on the family seated in the row in front of you.

52. Breaking into a car dealership, leaving your phone on the counter and waking up at a nearby airport.

53. Being driven home by your friend who's also drunk and crashes his car, leaving you stuck in a wheelchair, divorced, clinically depressed and obese.

54. Smashing your arm onto a desk until you deliberately break your wrist.

55. Going to a fancy dress party dressed as a Smurf and waking up the next morning on the ferry home dressed as Fred Flintstone.

56. Treading on a broken bottle and having a shard of glass go into your foot and up through the top of it without feeling a thing.

57. Throwing up in a toilet in Japan, accidentally hitting the bidet switch and getting hot water blasted in your face.

58. Ordering 50 bags of beef jerky, a slap chop, 26lb gummy bear, a vacation leaving from a different country, flashing LED toilet lights and an acre of land on the moon.

1001 REASONS TO STOP DRINKING

59. Passing out in a toilet stall, having water poured over you, then waking up in a hospital bed with an IV in your arm, hyperventilating and trying to pull the sheets off.

60. Waking up propped up against the bathroom wall next to the toilet with puke down your shirt thinking this is surely how death feels.

61. Losing your job as an engineer after being obliged to state you were convicted of a DUI on the forms you have to complete annually to maintain your license.

62. Falling onto a toilet tank causing water to leak through the apartment ceiling below.

63. Waking up in hospital with a dislocated shoulder and three broken ribs after winning a drinking contest at a club and jumping out of a moving SUV thinking you can fly.

64. Being removed from a plane, restrained in a wheelchair and charged with battery of a police officer and disturbing the peace.

65. Leaving a club without your pants because they are in the restroom covered in vomit.

66. Projectile vomiting through a McDonald's drive-thru window.

67. Waking up with a permanent limp, with no recollection of the night before.

68. Getting a tick shaped scar on the end of your penis after putting it into a desk fan set on high.

69. Falling and breaking your knee climbing over the automatic gate to your neighborhood having forgotten the entry code.

70. Waking up with a boxer's fracture to your right hand after punching a brick wall.

71. Forcing open the elevator doors, jumping into the void and clinging to the cables to slow your descent.

72. Going from having 40 good friends to none within an hour, with no idea what you did or said.

73. Waking up wrapped in cold wet sheets having peed the bed in your sleep.

74. Walking home four miles because you couldn't operate the Uber app on your phone.

75. Passing out in the middle of a golf course with people playing around you and being woken up early the next morning when the sprinklers come on.

76. Waking up in a barn surrounded by beer cans, shirtless and shoeless with a dead bird on your head.

77. Asking a friend to stub cigarettes out on your hand.

78. Being removed from a plane for throwing up in the galley and using people's heads to steady yourself on the way to the bathroom.

79. Getting pulled over for DUI after celebrating graduating from medical school, losing your residency program and being left with $250,000 in medical school loans.

80. Stripping naked and jumping into a bear cage at the zoo.

81. Climbing into an electric substation and peeing on top of a transformer.

82. Having your children taken into care because you are drinking 24/7.

83. Climbing out from the sunroof, sliding down the windscreen and onto the hood of a car going down a highway at 80 miles an hour.

84. Selling your company and retiring early, going on a bender overseas, getting arrested, sent to rehab and being divorced by your wife who takes the kids, money and property because everything's in her name.

85. Shooting yourself in the face and surviving.

86. Buying an octopus for $150,000.

87. Parking your car in the lot at a bar that neither you or your buddies remember being at and taking three days to find it.

88. Being woken up by the police banging on your door telling you they've got your clothes and ID because they found you bleeding, naked and passed out and took you to the ER after you tried to break into your own house.

89. Operating on a patient while severely hungover and killing them.

90. Falling off a hotel balcony and getting impaled on an umbrella pole.

91. Super gluing your teeth together.

92. Passing out in a dumpster, getting tipped into a compactor and waking up in a landfill site.

93. Peeing over the side of a canyon and falling into it.

94. Going to the emergency room with your breast firmly suctioned into a beer glass.

95. Being paralyzed from the waist down after climbing a drain pipe for a dare and falling off, breaking both legs, losing your management position at a big corporation and having to take a minimum wage job.

96. Being found on a sidewalk lying in a pool of blood and vomit four blocks from your hotel.

97. Falling out of an Uber and getting a brain injury.

98. Putting your full weight onto a sink while sitting to pee in it, landing on the broken pieces after it breaks and getting 50 stitches in your buttocks.

99. Sneaking onboard a fishing boat in Canada and waking up halfway to the USA.

100. Jumping into a river frothing with farm chemicals and being sick for a week.

101. Waking up on your first day of married life on hotel bedsheets stained brown from a mixture of sweat, piss and fake tan.

102. Walking into a sliding glass door, cutting your face open and super gluing it back together.

103. Passing out in the middle of the road in a fetal position, being awoken by a police officer and charged with disorderly conduct.

104. Burning holes in your clothes and getting blisters on your fingers from passing out with a cigarette in your hand every night.

105. Drunkenly slamming down a bottle of wine in a rage and slicing off the top of your finger.

106. Waking up in bed wearing different clothes, spooning a dwarf.

107. Riding your motorcycle with no helmet after storming out of the house during an argument, taking out four mailboxes and ending up with the mental capacity of a five-year-old.

108. Squatting to pet a small dog in the middle of a hotel foyer, accidentally peeing and blaming the dog.

109. Turning up to a job interview late, sweating, hungover and reeking of mouthwash.

110. Sitting on the pavement outside a 7 Eleven somewhere on Big Island, Hawaii with no idea where your rental house is and buying all the homeless people sandwiches and cigarettes while your phone charges inside.

111. Getting "Chug Life" tattooed on your foot and a smiley face tattooed on your chest.

112. Climbing up a giant elm in a graveyard, waking up covered in sticky tree sap and having to buy new bed sheets.

113. Falling down a flight of stairs, puking, passing out and going into cardiac arrest before being revived by paramedics.

114. Being thrown out of a nightclub for punching the coat check guy for stealing your jacket, only to find it in your bag later.

115. Falling out of your bedroom window while taking a piss then having to go back inside naked, bruised and covered in blood and snow.

116. Blacking out and waking up face down in the sand on a beach two thousand miles away from where you live.

117. Having your watch and credit cards stolen by a hooker while you're passed out naked in bed in a hotel room.

118. Running towards the hotel bar, falling down some steps and breaking your coccyx on the first night of your vacation.

119. Driving through the Air Force base gate, failing a breathalyzer, losing your rank, being demoted and losing out on $2,000 a month in additional pension for life.

120. Passing out on a beach and waking up with second-degree sunburn all over your body.

121. Talking non-stop on a great first date then wondering why your "ideal match" never contacted you again.

122. Waking up with a mouthful of broken veneers and sharp brown stumps where your expensive teeth used to be.

123. Falling off the bed and landing on a jar of mayonnaise, getting stitches in your buttocks and having to take a week off work lying on your side.

124. Coming to surrounded by firefighters, police and paramedics and getting rushed to the emergency room with severe alcohol poisoning after doing too many shots at a birthday party.

125. Crashing a 6,000-ton ship into a moored yacht and then into a bridge.

126. Waking up in the bathroom of a gay bar covered in dried blood and discovering to your horror that the head of your penis has been sliced off.

127. Attempting to chop the side mirrors off your car with a Samurai sword.

128. Losing $500,000 on blackjack during Super Bowl weekend and being unable to recall any of it.

129. Getting three years for vehicular homicide after killing a passenger while driving intoxicated.

130. Being too hungover to attend a meeting to sell your company for millions only for it to go bust a year later.

131. Falling down a flight of stairs and spending Christmas sitting on one butt cheek.

132. Being videoed touching yourself and saying "I like kids," then being blackmailed over it, fired from your job and kicked out of your house when the video goes public.

133. Waking up in handcuffs on the side of the road with your new car totaled.

134. Going out to celebrate having your alcohol monitoring ankle tag removed, leaving the bar and crashing your car into a utility pole.

135. Roller skating down some stairs and breaking your leg in two places.

136. Spray painting "I'm drunk" on the wall of a police station.

137. Being sexually attacked from behind while you're leaning over a bar throwing up.

138. Driving to the emergency room with your polyester shirt melted to your chest after accidentally setting yourself on fire.

139. Walking ten miles to a house you used to live in that you forgot you sold three weeks ago.

140. Jumping over a wall in front of a 25-foot drop and breaking both feet.

141. Falling asleep in a taxi and ending up at the driver's house sitting on the couch being brought coffee.

142. Doing cartwheels during a sobriety test.

143. Getting divorced and spending half your net worth on legal fees because you're so irrational and mood disordered your partner will only communicate via attorneys.

144. Punching a man blocking the entrance to the restaurant bathroom only to discover it's your reflection.

145. Starting off drinking in a London pub and waking up in the South of France.

146. Waking up handcuffed to a hospital bed and hooked up to an IV bag after drinking for 19 hours and passing out on a street in Las Vegas.

147. Putting wine glasses in the dryer, opening the door and having broken glass fly into your face.

148. Trying to open your hotel room by putting coins in the key card slot like a vending machine.

149. Falling into the hole dug for a coffin and landing on top of it while conducting a funeral service.

150. Spending nearly $500,000 partying over three years and being left with debilitating anxiety, no energy, no friends, no job and no money.

151. Spending the weekend drinking with friends in a log cabin in the mountains and deliberately chopping off your foot with a chainsaw for a dare.

152. Waking up in a ditch with a Jehovah's Witness telling you to find God, running off with one of their pamphlets, going to a nearby farm and stealing a tractor to get to work and being taken to jail to sober up.

153. Having to tell your boss you have to get an ignition interlock breathalyzer (a.k.a. "blow box") fitted to your company car and hoping you're not fired.

154. Trying to do a back flip off a slip and slide that's been set up on a roof, fracturing a vertebra, breaking some ribs and having to sleep upright for a year.

155. Smashing the train driver's cab with a fire extinguisher to tell him to slow down because the speed is making you sick.

156. Waking up by the side of an airport runway and telling the guys who direct the planes to put you on the next jet to the Bahamas.

157. Holding onto the grass to stop yourself falling off the earth.

158. Waking up in an unfamiliar bed wearing an 80s style jacket with a crawfish in the pocket.

159. Cutting a hole in your apartment door with a chainsaw because you locked yourself out.

160. The first thing you hear when you wake up is "Do you have a lawyer?"

161. Going out as a couple and waking up single, hungover and homeless.

162. Waking up in a field in your underwear surrounded by cows pulling at your clothes.

163. Having your jaw wired after breaking it in two places with no idea how it happened.

164. Vomiting out of a car with all the windows open and spraying puke over the passengers sitting behind you.

165. Gashing your brow down to the bone and getting a row of Frankenstein staples punched across your forehead after passing out and falling onto a gas cooktop.

166. Waking up with your shirt cuffs hanging around your wrists because you couldn't get your cufflinks out the night before.

1001 REASONS TO STOP DRINKING

167. Driving home and hitting a parked car a block from your home resulting in a DUI, a year's license suspension, a blow box for six months and about $10,000 in fines and legal costs.

168. Waking up with cut feet and seeing bloody footprints leading to the smashed window you climbed through.

169. Driving your Tesla on autopilot on the wrong side of the road, crashing into a police car, hitting an officer breaking her leg, being sentenced to 15 years in jail, losing your job and marriage and effectively destroying your life in under ten minutes.

170. Blacking out on a Zoom call meeting while watching porn on another screen.

171. Getting arrested after trying to open random apartment doors having forgotten which one you live in.

172. Cleaning your puke out of the crevices of your friend's car while suffering from a severe hangover.

173. Getting a DUI, spending over $10,000 in court fines and lawyer fees, having a mugshot and a license suspension plus a criminal record which everyone can see online.

174. Attempting to steal an unmarked police car with two officers inside.

175. Driving a golf cart down the center lane of an interstate highway.

176. Waking up in hospital after diving head first across a frozen parking lot, skinning your hands, elbows and face, putting your teeth through your lip and killing one of them at the root.

177. Waking up in jail wearing a hospital wristband with stitches in your chin and two broken front teeth, hoping they have your phone so you can figure out what happened.

178. Setting your armpit hair on fire with a can of deodorant and a lighter.

179. Running a red light, killing three people, breaking your child's leg and being sentenced to 65 years in prison.

180. Waking up lying on the ground to see police jumping out of their cars with guns drawn after climbing a security fence around a military tank building facility, falling off and dislocating your knee.

181. Opening up your printer, peeing on the glass, closing the lid and pressing the scan button to "flush."

182. Falling over and being so drunk you are unaware your eyeball has fallen out.

183. Calling someone and having a three-hour long conversation you remember absolutely nothing about the next day.

184. Arguing with your reflection in the coach window, trying to grope the tour guide and asking people to draw a campfire on your body to keep you warm on a trip across Europe.

185. Waking up in jail with your face in the breakfast tray.

186. Waking up in a strip club in Vegas to find $7,000 has been charged to your credit card at the Coach store in the nearby mall.

187. Stealing from your kids' piggy banks to buy alcohol.

188. Walking home from the bar and freaking out because your hands and legs have disappeared then realizing you've walked into a river.

189. Realizing your kids have never known you sober just angry, hungover, drunk, passed out, burning dinner, forgetting conver-sations and missing family events.

190. Calling the police to complain about the slow service at a fast-food restaurant and being charged with disorderly conduct.

191. Waking up covered in blood with two new nipple piercings.

192. Vomiting into a restroom sink, seeing it's full of ice, grabbing it to rub on your face and realizing it's broken glass.

193. Waking up covered head to toe in blood after pissing on your bathroom floor, slipping in it, slamming into the side of the bathtub and gashing your chin through to your mouth.

194. Falling off your fold-out chair into the river during a fishing competition.

195. Waking up in the emergency ward after accidentally tipping over a bar table, losing your balance and falling head first into the broken glasses.

196. Accidentally sending a sexually explicit message with a naked photo of yourself to a family group chat at 1:00 a.m.

197. Waking up on a park bench covered in vomit with your watch, wallet and phone gone.

198. Ordering $300 dollars-worth of remote-controlled vibrating panties and having them sent to an old delivery address where your ex-boyfriend lives.

199. Finding someone's false teeth on the dance floor and putting them in your mouth.

200. Being intubated and rushed to the nearest field to take a $35,000 helicopter ride to the trauma center after being found soaked in blood and urine after putting your head through a wall and lying unconscious on your kitchen floor for 24 hours.

201. Getting a ticket for public urination.

202. Waking up in hospital unable to move the hair out of your eyes because one half of your head is caked in dried vomit and the other in dried blood.

203. Waking up on a bus stop bench with your back pocket torn out, your money and phone gone and your buttocks on display.

204. Locking yourself out of your hotel room while naked and having to get another keycard from reception.

205. Going to the gym blackout drunk, dropping a weight on your head, setting off the emergency alarm and getting driven home by a member of staff.

206. Sleeping through the helicopter ride to the hospital then waking up in a neck brace with a nurse asking you if you can wiggle your toes after falling off a roof.

207. Being arrested after crashing your car and blowing three times over the limit, leaving jail to go drinking again, passing out on a

train station bench, jumping onto the tracks and getting taken to a psychiatric hospital.

208. Passing out in the snow, getting woken up by a police officer and giving him a Pizza Hut gift card when he asks for your ID.

209. Falling asleep over the drain outlet of the shower and flooding your house.

210. Booking interior rooms on cruise ships specifically to avoid drunkenly falling overboard.

211. Waking up at 4:30 a.m. in a Japanese strip club with the manager and two bouncers standing over you asking you to approve a $12,000 tab which includes three $900 bottles of champagne, leaving you in debt with a terrible credit score five years later.

212. Buying glasses in bulk because every night you drink outside on the patio until the whiskey tumbler falls out of your hand.

213. Having an outstanding GPA, drinking in your final college year, crashing your car into a house, being jailed and getting deported by ICE.

214. Having an accident on vacation and finding your travel insurance won't cover it because you were intoxicated.

215. Getting a girl that you were going to break up with pregnant at a party and having to pay 45% of your income in child support for a kid you didn't want for the next 18 years.

216. Becoming an incapacitated senior and leaving your daughter unmarried and childless because she has to take care of you her whole adult life.

217. Being just minutes away from being unrecoverable with hypothermia after stumbling through a creek and passing out with alcohol poisoning.

218. Sleeping in a carpark using the cement bumper as a pillow.

219. Being charged with six counts of involuntary manslaughter and assault with a deadly weapon using a car because driving while intoxicated is a considered a willful act.

220. Getting on a plane after three days of drinking, racing to the toilet and vomiting until the landing announcement comes on, then spending two hours throwing up outside the door of your car in the airport carpark, popping the veins in your eyes and destroying your voice.

221. Racking up a debt of over $2,500 in copays after being court mandated to get counselling following a conviction for aggravated DUI.

222. Jumping up and kicking the basement ceiling twice, crash landing on the floor both times and ending up with a hip that dislocates itself and a permanent limp.

223. Drunkenly proposing to a girl who accepts, then suffering two years of grief.

224. Punching a brick wall and breaking the bones in your hand and needing a plate and screws to fix it.

225. Chronically underperforming at work and being let go, with no retirement savings, laden with debt and on the brink of homelessness.

1001 REASONS TO STOP DRINKING

226. Inventing business trips that don't exist so you can sit alone in a hotel room and drink.

227. Buying so many porn subscriptions your credit card company calls to ask if you recognize purchases for Youjizz and Bang Bus.

228. Being sentenced to 20 years in prison after spending $70,000 on lawyers, with your family driving six hours to see you because you killed two people driving home from the bar.

229. Removing all your neighbor's car tires and getting charged with a misdemeanor.

230. Waking up covered in blood and vomit with your upper lip so swollen you look like a camel after falling headfirst into a garbage can full of broken blinds.

231. Ending up disabled for life after being rendered comatose then being minimally conscious for a year after falling asleep at the wheel.

232. Spending over $10,000 in lawyer's fees and fines plus $15,000 on surgery to save your dog's life after it ate a rope chew toy while you were jailed overnight for DUI.

233. Upon waking up your first thought is "Oh fuck I have to make a phone call and apologize."

234. Being tracked on Snapchat by your boss walking 12 miles home after a staff party.

235. Knocking your brand new 60-inch flat screen TV off its stand and destroying it.

236. Waking up at around 3:00 a.m. in the hospital with alcohol poisoning and a broken leg after going down a playground slide on a skateboard.

237. Staring into the mirror hungover one morning and seeing your alcoholic parent looking back at you.

238. Punching a brick wall, breaking the bones in your hand and taping it up with duct tape because you can't afford the copay on your health insurance.

239. Waking up in an ambulance holding your face together after being thrown from your motorcycle then suffering the shakes from alcohol withdrawal and feeling your skull bones twist back into place while you sober up in hospital.

240. Almost losing your leg after walking barefoot over feces covered broken glass at an open-air concert, then being left to sober up for eight hours in the emergency room by which time your foot has turned septic.

241. Having a great job, a partner you care about and being the happiest you've ever been, then driving home after three beers, getting into an accident that wasn't your fault but killed the passenger in the other car and going to prison for six years.

242. Renting an electric scooter and ending up with road rash on your face and seriously concussed after an hour-long journey home from the club that should have taken 15 minutes.

243. Searching through your text messages the next day, feeling like you want to crawl into a hole and die and deleting everything.

244. Waking up in your hotel room after choosing the "drink all you can in three hours" fixed price option at a bar in Tokyo with no memory of anything that happened after the first hour.

245. Going from having a good job working in the tech industry, an apartment in a nice neighborhood and long-term partner to being unemployed, living in your parents' spare bedroom and trying to rebuild your life in your 30s after punching someone in the face at a bar.

246. Having to get your mugshot taken five times because you can't keep your eyes open.

247. Soliciting guys at a bar to kill your husband for $10,000.

248. Being beaten up by two bouncers in a strip club for eating someone else's French fries, being handcuffed to a hospital bed and charged with petit theft, then getting a year of probation and a $500 fine in addition to the $7,000 in medical bills.

249. The DoorDash drop-off photo shows another delivery meal outside your door you forgot you had ordered.

250. Waking up on New Year's Day in the emergency room wearing a neck brace, with a lacerated mouth, chipped front tooth and black eye, after picking a fight with a drill sergeant.

251. Being suspended from your job as a flight attendant, being flown home the next day and then sent to rehab after showing up late for work still drunk from the night before.

252. Deliberately setting your shirt alight to see if liquor acts as a fire extinguisher and ending up with first, second and third-degree burns over 40% of your body.

253. Climbing a rotating beacon at the airport before passing out on the runway.

254. Getting hammered at a work event, offending your supervisor and getting fired after which you get divorced, move into a rental apartment and get to see your kids every other weekend.

255. Leaving your jacket containing your keys, wallet and money in a nightclub then being anally searched before you can fly home to get a new driving license.

256. Getting into a fight at 3.00 a.m., running at a police patrol car and cracking the windshield with your elbow then getting tasered and falling down, fracturing your wrist on the same arm as your broken elbow.

257. Getting pepper sprayed and punched in the face for hitting a nightclub bouncer, leaving you with a broken tooth, hole in your retina and loss of vision in one eye.

258. Climbing three stories up a building, descending down the palm tree next to it and getting multiple puncture wounds from the palm thorns.

259. Waking up on the side of a freeway with a fireman kicking you saying, "Get up, we're getting calls about a dead body."

260. Losing over $3,000 playing four online poker tables at once.

261. Passing out with your foot on the accelerator of a golf cart, hitting a tree and splitting your forehead open.

1001 REASONS TO STOP DRINKING

262. Having to buying plastic glasses and eventually a sippy cup for your wine because of all the breakages and cuts you get around glass.

263. Turning your life around after being an alcoholic, remarrying, getting a job and building a house in the country then getting bored, going back to drinking, getting divorced again, selling the house and blowing what's left of your money on drugs.

264. Cutting your head after falling in the shower, duct taping a maxi pad over it and putting a beanie hat on then calling an Uber and waking up in hospital with your head being stapled back together.

265. Falling and breaking your foot trying to scale a 10-foot fence to get to a train station even though there's an underpass right next to it; falling asleep on the train, missing your stop and waking up in a different country.

266. Having a beaten-up face in all your wedding photos.

267. Being sued for thousands with security camera foot-age showing you emptying a huge bucket of paint on the road outside your house which didn't dry overnight due to damp weather, so drivers splashed through it spraying paint all over their vehicles.

268. Falling asleep in your car at a gas station and waking up with a needle in your arm in the back of an ambulance after being arrested for DUI.

269. Waking up being gang raped in the back of a truck.

270. Leaving your girlfriend in a pub in Latvia without the address of your hotel and waking up covered in snow in a churchyard.

1001 REASONS TO STOP DRINKING

271. Getting blackout drunk on a flight school trip, throwing bricks through a window, then being put in the military's alcohol treatment program and assigned a different job in the Air Force after being near the top of your class.

272. Celebrating your 18th birthday by sliding down a lamp post, scraping the flesh off your penis and de-gloving it, leaving just a couple of inches of urethra covered by a thin layer of bloody pulp.

273. Sleepwalking over to your chest freezer, pissing in it and sleep walking back to bed.

274. Taking out a $300 payday loan to buy alcohol and taking four years to pay it off.

275. Going to a bar during the first cruise port stop and being driven back to the ship on a golf cart three hours later with a broken foot.

276. Your support dog is taken to be euthanized by animal control after trying to eat you after licking your wounds and getting a taste for blood as you laid unconscious having fallen into a store's glass display cabinet.

277. Losing thousands of dollars, multiple cars, almost every relationship, your apartment and job and disfiguring your face, leaving you depressed and burnt out at 25.

278. Contacting someone on Tinder, giving them your address, having blackout drunk sex, then waking up to find your purse has been stolen and later testing positive for type 2 herpes.

279. Shattering both heels jumping off a wall, being crippled for months, suffering constant pain and having to use a walking stick from your mid-20s onwards.

1001 REASONS TO STOP DRINKING

280. Going from having the partner of your dreams, a good job and a condo to being fired, evicted and losing your fiancé after crashing your car into some parked vehicles, getting your stomach pumped, becoming psychotic and being sent to a psych ward.

281. Feeling horrendous guilt because all you can do is play video games with your kid all weekend due to a severe hangover even though the weather outside is beautiful.

282. Realizing you have screwed up every relationship due to alcohol, are too old to have kids and will probably never get married.

283. When the trash cart tips out your recycling bin it sounds like a Tasmanian devil whirling through a bottle factory.

284. Leaving a club to go home without telling your friends (a.k.a., making an Irish exit), getting into a convertible with two random men, driving 10 miles to another bar, tripping over a step and chipping off half your front tooth.

285. Ending up $250,000 in medical debt after falling asleep at the wheel, smashing your car into a tree and being put in a medically induced coma for a month.

286. Showing up to work with Nazi symbols drawn on your forehead, your pants on inside out and peanut butter on your neck, then being sent home and sleeping for two days.

287. Spending 30 days in jail after being found guilty of DUI and 12 reckless endangerment charges, one for each of your bus passengers.

288. Blacking out, then waking up and only being able to speak in Spanish.

289. Going from having a paid off house, your own business and a loving wife to sitting on the sidewalk with no job and no memory of recent events, wearing wet shoes.

290. Passing out in a remote valley in Hawaii during a rainstorm, almost drowning crossing a river and getting hypothermia trying to get back to your hotel.

291. Trying to kick down your own front door at 4:00 a.m. only to have it opened by a police officer who tells you he suspects you're drunk to which you reply, "No shit Sherlock."

292. Your 13-year-old can't bring her friends over because you're laughing one minute and crying the next, passed out snoring or awake and vomiting.

293. Being banned from the only bowling alley in town for puking in the bathroom for an hour.

294. Revealing private details about yourself and your partner to a table full of fellow passengers on the first night of a week-long Rhine River cruise, then feeling mortified the next morning and begging to go home.

295. Shattering your cheek and getting a brain hemorrhage after falling off a balcony wearing a bear suit.

296. Getting into a brawl for throwing trash in the sea, injuring several waiters and two Spanish policemen and paying to be released on bail 48 hours before your wedding.

297. Your dogs start avoiding you because you trip over them, push them away or scream at them when you're drunk, despite caring for them most of the time.

298. Getting an email telling you not to come to work anymore after jumping into a swimming pool, fighting with the best man, calling your ex and asking her to marry you, then crying and apologizing to everyone at your boss's wedding.

299. Driving a friend's car a couple of blocks to stop it being towed and getting a DUI, which derails your career plans and leaves you with untreated depression and drinking a 12-pack of beer every evening.

300. Despite being married for 15 years and having four kids, both you and your partner have been to prison for stabbing each other because you both drink every day.

301. Going from, having zero debt, sports cars, flying first class anywhere on a whim, eating at Michelin star restaurants, running five miles a day and being able to perform sexually to losing your friends, job, money, health, reputation and marriage and living in a tiny apartment with only a laptop, cellphone and an old bed to your name.

302. Accepting a free limo ride to a strip club in Vegas then signing for over $2,500 in lap dances.

303. Forgetting the passwords to your most used online accounts, changing them all and repeating the process the next day.

304. Ending up in the burn unit with a foot long catheter in your anus, having skin grafts to reconstruct your testicles and having to lie on your stomach for months after letting someone light a firework in your ass.

305. Waking up feeling something cold against your shoulder, realizing it's a jail floor; then discovering your partner has pressed charges against you for beating her with a bag of nuts.

306. Losing a job for getting drunk, being fired from the next one for taking time off for a hangover, then doing a shot in your lunch break to celebrate being hired again and losing that job three hours in.

307. Living alone as a bitter old curmudgeon, disowned by your kids, bloated and barely mobile with hypertension and bad knees, with a sports car in your driveway you can no longer drive.

308. Going up to a girl in a bar and giving her $20 for being pretty.

309. Crashing your bike while blackout cycling and being unable to eat solid food for three weeks.

310. Waking up in a hotel propped up against a hallway wall, naked from the waist down, surrounded by housekeeping staff.

311. Trying to clear a very tall spiked wrought iron fence, impaling your balls and not getting to keep them.

312. Becoming a homeless panhandler, living in a squatter's trailer and making your own booze in a discarded bathtub.

313. Losing your top-level security clearance and ruining your Navy career as a cryptologic technician, ending up 50lbs overweight, unemployed and depressed.

314. Spending hundreds of thousands of dollars over the years on lavish parties, wild evenings out and expensive vacations, almost none of which you can remember now.

1001 REASONS TO STOP DRINKING

315. Snapping your wrist while joking around on a bench press, going for a follow up hospital exam and seeing the words "drunk broad" written on your X-ray folder.

316. Drinking the last of the beer while packing up from a weekend's camping trip, driving home and hitting a utility pole, paralyzing your 13-year-old daughter from the neck down.

317. Spiraling down into becoming a full-blown alcoholic after failing your last semester of college and missing out on a degree after years of excellent academics.

318. Checking your wife's Facebook page in the morning so you can fake remember what you did the night before.

319. Taking the bus to do a minimum wage job having lost your high earning career of 20 years by hitting four vehicles while driving over the limit and spending two years in jail.

320. Almost dying while being blackout drunk after taking a pill from someone you just met on the street which turns out to be loaded with fentanyl.

321. Waking up with broken glass everywhere, your favorite makeup palette embedded into the carpet and your 5-year relationship down the drain.

322. Being on your computer one minute then naked in jail the next, with no memory of what happened in between, including how you got to the parking lot where you were arrested or why you left your house.

323. Drinking so much you neglect your cat and your apartment gets infested with fleas, after which the bites on your legs get infected and you get sepsis and almost die.

324. Sexually assaulting someone "as a joke," losing your job and ending up depressed and suffering from so much stress your face swells up from angioedema.

325. On your first day in prison for your second DUI you are told you have fucked up your life, are no longer a person but a number and must respect the officers and comply with their orders or you'll be sent to solitary confinement otherwise known as "the hole."

326. Going on a free five-day cruise for two and ending up with a $1,300 liquor bill.

327. Arriving home after being in hospital with an alcohol-related problem to find your relatives have cleared out hundreds of empty bottles from your closet and left a bottle of B vitamins and this book on your kitchen countertop.

328. Peeing your pants while trying to cook a whole unpeeled onion in a frying pan, then falling asleep on the floor after your eight-year-old begged you not to drink.

329. Celebrating passing your bar exam then driving home, getting a DWI, being disbarred, losing your law firm job offer and working in a grocery store to pay off $10,000 in legal costs and your six-figure student loan.

330. Drunk cooking, then passing out watching TV after leaving the gas burner on but unlit and giving yourself carbon monoxide poisoning.

331. Waking up unable to see or move, screaming death threats and being restrained in a hospital bed with a catheter in after being found passed out in the street while on a bachelor party weekend in Spain.

332. Stealing from your family so you can pawn their stuff for liquor, with no friends or kids and nobody around you except a girl at the club who stops talking to you once you run out of money.

333. Taking a private jet from your country club to Las Vegas, gambling away $3.2 million then calling the club the next day to ask, "What the fuck happened?"

334. Losing everything after being sentenced to 30 days of rehab, 30 days of probation and 36 hours of anger management classes for misdemeanor third-degree assault and criminal mischief after attacking your partner in a drunken rage.

335. Ordering $500 worth of New York Yankees memorabilia despite living in Scotland and not being a hundred percent sure what the sport is even about.

336. Becoming quadriplegic after being lifted into a sitting position for an X-ray, because the numbing effects of alcohol left you unable to feel or express pain.

337. Giving one of the worst national anthem renditions ever performed at a major sports event broadcast live on national TV and checking into rehab the next day.

338. Threatening suicide, being pink slipped by a police officer then taken to a psychiatric hospital where you are stripped of everything and left in a room wearing scrubs and have to drink hospital ginger ale for three days.

339. Dropping a glass of wine and watching it soak the piece of artwork your kid made for you at school.

340. Peeing on an electric fence and knocking yourself out.

"Please list reasons to quit and even scare me if you can. I need a scare. No matter how much my stomach hurts and my mental health declines I can't stop. I can feel that alcohol is claiming me slowly and taking my personality and health away.

PLEASE scare me straight!"

From a desperate 27-year-old

Real-life examples of the distressing, shocking and unforeseen health problems caused by excessive drinking

341. Waking up in the early hours with "hangxiety," a.k.a. "The Fear," with a racing heart, feelings of panic and deep sense of dread because your brain is flooded with excitatory stress hormones to counteract alcohol's sedative effects.

342. Your hangover is so bad you drink the water out of your steam iron because it's the nearest thing you can reach.

343. The room feels like it's spinning when you lie down because alcohol temporarily lowers your blood pressure and affects the fluids in your inner ear, making you feel disorientated and nauseous.

344. Being rude, impulsive and generally behaving like an asshole even when you're not drinking due to alcohol-induced frontal lobe brain damage.

345. An ultrasound to find out what's causing the pain in your right upper abdominal area shows you have an enlarged fatty liver[1] (alcoholic hepatic steatosis) that's in danger of becoming inflamed (alcoholic hepatitis) and turning into a shrunken mass of hardened scar tissue (alcoholic cirrhosis).

346. Your liver is bigger than normal from storing too much fat, because alcohol that isn't used for energy is metabolized down to

---

[1] Sober Synthesis
https://sobersynthesis.com/2024/07/05/alcohol-liver-disease/

produce fats like cholesterol, plus alcohol releases triglycerides from other parts of the body which end up in the liver.

347. Gaining weight because the fattier your liver gets the less able it is to process and remove fat from the rest of your body.

348. Getting blackout drunk, because alcohol stops the nerve cells in your brain's hippocampus – the bit that makes new memories – from firing properly, leaving you with no recollection of anything you did past a certain point even though you seemed physically awake.

349. Becoming one of the huge number of people in their 20s and 30s with full-blown cirrhosis after developing a serious drinking problem during the Covid lockdowns.[2]

350. Gaining weight because alcohol crashes your blood sugar levels leaving you ravenously hungry.

351. Your smartwatch says you went running at 3:00 a.m., because all the alcohol increased your blood pressure and crashed your blood sugar levels, causing your heart to race.

352. Being confined to a care home in your 50s with frontal lobe dementia and the memory of a goldfish with your CT scans citing, "diffuse brain atrophy due to chronic alcohol exposure."

353. Hallucinating, shaking, vomiting and sweating for days due to alcohol withdrawal.

---

[2] Increased alcohol use during the COVID-19 pandemic: The effect of mental health and age in a cross-sectional sample of social media users in the U.S.
https://pmc.ncbi.nlm.nih.gov/articles/PMC9063034/#:~:text=Proportionally%20more%20women%20reported%20an,aged%2060%20years%20or%20over.

354. Puking so hard you pop the blood vessels in both eyes.

355. An ultrasound shows you have a fatty pancreas[3] as well as an almost completely white fatty liver (it should look black on sonography) due to an accumulation of cholesterol and triglycerides that are produced when your body breaks down alcohol.

356. You have morphed into the Despicable Me character Gru, with a pot belly and alcoholic skinny legs and arms.

357. Being told by a hepatologist (liver doctor) that every time you drink, some of your liver cells die, and although it can make new ones eventually it will stop regenerating.

358. Losing your mind, because your liver can't filter out toxins like ammonia to be eliminated in your poop, so they end up in your brain, making you confused, angry and forgetful: a condition called hepatic encephalopathy.

359. Vomiting, dry heaving and having diarrhea every morning then having to drink, because alcohol has become the normalizing agent that relieves these withdrawal symptoms.

360. You have a hard time walking properly and feel confused because alcohol makes it harder to store vitamin B1 (thiamine), without which your brain cells can't produce enough energy to function and die: a condition called Wernicke-Korsakoff syndrome.

---

[3] Ethanol toxicity in pancreatic acinar cells: Mediation by nonoxidative fatty acid metabolites
https://www.pnas.org/doi/full/10.1073/pnas.0403431101

361. Gaining weight because your body is using alcohol as its main energy source instead of your fat stores.

362. The bloating and dull ache on your right side under your rib cage you thought were due to indigestion turn out to be symptoms of grade 3 fatty liver disease, which is the most advanced stage before inflammation and cirrhosis set in.

363. Being shocked to hear there's something wrong with your liver when you're being tested for something else, because the symptoms of liver damage often don't show up until over 80% of its tissue function has gone.

364. Suddenly quitting booze and having severe tremors, terrifying hallucinations (alcoholic hallucinosis) and a grand mal seizure three days later: a phenomenon called delirium tremens.

365. Being hospitalized after taking seven shots in a row and being warned by a doctor that the death rate among women who drink excessively is double that of men.

366. Being locked in a psych unit room having lost your brain function overnight due to alcohol-induced brain damage: a condition called Wernicke-Korsakoff syndrome, which is a combination of brain swelling (Wernicke's encephalopathy) and severe confusion (Korsakoff psychosis).

367. Craving junk food and sugar because alcohol sends blood sugar levels soaring after which they drop dramatically, creating a crash and crave cycle.

368. Pressure builds up in your portal vein – the main vein that supplies the liver with blood – because your liver is stiff with scar tissue, which means blood can't flow through it easily.

369. There's blood in your poop due to a combination of acetaldehyde – the toxic breakdown product of alcohol – irritating the lining of your rectum, coupled with chronic high blood pressure.

370. Your cancer risk is increased because acetaldehyde (which is actually used as an industrial solvent) causes DNA damage.

371. Going to urgent care with severe back pain, yellow eyes and swollen feet and being devastated to hear you are in liver failure in your 20s.

372. Waking up with excruciating pain in your leg due to a blood clot caused by years of hardcore drinking, zero exercise and eating crappy food.

373. The constant dull pains in your right side turn out to be caused by your inflamed liver (which has no pain receptors) pressing on the surrounding tissue called fascia which is packed with pain-sensitive nerves.

374. Having to drink a beer before work to stop the shakes and drinking on your breaks so you don't get withdrawal seizures.

375. Every morning you lunge towards the bathroom and fall against the walls like you're on a pitching ship in a storm because you're still drunk from the night before.

376. Because your blood can't get through your hardened liver you get varicose veins called varices in your stomach and esophagus.

377. Having a life-threatening seizure because you suddenly stop drinking and deprive your brain of the alcohol it has been forced to adapt to, leaving it in a highly over-stimulated state.

378. Vomiting "coffee grounds" (blood that has been partially digested by stomach acid) due to the varices in your gastrointestinal (GI) tract bursting and bleeding out into your stomach.

379. Ending up with withdrawal seizures caused by a severe overload of excitatory brain chemicals[4] – namely adrenaline, cortisol and glutamate – because your brain is no longer balancing out the sedating effects of alcohol.

380. Needing dialysis because your kidneys have been forced to compensate for your semi-functioning liver which normally filters out toxins, and now they're damaged from having to work so hard.

381. An all-day headache[5] caused by alcohol making you pee out four times more liquid than you consume and forcing your organs to steal water from your brain which makes it shrink and pull on the membranes that attach it to your skull.

382. Waking up with no idea where you are, slurring your words and shaking uncontrollably due to a build-up of ammonia in your brain, because your liver is no longer able to send it to get peed out in your urine.

383. Spending three days in the intensive care unit ICU after almost bleeding to death due to a ruptured ulcer caused as a result of drinking a handle of vodka every day for two years.

384. Feeling suicidal because your brain has adapted to constant alcohol-induced serotonin and dopamine overloads by making less

---

[4] Adrenergic storm
https://en.wikipedia.org/wiki/Adrenergic_storm
[5] How Hangovers Work
https://health.howstuffworks.com/wellness/drugs-alcohol/hangover2.htm

of these happy chemicals and speeding up their removal, leaving you feeling severely depressed and hopeless when you are sober.

385. Going from being told, "Hey your eyes look a little yellow" to having words like "end stage" and "mortality" thrown at you while you're lying in an emergency room bed.

386. Developing a huge, firm, bloated belly as a result of your hardened liver having formed a bottleneck in your circulatory system which has created high pressure in your portal vein and pressed the fluid component of your blood called lymph out into your abdomen: a condition known as ascites.

387. Waking up with migraine-level pain, sweating yet feeling cold, feeling extremely nauseous and then vomiting for the next eight hours due to alcohol poisoning.

388. Causing lifelong harm to your unborn baby because alcohol crosses the placenta and diffuses into the fetus's blood, brain and vital organs, disrupting their development.

389. Getting migraines because alcohol makes you pee too much, dilates the blood vessels in your brain and reduces the level of fluid around it.

390. Waking up with red teeth and blood pooling in your mouth because one of your esophageal varices started leaking overnight.

391. Flatlining three times before the age of 35: twice from alcohol poisoning and once from alcohol withdrawal.

392. You develop "lost key syndrome" in your 40s, with a worsening memory and the inability to focus due to alcohol's brain aging effects.

393. Sections of the walls of the veins in your throat that are thin and bulging (due to pressure caused by your blood being unable to flow through your liver) are suctioned up and tied off with rubber bands, causing these areas to die and be replaced with tougher scar tissue: a procedure called variceal banding.

394. Your diseased liver can't process the orange substance made from your broken-down red blood cells called bilirubin, so it builds up in your blood and diffuses into your skin and eyes turning them yellow: a condition called jaundice.

395. Having puffy eyelids and looking bloated because alcohol dehydrates the body causing the skin to hold onto water and also increases cortisol levels which leads to extra fat being stored around your face and neck.

396. You end up in the hospital for five days with alcohol-induced gastritis (stomach inflammation) and ischemia (tissue death) which results in you pooing out mucus and blood, gagging constantly and being unable to eat.

397. Spurting half the blood in your body out of your mouth while you're on vacation when the varices in the veins of your esophagus explode due to a combination of heat, high blood pressure and all-day drinking.

398. Straining your vomit and drinking it when you run out of alcohol because you're so desperate to avoid the effects of withdrawal.

399. Not being able to lift anything over 10lbs because of the risk of blowing out your varices.

400. Waking up in the ICU with a feeding tube down your throat because your liver is dying and your kidneys are shutting down.

401. You need a TIPS (transjugular intrahepatic portosystemic shunt) procedure, where a surgeon connects your portal vein to a lower-pressure blood vessel using a Teflon tube.

402. Being given a "Model for End-stage Liver Disease" (MELD) score, which is a combination of your lab test results, kidney function and age, to see how likely it is you will die within the next three months without a liver transplant.

403. Being admitted to hospital with aspiration pneumonia and needing a tracheotomy to save your life after passing out lying on your back and inhaling vomit in your sleep.

404. Not knowing which new health concern is coming next because the liver does over 500 things, so when it's not working properly problems can crop up anywhere in the body.

405. Having to be two seconds away from a toilet because you've been prescribed lactulose – a very strong laxative – to flush the food through your system before it's fully digested to avoid ammonia building up in your brain, because your hardened liver can't process it properly anymore.

406. Aspirating vomit into your lungs then spending two weeks in the ICU, which leaves you with a permanently raspy voice from having a tube put into your windpipe so you can breathe: a procedure called intubation.

407. Discovering the frontal lobes of your brain have less white matter mass compared to other people aged 40 according to the results of an MRI for an unrelated health issue.

408. Ending up in the ICU with your throat burning from vomiting stomach acid, having come close to a heart attack due to alcohol poisoning and alcohol-induced hypertension.

409. Squirting "ass piss" or "ass soup" instead of solid poop because the chronic inflammation in your liver's bile ducts has stopped them from being able to deliver the bile salts that are needed to properly digest food.

410. Forgetting why you're going into a room, what you just read or saw on TV, talking to yourself, going to sleep mid conversation, getting lost and having to write everything down due to hepatic encephalopathy.

411. Knowing the names of three other brands of adult diaper other than "Depends."

412. Feeling fine one day, and screaming in agony the next with pain in your abdomen that radiates to your back, because the acetaldehyde from alcohol has reacted with the enzymes in your pancreas and blocked its ducts, leaving the digestive enzymes unable to go anywhere so they start "digesting" your pancreatic tissue: a condition called pancreatitis.

413. Getting a $4,000 ER bill for a "heart attack" that was actually a massive hangover coupled with a withdrawal-related panic attack, because your excitatory brain chemicals were out of whack from trying to balance out the numbing effect of the alcohol.

414. Waking up shaking, unable to use your phone or laptop or put a glass of water to your mouth because your body has become so dependent on alcohol you can't function without it.

415. You have sharp pains under your ribcage on the right-hand side because the alcohol has stimulated your liver into producing too much cholesterol which has made "stones" in your gallbladder (where bile is stored and produced) and blocked its ducts, making it inflamed: a condition called cholecystitis.

416. Worsening menopause symptoms, including hot flashes, night sweats and insomnia, because your liver has prioritized dealing with alcohol instead of processing hormones.

417. After being confused and having hallucinations you are diagnosed with Korsakoff syndrome because your liver isn't producing enough bile to digest your food properly, leaving you with a lack of vitamin B1 which your brain cells need to function.

418. Suffering gradual hearing loss due to alcohol's by-product acetaldehyde destroying the hair cells in your inner ear.

419. Being on a salt and sugar restricted diet, living on yoghurt and protein drinks and having to use a walker and oxygen after being discharged from hospital with liver failure with just a few months to live.

420. Bloodshot, watery eyes caused by alcohol dilating and irritating their blood vessels.

421. Ending up with varices covering all of your organs, as well as blood clots in your portal vein, which means the liver transplant team can't operate because you're too high risk.

422. Hearing a doctor advise your family to sign a do-not-resuscitate order while you're in a medically induced coma with double pneumonia, sepsis and advanced liver disease.

423. Muscle weakness, cramping and an abnormal heart rhythm due to a lack of potassium – which is vital for proper nerve and muscle function – because your kidneys have been working overtime getting rid of the alcohol and you've peed it all out.

424. Ending up in a geriatric psychiatric ward in your 40s with the speech level of a five-year-old, prematurely aged, unable to remember anything you're told after a few seconds and living in a world where the past does not exist, due to alcohol-induced Korsakoff syndrome.

425. Needing a hip replacement in your 30s because you don't have the vitamins and minerals your body needs to create new bone cells, due to a combination of not eating properly, faster nutrient excretion, gut inflammation and excess stomach acid.

426. Having to switch careers because you can no longer cope with complex tasks, handle stress or communicate properly because of brain deterioration caused by drinking hard liquor every day for the last 20 plus years.

427. Becoming an insulin injecting diabetic because drinking has damaged your pancreas.

428. Falling into a coma, getting sepsis and needing to have your arms and feet amputated following a three-day binge.

429. Burning, tingling and numbness in your hands and feet caused by a B vitamin deficiency and acetaldehyde-induced damage to the protective myelin coating (like the plastic around electrical cords) of your nerves: a condition called peripheral neuropathy.

430. Losing your career in aviation and ending up working at a car wash after going into seizures, falling into a coma and having to be

ventilated and tube fed for six months after suddenly quitting alcohol without medical advice.

431. Being hit with the news that you are in the early stages of cirrhosis despite there being no prior warning signs that alcohol was destroying your liver.

432. Realizing that your life could end before you reach 30 with a bunch of your friends telling stupid drinking stories at your funeral.

433. Feeling constantly short of breath because alcohol's toxic effect on your bone marrow plus a lack of B vitamins has stopped healthy oxygen-transporting red blood cells from being made and the ones that are being produced are too big and break down faster: a condition called alcoholic macrocytic anemia.

434. You become nothing more than a walking, drooling skeleton with less than half your IQ left because your brain has shrunk so badly from alcohol abuse.

435. Having your leg amputated just below the knee after contracting a leg infection as a result of complications from alcohol-induced peripheral artery disease.

436. Tossing and turning at 3:00 a.m. fretting over everything you'd blocked from your mind because your brain is full of cortisol, adrenaline and glutamate now the alcohol has worn off.

437. Red spots with little blood vessels that look like spider's legs – called spider angiomas – start appearing on your face due to an over-abundance of estrogen which is normally metabolized by the liver.

438. Developing a huge beer belly because the constant drinking has left you with too little testosterone, too much estrogen and too much fat around your organs.

439. Going to the hospital with stomach pain, being discharged and then getting a phone call from a panicked doctor saying your creatine kinase level is sky high (a sign of heart, brain, or muscle damage) and your liver is so huge and fatty it looks like it belongs to someone in their late 60s not a 25-year-old.

440. The walls of your heart are thin and saggy and can't pump blood properly due to the deadly effect of acetaldehyde on the heart cells and the tissue that's left having to stretch to compensate: a condition called cardiomyopathy.[6]

441. Your sex drive has disappeared because alcohol's toxic by-products have damaged the Leydig cells in your testes that produce testosterone and destroyed the nerves and blood vessels in your penis, making it hard to get and maintain an erection.

442. Huffing and puffing and getting into weird positions to put your socks on and tie your shoelaces because your beer belly is in the way.

443. You start growing breasts – a.k.a. man boobs – due to alcohol's ability to destroy the enzymes that are needed to make testosterone and convert testosterone into estradiol, the most potent form of estrogen.

444. You need a hip replacement in your 40s due to your blood's high fat content (alcoholic hyperlipidemia) blocking the blood vessels going to the spherical ball joint at the end of one of your thigh

---

[6] Alcoholic cardiomyopathy: Pathophysiologic insights
https://pmc.ncbi.nlm.nih.gov/articles/PMC4177522/

bones and causing the bone tissue to die: a condition called avascular necrosis of the femoral head.

445. Being driven to the emergency room with high blood pressure and a racing heart – a condition called supraventricular tachycardia[7] – caused by low electrolyte levels (from peeing too much) and an adrenergic storm reaction to binge drinking alcohol.

446. You're always tired and have little interest in sex because your liver is unable to help regulate your hormones, leading to an overload of estrogen and deficit of testosterone, which lowers the sex drive in both men and women.

447. Eating antacids like candy due to persistent acid reflux, because alcohol relaxes the muscle between the esophagus and stomach allowing its contents to move up into your throat.

448. Repeatedly getting fired and destroying relationships by yelling and storming off all the time – a condition called intermittent explosive disorder – because drinking has damaged the frontal lobes of your brain which handle impulse control and social behavior.

449. You break your arm playing with your grandkid due to alcohol-induced osteoporosis, because alcohol stops the body from absorbing calcium and vitamin D which are needed for bone strength and creates hormonal problems that cause the bones to break down.

---

[7] Presumed Alcohol-Induced Ventricular Tachycardia Storm: A Case Report https://pmc.ncbi.nlm.nih.gov/articles/PMC7292685/

450. Sitting in your car outside your lawyer's office unable to go in to sign some forms because your hands won't stop shaking from alcohol withdrawals.

451. Waking up with crippling anxiety after a binge, with paranoia and catastrophic thoughts, because alcohol elevates cortisol levels which drains your brain of dopamine and gamma-amino-butyric acid (GABA) – the calming chemical – leaving you unable to feel positive or at peace for hours.

452. The palms of your hands are red (known as "liver palms") because your blood vessels are wider than normal due to the changes in blood pressure and blood flow caused by liver disease.

453. Loading a gun with the intention of killing yourself, then calling your buddy who's an ER doctor who tells you suicidal depression from heavy drinking is quite common and they call it "drunkacide" at the hospital.

454. Racking up a massive medical debt from being tested for colon cancer, heart disease, kidney failure, multiple sclerosis and tuberculosis, then discovering all your symptoms are related to drinking.

455. Being unresponsive nine hours after being admitted to hospital with a BAC (blood alcohol concentration) of .48% and not being expected to pull through without significant brain damage.

456. Losing the strength in your muscles, falling over, having slurred speech and difficulty staying awake due to the multiple effects of advanced liver disease.

457. Being super swollen and in pain from fluid build-up in your legs – a condition called peripheral edema – caused by water retention in

response to alcohol's dehydrating effect and lack of vitamin B1 (thiamine).

458. Getting out of bed with pain in your knees and lower back because alcohol-induced muscle loss has put stress on your joints.

459. You are diagnosed with coronary heart disease because processing alcohol diverts the liver from metabolizing fatty acids which has caused a build-up of fatty deposits on your coronary artery walls and made it hard for blood to reach your heart muscle.

460. You have a genetic health condition called Alpha-1 antitrypsin (AAT) deficiency (which is more common in European populations), where the body doesn't produce enough of the protein that protects the liver from damage, so any amount of alcohol makes you more prone to cirrhosis.

461. Having a withdrawal seizure and lying undiscovered for days, during which time you develop rhabdo – short for rhabdomyolysis – which occurs when damaged muscle tissue releases toxins into the blood.

462. Spontaneously emptying your bowels and suffering frequent diarrhea due to alcohol-induced damage to your autonomic nerves: another variation of alcoholic neuropathy.

463. Perpetuating and worsening your depression because your brain has adapted to the unnatural spike of dopamine alcohol provides by producing less of this "happy chemical" and more transporter proteins to clear it away.

464. Your stage two cirrhosis turns into an aggressive form of cancer which keeps returning even when the tumors are removed, prompting your surgeon to recommend a liver transplant.

465. Racking up over $250,000 in medical bills from repeated hospital stays due to alcohol-related pancreatitis made worse by stress, smoking and mostly eating carbs for your meals.

466. People comment that you don't sound or look intoxicated when you're wasted, because drinking so much has forced your brain to shut down most of its GABA receptors (GABA gives you that numbed out, drunk feeling) and made the liver produce more enzymes to metabolize it: a phenomenon called tolerance.

467. Being shocked back to life by paramedics after passing out and not breathing, then waking up in the ICU three days later having drunk yourself to a blood alcohol concentration of .42.

468. Going into cardiac arrest, being intubated and having to be chemically and physically restrained on a hospital bed due to the most severe form of alcohol withdrawals called delirium tremens.

469. Your arthritis pain is getting worse because alcohol's dehydrating effect means there is less lubrication between your joints.

470. Taking a shit is so painful because of tears in the lining of your anus called anal fissures caused by years of alcohol-induced diarrhea.

471. The walls of your colon are stained black, which the gastroenterologist thinks is due to taking laxatives, but it's really because of all the red wine.

472. Ending up a collection of bones with yellow skin on top, being tube fed tube and having your belly periodically drained of fluid with a large bore needle due to irreversible liver failure.

473. At the age of 38, after 14 plus years of drinking your portal vein is permanently inflamed and putting pressure on your pancreas which causes pain.

474. Even though your dementia is worsening, your physical health is improving because Wernicke's encephalopathy causes memory loss, so you forget to drink.

475. During your autopsy the medical examiner says your organs look like they were microwaved on high for twenty minutes with your liver resembling a blackened piece of meat.

476. Smelling like trash in a dumpster on a hot day because your body is trying to sweat out the toxins your liver can no longer handle.

477. The side effects of your prescription drugs are amplified because your damaged liver is unable to filter them out, so they build up in your blood and act longer than they should.

478. Because bile is unable to flow through your liver it collects under your skin where it irritates the nerve endings making you feel like you're rolling around in fire ants: a condition called pruritus.

479. Shitting yellow liquid up to five times a day and suffering from malnutrition because all the alcohol has damaged the walls of your intestines.

480. Going into cardiac arrest after having ten liters of fluid drained from your abdomen, causing a steep drop in the amount of blood going to your heart, a situation known as hypovolemic shock.

481. Losing over 50lbs in two months because you are scared to eat in case it triggers another agonizing bout of pancreatitis.

482. Feeling lethargic, depressed and mentally slow because alcohol has killed your good gut bacteria, with the knock-on effect that your immune system is weaker and your brain function is reduced.

483. A well as having an inherited blood clotting problem called MTHFR (which affects nearly half the population[8] but usually goes undiagnosed) you are more susceptible to fatty liver disease because your homocysteine levels are too high.

484. Your hands twist into claws, you start foaming at the mouth and your face turns purple while seizing during alcohol withdrawal.

485. Staying awake for days, hearing and seeing things and writing songs in your head because your brain is so messed up from alcohol if you suddenly take it away it starts inventing things due to a severe chemical imbalance: a condition called alcoholic hallucinosis.

486. Having your stomach pumped then needing a banana bag IV (so-called due to its yellow color from the B vitamins) after giving yourself alcohol poisoning.

487. Having a sibling with fetal alcohol syndrome and noticing how they are smaller, look facially different, struggle in school, are impulsive and can't focus.

488. Walking with leg braces and a cane and only getting around the house if there's something to grab hold of, because the nerves in your feet and legs have been permanently damaged by peripheral neuropathy.

---

[8] MTHFR Gene: All About the Genetic Mutation That Affects 40% of the World
https://drwillcole.com/brain-health/do-you-have-the-gene-mutation-that-affects-40-of-the-world

489. Having an uncontrollable urge to pee and a burning feeling when you do, with just a couple drips of "acid" coming out, due to alcohol-induced prostate inflammation, known as prostatitis.

490. Your esophagus collapses from only consuming alcohol and not eating for months and has to be replaced with part of your stomach shaped into a tube.

491. Vomiting blood because your esophagus is torn from alcohol-induced acid reflux, leaving you unable to eat solid food and having to sit up straight for a month, even while sleeping.

492. Despite puking all week you've put on 10lbs with all the fluid accumulating in your abdomen, due to the build-up of blood pressure in your liver's portal vein.

493. Having severe back pain and difficulty peeing as a result of alcohol-induced prostate cancer which spread and metastasized quickly because of your high blood estrogen level.

494. Overhearing someone say they would be devastated but not surprised to hear you have died.

495. A few weeks after having a pancreatitis attack, the fluid leaking out from your pancreas has created a large "pseudocyst" which has to be endoscopically drained.

496. Your ankles swell to almost double their size due to alcohol-induced edema.

497. Spending vast sums on mobile IV services to counter the effects of alcohol poisoning and hangovers.

498. Sweating, feeling sick, having a headache and being red faced after drinking because your liver enzymes metabolize alcohol too quickly creating an immediate build-up of toxic acetaldehyde: a condition called "Asian Flush"[9] because this reaction primarily affects Japanese and Korean people.

499. Having a dry mouth and foul-smelling breath in the morning due to a combination of a lack of saliva and a build-up of bacteria, because you rarely brush your teeth before passing out drunk.

500. Vomiting in your sleep a couple of hours after your last drink because that's when your blood alcohol level reaches its peak.

501. Suffering a stroke because alcohol caused your heart muscle to quiver or fibrillate instead of contract and relax, so the blood stagnated in one of your heart's chambers and formed a clot which got dislodged and blocked the flow of blood to your brain.

502. Being admitted to a psych ward with alcoholic hallucinosis while going through alcohol withdrawal, having called the police to say there are helicopters in your backyard and aliens sitting around your kitchen table.

503. Blood is spurting out of both ends because your hardened liver has forced it to flow into the thinner walled veins of your esophagus, stomach and rectum, creating an explosive build-up of pressure.

504. Suddenly losing your sight – which you're told could be permanent – because the enzymes from your inflamed pancreas have damaged the retinas of your eyes.

---

[9] Why some people get 'Asian flush,' hives and headaches when they drink alcohol
https://www.abc.net.au/news/2019-08-11/understanding-asian-flush/11387696

505. Being unable to get pregnant because alcohol has messed up your hormones and you are no longer ovulating or having regular periods.

506. Due to the lipid generating effects of alcohol your blood looks like it's topped with a layer of cream after it has been drawn and left to settle in the test tube.

507. Vomiting blood halfway through a flight when the varices in your esophagus burst due to the added stress of the cabin pressure.

508. 15 years after quitting alcohol you are diagnosed with cirrhosis because you drank a ridiculous amount up to the age of 30 and then swapped alcohol for candy and sugary drinks.

509. Only being able to wear flip flops because your feet are so bloated from fluid retention.

510. Your urine is the color of Coca-Cola due to liver inflammation (called hepatitis) which means your blood isn't being filtered properly, which has caused a build-up of bilirubin.

511. Suffering from chronic back pain because alcohol has dehydrated the gel-like discs in your spine that cushion the bones in your vertebrae.

512. Having to sell your house after racking up a massive insurance copay debt following a $2.6 million liver and kidney transplant.

513. Breaking the bones in your feet and continuing to walk on them because you've lost all feeling from your ankles down due to a combination of alcohol-induced nerve damage and vitamin B1 deficiency.

514. Propping yourself up with pillows every night so you can burp safely without choking on your vomit.

515. Losing things, forgetting the topic of conversation and not knowing what day it is because the parts of your brain that make and retrieve memories no longer work due to alcohol-induced brain atrophy and vitamin B1 deficiency.

516. Needing regular scans despite your liver disease having stabilized, because now it is growing new cells which can lead to errors in replication, plus having a fibrotic liver reduces folate and vitamin B12 levels, all of which increases your risk for liver cancer.

517. Waking up with painful, throbbing teeth and sore gums from grinding your teeth due to the alcohol-induced release of stress hormones hyperactivating your jaw muscles.

518. Lying on your back and applying pressure to your groin to stop the blood flowing out of the enlarged veins in your testicles which have ruptured due to the knock-on effects of portal hypertension.

519. Your hepatologist describes your liver as "pretty much all useless rope and fiber" because it has barely enough functionality to keep you alive.

520. Your face is permanently bloated because your body is storing water in anticipation of another episode of alcohol-induced dehydration.

521. Hitting your phone's emergency button when blood starts spurting out of your mouth and butt, being helicoptered to hospital and being told there's a cancerous tumor the size of a walnut on your liver ten years after you were diagnosed with cirrhosis.

522. Swallowing becomes painful and your chest hurts when you eat due to the constant backwash of acid from your stomach having eroded the lining of your esophagus: a condition called alcoholic esophagitis.

523. Uncontrollably tapping your leg up and down due to low levels of potassium (an electrolyte that regulates nerve impulses) because the alcohol has caused you to pee and sweat it out.

524. Constantly suffering from bloating and diarrhea due to alcohol-induced damage to your stomach lining which has led to the build-up of bad gut bacteria which is preventing you from digesting your food properly.

525. Being told your cirrhotic liver looks like a pineapple and you need to get on the transplant list.

526. Feeling super tired but unable to sleep at 3:00 a.m. because your brain's excitatory "fight or flight" chemical neurotransmitters have outlived alcohol's sedative effects.

527. Being kept in the ICU for five days and given the legal maximums of fentanyl and ketamine to manage your pain and looking like a prisoner of war because you've lost so much weight due to necrotizing pancreatitis.

528. Your breath literally smells like shit – called fetor hepaticus ("liver stench" or "breath of the dead") – a foul odor caused by the accumulation of metabolic waste products in your blood because your liver is no longer processing them.

529. Getting a brain bleed – or hemorrhagic stroke – when a blood vessel bursts due to alcohol having thinned your blood and increased its pressure in your circulatory system.

530. Suffering severe abdominal pain and violently throwing up due to alcohol-induced kidney failure, then having to get your blood cleaned by a dialysis machine three times a week.

531. Your doctor warns you that every drink you take is gradually turning your brain into Swiss cheese.

532. Developing symptoms of diabetes, chronic fatigue and IBS due to nutrient deficiencies because alcohol lowers digestive enzyme levels, damages the cells in the digestive tract and causes dehydration, all of which are bad for proper digestion.

533. Having to be restrained and sedated due to extreme pain and having four drains sutured to the sides of your stomach to remove the toxic fluids from an infection caused by your dying pancreas.

534. Having almost no normal looking sperm in the few that are seen under a microscope, because the toxic breakdown products of alcohol have inflamed your testes and killed your sperm cells.

535. Passing stools that float and are almost white due to a lack of liver-derived bile salts which contain bilirubin (the substance made mainly from broken down red blood cells) which gives poop its brown color.

536. Being hospitalized with a potassium level so low it's classed as life-threatening and requires you to have an emergency IV infusion: a condition called hypokalemia.

537. Almost dying from pancreatitis then spending 30 days in hospital being fed intravenously and developing a blood clot where the central line was inserted.

538. Wearing a backpack with a couple of pillows in it to keep yourself upright in bed to stop yourself inhaling your stomach acid while you're asleep.

539. Waiting for your hemorrhoids to stop bleeding and your eyeballs to turn white again after a New Year's Eve bender.

540. Throwing up a thick black substance that looks like coffee grounds and tastes metallic, which your doctor says is digested blood (made up of iron mixed with stomach acid) from the variceal bleeding in your GI tract.

541. Waking up naked in an ambulance with a gash on your head and a broken arm and being asked what year it is after having a tonic-clonic seizure in the shower ('tonic' being when your muscles clench and 'clonic' being the shakes).

542. Waking up lying in a puddle of blood because one of the veins around your belly button has burst: another side effect of portal hypertension.

543. Going from being attractive and healthy looking to blotchy, greasy-haired, broken-veined and puffy faced within two years.

544. Being unable to solve simple problems at work in your 30s as a result of abusing alcohol in your 20s.

545. You have a round "moon face," feel depressed and anxious and your blood pressure is high due to increased levels of adrenaline, cortisol and glutamate and low serotonin and dopamine levels: a condition called alcohol-induced pseudo-Cushing syndrome.[11]

---

[11] Alcohol-induced Cushing syndrome: report of eight cases and review of the literature

546. You have leaky gut syndrome with bloating and loose bowel movements because your gut bacteria are out of whack and your gut lining is damaged, so small food particles can get through it, triggering an inflammatory immune reaction.

547. Being diagnosed with stage 3 melanoma on your chest and back after drinking excessively every day for years and unknowingly increasing your skin cancer risk.

548. After having your gall bladder removed you are told by the surgeon that it was difficult to get out due to the stiffness of your liver.

549. Throwing up and having severe stomach pains because alcohol has inflamed the protective mucous covered membrane inside your stomach: a condition called gastritis.

550. Feeling a painful burning sensation when you try to pee because your dehydrated urine is so concentrated and acidic it has inflamed your urinary tract and bladder.

551. The burger you just ate goes straight through mostly undigested in what looks like yellow bile due to a lack of digestive enzymes.

552. Waking up multiple times at night gasping for air with your heart thundering because alcohol has left you congested and caused your throat muscles to relax and sag into your airway: a condition called sleep apnea.

553. Living the rest of your life needing 24/7 nursing care in your 30s, having lost your eyesight and much of your brain function due to Wernicke-Korsakoff syndrome because drinking affected your

---

https://www.frontiersin.org/journals/endocrinology/articles/10.3389/fendo.2023.1199091/full

digestion so your brain cells couldn't get the vitamins they needed to operate, combined with repeated build ups of brain damaging ammonia.

554. Suffering from bloating and diarrhea because drinking has caused a deficiency of lactase, the enzyme that breaks down milk and dairy products.

555. Learning that you have gingivitis because you hardly ever brush your teeth when you're drunk or hungover.

556. Your sweat smells like cat pee because your liver can't clear all the ammonia from your blood and your body is eliminating it through the pores of your skin.

557. You are diagnosed with hyperlipidemia which means you have high levels of fat in your blood, because the liver breaks down any alcohol that is not burned for fuel and rebuilds it into triglycerides and cholesterol.

558. After having an ultrasound, you are told the length of your liver is almost eight inches at its widest point, which is around two inches bigger than average, due to advanced fatty liver disease.

559. You have blood-stained semen caused by a blood vessel bursting in your prostate due to alcohol-induced hypertension.

560. Gaining over 100lbs and increasing your already high cholesterol and triglyceride numbers due to the binge eating that always happens when you're drunk.

561. Your brain has shrunk because chronic heavy drinking has dehydrated your brain cells.

1001 REASONS TO STOP DRINKING

562. Being in and out of the ICU for months after severe pancreatitis and becoming a diabetic for life at the age of 32.

563. Having black poop and losing sleep worrying that it's due to internal bleeding, then realizing it's because of the Pepto Bismol you're taking for your alcohol-induced heartburn.

564. Being admitted to the emergency room with a BAC of .46 with the doctor telling you what scares him most is how coherent and normal sounding you are.

565. Having to wear shorts because your legs are so swollen with edema your jeans don't fit anymore.

566. Ending up in hospital with a stomach that looks like a yellow balloon and a life expectancy of less than six months, having spent most of your life either drunk and obnoxious or sober and bad tempered.

567. The multitude of alcohol-induced cortisol spikes you have subjected your brain to over the years has destroyed your memory.

568. Your ascites fluid has to be drained with a catheter: a procedure called paracentesis or "being tapped."

569. Because alcohol is vasodilator the blood vessels in your nose have burst: a condition called rhinophyma.

570. Being too wasted to look after your teeth, resulting in eight of them having to be replaced with an expensive bridge and frequent dental cleanings to prevent further infection.

1001 REASONS TO STOP DRINKING

571. The high LDL cholesterol and triglyceride numbers you have been ignoring all these years turn out to be markers of a fatty liver which has now become painful and inflamed.

572. Inhaling your vomit and making your trachea slam shut, effectively asphyxiating yourself.

573. Waking up in hospital after passing out with a BAC of .25, then getting a bill for $4,000 for two glasses of apple juice, a 10-minute doctor visit and a two-mile ambulance ride.

574. You are diagnosed with a low white blood cell count (leukopenia) due to alcohol-related portal hypertension, where reduced blood flow through the spleen has caused it to store up white blood cells and take them out of circulation.

575. After a few glasses of wine, your smart watch always says your resting heart rate at night is 10 to 15 bpm higher than usual.

576. Not realizing you were pregnant, continuing to drink and having a miscarriage at 10 weeks because alcohol stopped the placenta growing and prevented the embryo from implanting into your uterus wall.

577. Spending a year in hospital after a massive stroke leaves you paralyzed on one side, then continuing to drink after you're released, having two heart attacks and being told you have late-stage kidney and liver disease in your 50s.

578. Spending hours attempting to solder a cable to a circuit board, only to burn yourself due to hepatic encephalopathy – otherwise referred to as "the HEs" – which makes you clumsy and unable to focus when your ammonia levels get too high.

579. You have corroded, yellow "Prosecco teeth" from the wine's high sugar content and acidity which has destroyed your tooth enamel.

580. The doctor describes your liver as looking like a squishy stress ball inside a mesh bag with blobs protruding through the netting when it's squeezed, only the mesh is the fibrosis/scar tissue and the ball squishing through it is your unscarred liver tissue.

581. After years of daily drinking your testosterone has dropped dramatically, leaving you with depression, almost no libido, a pot belly and erectile dysfunction.

582. Going to the emergency room vomiting, sweating and in extreme pain and waking up in the ICU nine days later because your pancreas has ruptured after years of heavy drinking.

583. Having a "varices episode" and bleeding so much you have a sudden drop in blood pressure causing you to go in and out of consciousness.

584. Spending the day lying in bed having brain zaps and panic attacks because your brain is in an adrenergic, hyper-stimulated state after going on a weekend bender.

585. Starting with "just one beer" then moving on to liquor and almost exclusively drinking for a week; then vomiting and having traumatizing hallucinations before going to hospital and being attached to an IV drip.

586. Feeling like you're wearing thick gloves when you try and pick things up due to alcohol's corrosive effect on the nerve endings in your hands.

587. You get worse withdrawal symptoms every time you start drinking and then quit again because your brain is more sensitized to the process: a phenomenon called kindling.

588. Not being sure if you're awake or sleeping, feeling cold, forgetting where you are and what you're talking about because you're in the first stages of Wernicke's encephalopathy (which can be reversed if it's diagnosed and treated in time).

589. The surgeon tells you that your liver is hard and grey instead of being pink and flexible.

590. After years of moderate daily drinking with the occasional binge, you have anxiety, chest pains, heart arrythmia, high blood pressure, high cholesterol and the beginnings of neuropathy in your feet at the age of 43.

591. Being told that your alcohol-induced pancreatic cancer has spread to your liver and lungs and you have six months to a year left.

592. Waking up on a bloody pillow having taken and a bite out of your tongue while having a seizure in your sleep.

593. Getting drunk on a small amount of alcohol because your crippled liver can no longer produce the enzymes that are needed to process it: a condition called reverse tolerance.

594. Passing out after a binge, going to hospital and being told your liver enzymes are elevated, your liver is enlarged and you have diabetes.

595. Becoming progressively more antisocial because the more you drink the more unstable, irrational, self-isolating and resistant to change you become.

596. Becoming constipated due to dehydration, because alcohol stops the hormone vasopressin from telling your kidneys to store water and tells your brain you need to pee instead.

597. Inadvertently giving yourself a chemical lobotomy – a.k.a., alcoholic frontal lobe atrophy.

598. Watching the large plastic bottles fill with liquid when you have your ascites drained every week and hoping they don't nick an organ with the long needle.

599. Your poop looks like tar because the scar tissue in your liver has increased the pressure in your blood vessels, causing one of them to burst in your GI tract and the blood has turned black after being digested by enzymes.

600. Thinking you must have broken the bones in your big toes because you are in so much pain due to a build-up of glass-like uric acid crystals in your joints: a condition called gout.

601. Discovering you are anemic after fainting, due to alcohol's ability to suppress red blood cell production and cause defects in those that are produced.

602. Your testicles are the size of two grapefruits because some of the fluid in your abdomen has made its way into your lower body causing edema.

603. Overhearing someone comment as they walk past your hospital room, "Hey, did you see that guy in 49? He looks like a highlighter!"

604. Losing your voice box after a total laryngectomy and having to breathe through a stoma in your neck due to DNA damage to the

cells of your throat caused by acetaldehyde, the carcinogenic breakdown product of alcohol.

605. Being housebound with depression, severe anxiety and panic attacks during a second phase of withdrawal that can happen a few weeks after quitting alcohol when the brain is still recalibrating its hormones and neurotransmitters: a phenomenon called Post-Acute Withdrawal Syndrome (PAWS).

606. Having an enormous nosebleed which doesn't stop for three hours due to a lack of platelets – the cells that stick together to stop bleeding, because your liver has stopped telling your bone marrow to make them.

607. Seeing most of your older family members end up in care homes with alcohol related dementia or dying earlier than normal from drinking related diseases.

608. Waking up exhausted with your head pulsating, replaying what you can recall of the previous night's events, then having random waves of anxiety and doom-laden thoughts that last for two days.

609. You can no longer walk because of the shooting pains in your lower legs, wear adult diapers and rarely leave your bed because of severe alcohol-related neuropathy.

610. Your tongue is bright red and smooth due to alcohol-induced vitamin B deficiency.

611. Your doctor explains that NOT having hangovers or shaking in the mornings is a bad thing because it means your body has developed a tolerance to large amounts of alcohol and the amount you will need to drink to function and avoid these symptoms will just keep on increasing.

612. Feeling exhausted and cranky due to chronic malnutrition caused by alcohol-induced gut inflammation and because your body isn't getting enough nutrients due to your digestive enzyme levels being too low.

613. The oily foul-smelling tar you've been shitting turns out to be your stomach lining.

614. Taking large amounts of acetaminophen in the form of paracetamol or Tylenol for your hangovers, unaware that liver failure due to acetaminophen poisoning is more common than liver failure due to drinking.

615. Waking up with swelling in your genitals and one of your legs caused by the fluid accumulating in your veins and being forced out into the surrounding tissue (a condition called edema) because your heart isn't pumping enough blood out of its left ventricle due to alcohol-induced cardiomyopathy.

616. Drinking mouthwash because you're afraid you'll die from withdrawals before the liquor store opens, then vomiting so hard you throw up chunks of flesh from the lining of your throat and end up in hospital for a month.

617. Having excruciating pains in your belly and taking a crap that looks like someone poured tar in the toilet due to acetaldehyde-induced stomach cancer.

618. You develop an inability to focus, have obsessive thoughts, anxiety, hallucinations (including hearing things) and chronic insomnia due to alcohol-induced vitamin B deficiency caused by liver damage.

619. Having oily diarrhea, feeling thirsty and rapidly losing weight due to type 3c diabetes caused by a single episode of alcohol-induced pancreatitis.

620. Getting peripheral nerve and liver damage despite drinking half as much as your partner, because being a woman you are more vulnerable to alcohol-related diseases.

621. Spending six days in the ICU with excruciating, "worse-than-kidney-stones pain" in your belly that radiates to your back with an IV morphine drip barely touching it due to alcohol-induced pancreatitis.

622. Your poop is a light beige color due to the lack of bile being produced because of late-stage fatty liver disease and being told by a doctor, "the greater the liver damage, the lighter the stool."

623. Experiencing heavy bleeding from your butt due to stage 2 rectal cancer because, as your doctor explains, "alcohol carpet-bombs the GI tract."

624. You have uncontrolled bloody diarrhea due to the blood pouring into your stomach from your esophageal varices which acts like a bowel stimulant.

625. Falling to the floor, with your jaw clenched, arms and legs stretched out, eyes rolled back, shaking and foaming at the mouth while having a seizure from sudden alcohol withdrawal.

626. Six months after a normal blood panel you are diagnosed with cirrhosis, because even if the liver is only 60% efficient it can still function "normally" and produce within range blood values.

627. Developing ulcers in your GI tract from regularly vomiting up bile.

628. Trying to remember simple usernames and passwords to online accounts you use all the time while in the early stages of hepatic encephalopathy.

629. Waking up thinking you are having a heart attack, going to the emergency room where you are given a Xanax for hangxiety and racking up an enormous bill that you are still paying off a year later.

630. People start avoiding you because of your abusive outbursts, childlike behavior and lack of empathy, which are symptoms of alcohol-induced frontal lobe brain damage.

631. Having multiple blood transfusions and surgery to stop the internal bleeding from your varices and being kept alive in the ICU for a week so your eyes and other useable body parts can be donated.

632. Waking up with a hugely inflated stomach with your alcohol-damaged liver floating in liters of fluid because it can't make enough of a protein called albumin which your blood needs to regulate blood pressure and stop its blood vessels from leaking.

633. After surgery to remove lesions from your liver you're told your stomach looks like hamburger meat.

634. Collapsing face first, breaking your jaw and biting off a piece of your tongue while seizing, all within the space of 30 seconds.

635. After a year of no alcohol, you have one drink which turns into two, then shots, then a weekend of drinking which turns into a 14-month bender at the end of which you are admitted into hospital with seriously elevated cardiac markers.

636. You develop what looks like severe bruising with uniformly purple skin on your arms, due alcohol's damaging effect on your blood platelets: a condition called alcohol-induced thrombocytopenia.

637. Developing a mass which turns out to be stage 2 breast cancer, because breast tissue is especially vulnerable to the effects of acetaldehyde and the elevated estrogen levels alcohol induces.

638. Coughing up blood on the way to the bar and being taken to hospital where you're told you have atypical pneumonia brought on by liver failure.

639. Being refused emergency surgery for an abscessed tooth while you are sitting in the dentist's chair because your blood pressure is too high, which makes you a bleed, stroke and heart attack risk.

640. After weeks of painful eating and hiccups you are diagnosed with esophageal squamous cell carcinoma as a result of decades of drinking hard liquor.

641. Drinking yourself into a state of hyperglycemia to the point your blood sugar is in the 500s.

642. Getting advanced liver disease despite normal liver function results because the markers of injury do not always show up in "compensated" cirrhosis where there are still enough functioning liver cells to compensate for those that have been replaced by scar tissue.

643. Forgetting how to drive and veering off the road because your diseased liver can't process ammonia so it has built up in your body and brain causing intermittent memory loss and confusion.

644. After a few years of heavy drinking, you develop a pain in your ear due to a cancerous tumor at the base of your tongue, half of which has to be cut away at the age of 24.

645. Staggering around and slurring your words like you're drunk, almost falling when trying to get into a chair and losing your balance – a condition called ataxia – caused by the degeneration of white matter in your brain's frontal lobes and cerebellum.

646. After drinking non-stop and barely eating for six weeks you start shaking, sweating and vomiting blood and are told you have jaundice, portal hypertension and esophageal varices at the age of 32.

647. Peeing in your sleep, because alcohol increases urine production and stops your brain communicating with your bladder wall's detrusor muscle that signals when you need to urinate.

648. Two years after being hospitalized with alcoholic pancreatitis you are diagnosed with type 3c diabetes and pancreatic cancer and are seriously considering suicide.

649. Giving up on sex in your 50s due to impotence caused by irreversible damage to the nerves in your penis as a result of alcoholic neuropathy and nutrient deficiencies.

650. Giving birth to a small, underweight baby because drinking, especially in the first trimester, restricts the amount of nutrients going through the placenta to the fetus.

651. The cashier has to swipe your credit card for you because your hands are shaking so badly from alcohol withdrawals.

652. Ending up with an irregular heartbeat, palpitations, shortness of breath and fatigue due to a mild adrenergic storm after a weekend of binge drinking: otherwise known as "holiday heart syndrome."[12]

653. Developing colon cancer because acetaldehyde promoted the development of polyps in your colon and they have turned cancerous.

654. Having a permanently red face because the enlarged capillaries have risen closer to the surface.

655. Overnight you develop jaundice, your abdomen swells up with ascites and your pee turns brown because of cirrhosis.

656. Paying for tests to find out why you have fatigue, hair loss and can't lose weight and being told it's likely due to alcohol's damaging effect on your thyroid gland leaving you with a lack of thyroid hormones.

657. Despite your lab results and liver enzymes being within range, an ultrasound shows that you have a "large focal fat mass" in your liver as well as "starry sky diffuse liver fat."

658. Ending up as a "high functioning" Wernicke-Korsakoff patient, able to toilet yourself, change your bed sheets and watch the other patients, but with no memory of ever being married, having children or your job as a college lecturer.

659. Developing chronic obstructive pulmonary disease (COPD) because the system which clears mucous and other contaminants out of your airways and sinuses has been damaged from all the

---

[12] Alcohol Binge-Induced Cardiovascular Dysfunction Involves Endocannabinoid–CB1-R Signaling

alcohol, which has also depleted your immune response, leaving your lungs unable to fight off infections.

660. Drinking your calories instead of eating proper food so you can stay drunk and skinny: a mindset commonly called "drunkorexia."

661. Waking up with a racing heart and pounding headache and looking for something to vomit into as your body tries to evacuate the toxins it has produced from metabolizing all the alcohol.

662. Your pancreas, spleen and gallbladder have to be removed after multiple episodes of acute alcoholic pancreatitis, leaving you dependent on an insulin pump, artificial enzymes to digest your food and medications costing over $5,000 a month to keep you alive.

663. The palms of your hands have symmetrical bright red blotches – a condition called palmar erythema – from alcohol-induced elevated estrogen levels and changes to your blood flow.

664. Waking up feeling nauseous and throwing up, then vomiting anything you try to eat and seeing streaks of blood in it due to combination of heartburn, acid reflux and gastritis.

665. Loud, almost painful ringing in your ear that stops you thinking and sleeping because alcohol has permanently destroyed the hair cells of your inner ear and given you tinnitus.

666. Spending hours a day in a hot bath because you're freezing cold and in pain, then occasionally watering the plants and watching TV while you live out your last days at home with end stage liver disease.

667. Being unable to remember specific words (anomic aphasia) and having poor self-deficit awareness (being unable to recognize your limitations) due to damage to your brain's frontal lobes.

668. Gaining a beer belly because alcohol stops your body burning other forms of energy, is high in calories, triggers cravings for sugar and junk food, makes you less active and spikes your cortisol levels – all of which promotes belly fat storage.

669. You wake up one morning and your stomach looks like a watermelon, your pee is rust colored and the whites of your eyes are yellow after drinking for three decades.

670. Losing your vision due to cataracts caused by the toxic byproducts of alcohol damaging the lens cells of your eye and making proteins in the lens clump together.

671. Hearing your doctor explain that a diseased liver is a bit like a sinking ship; once it has sunk it can't send out any more distress signals, which means your liver enzyme levels can be low even when your liver is badly damaged.

672. Your skin turns green – the next stage after yellow – due to a build-up of a bile pigment substance called biliverdin.

673. Having several esophageal varices blow at once, puking and filling a two-liter bucket with blood, then losing consciousness from blood loss.

674. Lapsing into a hepatic coma for two weeks during which time you are given lactulose enemas every few hours to reduce your ammonia levels.

675. Being diagnosed with type 2 diabetes and abnormally high blood sugar levels because your liver can't respond properly to insulin, which means less glucose is taken up by the liver and your pancreas wears itself out trying to release enough insulin to increase glucose uptake.

676. Being kept alive for two weeks after your lungs filled with regurgitated alcohol while you were sleeping on your back: a condition called aspirate-induced pulmonary pneumonitis.

677. Having to keep your hands under the table during meetings at work so people don't see them shaking.

678. Having an infected sore on your foot and not being able to stop drinking long enough for the antibiotics to work, thereby losing your toes after the first surgery and your foot and ankle by the third.

679. After decades of drinking your testicles have irreversibly shrunk and are barely visible due to the toxic effect of alcohol on their membranes and tissue: a condition called testicular atrophy.

680. After feeling depressed and starting to lose your memory and hearing you are diagnosed with folate deficiency syndrome and a lack of Vitamin D2 because all the alcohol has blocked your folic acid receptors and prevented your body from absorbing nutrients.

681. Looking and feeling prematurely old because alcohol wrecks collagen production and damages the end caps of your cells, called telomeres, which speeds up biological aging.

Please tell me all the ways your life got better after you quit. I have to stop drinking but my brain doesn't want me to."

From a 36-year-old drinker who isn't sure
there really is life after alcohol

Real-life examples of the life improving benefits of not drinking

682. Waking up after a night of restful sleep feeling clear headed and ready to go because your hormone levels are balanced and your circadian rhythm is back on track.[13]

683. Going from being homeless and drinking every night to having a part time job, graduating law school and becoming a law clerk seven years later.

684. No more looking in the toilet bowl and thinking, "That's probably not good."

685. Six months in, your doctor clears you to taper off your medications for gout, insomnia and heartburn.

686. Prioritizing your health and eating better means you no longer have the nutrient problems and blood sugar swings that were keeping you stuck in a crash and crave cycle.

687. No longer suffering the "wanting to crawl into a hole and die" feelings you always got after a binge.

688. Taking up mountain biking and weight training in your 60s and feeling more energetic than you did in your 20s.

---

[13] Better sleep is one of many benefits to alcohol abstinence
https://www.healio.com/news/primary-care/20240131/better-sleep-is-one-of-many-benefits-to-alcohol-abstinence

689. Looking at yourself and thinking, "Damn!" instead of "damn…"

690. No more paralyzing hangovers trying to figure out which is worse, your nausea or pounding headache.

691. The "IBS" that was making you feel weak and tired and has cost you thousands in tests, colonoscopies, supplements and special diets miraculously disappears.

692. You wake up bright and early in the morning instead of slowly regaining consciousness.

693. Having less mosquito bites, because alcohol makes your body produce more carbon dioxide and makes your sweat more concentrated, all of which attracts them.

694. Being able to drive to collect your kids or take your dog to the vet whenever you have to.

695. No more lying on the phone that your drinking is under control as you quietly open a bottle of wine mid-conversation.

696. Going to a conference where everyone gets shit-faced, waking up early the next day and being told by your boss you're the most engaged salesperson out of the 100-plus employees at the event.

697. You have the presence of mind and improved mental stability to resist the "the fuck-its" and not pour yourself a drink whenever you're stressed.

698. Choosing when and where you sleep instead of passing out unconsciousness wherever you happen to be.

699. Completing a journalism course and working on a novel two years after you were put into a care home and expected to die from liver disease at the age of 57.

700. The daily disappointment in yourself is a thing of the past.

701. Drinking water instead of booze and discovering it works like an antidepressant by increasing blood flow and oxygen to the brain.

702. Your brain starts to heal and repair itself after about a week in a process called neurogenesis.

703. No more worrying about the dreaded sweating, shaking and hallucinations the day after a bender.

704. Less missed days of work, better mental clarity, improved memory and better decision making.

705. After a week or so you experience something called "pink cloud syndrome" which is a feeling of euphoria when your brain starts rebuilding itself.

706. You inspire others not to drink when they see how great you look and how much your life has improved.

707. The airport security officer doesn't recognize you from your passport photo which was taken six years ago when you were bloated, overweight and miserable.

708. No longer having to plan your day around drinking, hangovers and withdrawals.

709. Getting on a plane for the first time in 20 years and going on a dream trip to Europe thanks to all the money you've saved over the past couple of years.

710. Generally feeling happier because alcohol forces the body down-regulate its own production of dopamine and serotonin, but now these levels are normal again.

711. Being less worried about almost everything that would upset you before.

712. Feeling mentally and physically better every day as your body starts eliminating the fat in your liver, with the knock-on effect that your blood is better purified so your brain chemicals start balancing out.

713. Experiencing the quiet pleasure of "hangover schadenfreude" on your way down to breakfast in a hotel elevator full of hungover people complaining about the smell of food.

714. Four months after getting sober your liver function tests are normal and your pancreas is no longer inflamed.

715. You become "that dependable guy" on high profile projects.

716. Your blood pressure drops around 5 to 10 points each day until it reaches normal levels because alcohol is no longer hyperactivating your central nervous system.[14]

---

[14] Alcohol-induced hypertension: Mechanism and prevention
https://pmc.ncbi.nlm.nih.gov/articles/PMC4038773/

717. Being able to deal with pressure at work without thinking, "God I need a drink."

718. No more drunken, paranoid fights with your partner, imagining what they are thinking, feeling or doing.

719. Your online chess score – or "graph of intelligence" – increases having been stuck at the same level for years.

720. No longer needing a CPAP machine because sleep apnea has gone.

721. Having money now that every cent isn't accounted for in bottles and bank charges for unauthorized overdrafts.

722. Feeling low at the beginning, but realizing that's a good thing because when you were drinking your brain wasn't making its own dopamine and serotonin and now it will have the chance to produce its own "happy chemicals" again.

723. Making and keeping memories of social events instead of them being moments in your life that are best forgotten.

724. Your cholesterol has dropped by 60 points in six months and all your other bloodwork is heading back to normal including your liver enzymes.

725. People can't wind you up for their own amusement anymore because you are far less reactive.

726. Feeling confident and able to resolve your problems rather than using alcohol to tolerate them.

727. You don't get sunburn as easily because it takes more UV light exposure to burn your skin when you don't drink.

728. Going from being in the ICU with hallucinations and high blood pressure to being pretty healthy within a couple of years.

729. Vitamin supplements and medications work more effectively because they're better absorbed.

730. Quitting your job and starting a tech company that you've wanted to do for three years, becoming massively successful and expanding so you now have eight employees.

731. Vastly improved mental health with less mood swings and feelings of despair.

732. People can't take advantage of your lapses in memory anymore.

733. You get out of bed and go to the bathroom to pee at night instead of waking up in cold, wet sheets.

734. Being able to drive out to get carpet cleaner when your dog has diarrhea late on a Friday night.

735. Your problems are now normal people's problems, not crazy, spiraling train wreck problems.

736. You can clean your teeth without gagging.

737. Dealing with things such as emails, bills, health checkups, car repairs, cleaning and laundry instead of letting everything pile up.

738. Getting up early and absorbing every second of your children's joy on Christmas morning instead of staying in bed until your hangover wears off.

739. Waking up knowing where your phone, wallet and keys are.

740. Your idiopathic (meaning unexplained) urticaria, with symptoms of anxiety, hives and swelling, magically goes away within six months.

741. Not having to lie to save your relationship, keep your job and stay in your apartment.

742. No longer feeling like you have a horrible chronic illness.

743. Your baseline cortisol level is now normal, which means you feel less anger, fear, frustration and annoyance.

744. No longer thinking about killing yourself, self-harming or being institutionalized for attempted suicide.

745. Feeling like someone has mentally turned the lights back on when you hit the 4-month mark of being sober.

746. Being asked to write wedding place setting cards and your handwriting is neat and even instead of shaky and illegible.

747. You aren't passing out, lashing out, blacking out or making a fool of yourself anymore.

748. The inflammation level from your seasonal allergies is lower and your sinuses have improved.

749. Hearing your 5-year-old ask, "Why are mommy and daddy so happy all the time now?"

750. Getting your driver's license back, finding a job and having your kids come visit you again.

751. Your ALT, AST, GGT liver enzymes and triglyceride blood work numbers fall within normal range after a couple of months of not drinking and eating right.

752. You start dating again and are no longer living like a monk due to erectile problems and perpetually being tired and hungover.

753. Having great liver panel and endoscopy results when eight years prior you were diagnosed with stage 4 cirrhosis at the age of 30 and told it would be a miracle if you made it to your 31st birthday.

754. A tooth that was slightly loose has become solid and stable because you no longer have gum disease and the tissue has regrown.

755. You are calm, happy and driven and have a purpose; instead of wasting your time, failing at relationships and self-destructing.

756. You can see your junk again; your erections are more erect and your dick looks bigger.

757. Waking up with a clear head and being able to function instead of spending the day in bed feeling like death.

758. Your liver shows signs of softening, proving that you doctor was right when he said as long it's not a puddle of mud or looks like cigarette ash it can bounce back.

759. No longer flinching at the sound of the hailstorm of glass when your recycling bin is emptied.

760. You can be romantic, charming and funny without people thinking it's just the drink talking.

761. You walk past a window and notice you're not slumping or looking at the ground because now you walk tall with your head high.

762. No more waking up at 3:00 a.m. when your blood alcohol level drops and your brain is overloaded with panic-inducing adrenaline, cortisol and glutamate.

763. Not having to constantly make the effort to pretend to be sober.

764. Always being able to trust a fart.

765. Enjoying everything there is about food: shopping for it, cooking it and savoring its flavors after all the alcohol had dulled your tastebuds.

766. Your stamina lasts for the whole entire day every day.

767. After eight months you're £1,400 better off, haven't drunk the 1,050 beers you would have, are 45lbs lighter, have more muscle, look more handsome and even got called "young man" at the age of 46.

768. You are far less reactive to life because your stress threshold and ability to deal with stress is far higher.

769. The cystic acne, with the deep lumps you can't squeeze disappears because your body is no longer pushing out the toxins from alcohol through your skin or weakening your immune system, leaving you prone to infection.

770. Your skin tans better because your body's vitamin B stores are no longer being used up processing alcohol.

771. Discovering that exercising when you're stressed sweats out the cortisol and calms you down far longer than drinking does.

772. No more ruined carpets, rugs, furniture, mattresses, sofa cushions or clothes.

773. You don't need to wear sunglasses to open the fridge door in the morning.

774. Being able to drive your kids to after school activities.

775. Having vivid, memorable, movie-like dreams because you are getting deep REM sleep.

776. Losing weight because you are no longer binge drinking and compulsively eating an extra 2,000 calories every few days.

777. Regaining IQ points with improved recall, sharper thinking, improved mental agility and better focus.

778. Having the clarity of mind to address your mental health struggles instead of constantly trying to numb them out.

779. Your rings, bracelets and shoe straps aren't tight any more.

780. You get more quality rest from four hours of sober sleep than eight hours of being passed out drunk.

781. Going from fighting to keep your job to managing a staff of 30.

782. Not having to get a liver transplant.

783. Instead of churning through partners, you are kinder, more present and more capable of having a happy, healthy, functioning relationship.

784. Being able to get pregnant after years of trying and failing because your hormones were out of whack.

785. Three months after being diagnosed with fatty liver while you were in hospital for alcohol withdrawals, your liver is practically healed.

786. Discovering morning sickness is child's play compared to the nausea and head-crushing hangovers you used to get from booze.

787. No longer having to write down a list of the lies you've told so you can repeat them accurately.

788. After a month, your knee, back and elbow pains from prior sports injuries are about 90% gone due to the absence of systemic inflammation.

789. No longer needing prescription sleep medications.

790. No more night terrors or waking up with a racing heart thinking you're going to die.

791. Your loved ones are no longer heartbroken and helpless watching you drink yourself to death.

792. Your resting heart rate goes from 92 to 66 within ten days.

793. Getting a better job because you found the time and had the focus to do some extended learning.

794. Not shitting and pissing blood every day.

795. Your dad cancels the life insurance policy he took out to pay for your funeral.

796. No longer feeling guilty, ashamed or depressed about constantly getting black-out drunk.

797. Getting far more done, far better, in less time.

798. No more kissing, groping or having sex with people you are not attracted to or don't even like.

799. After setting a hospital record for the amount of fluid drained from your abdomen, your liver damage is at stage 2 – down from stage 4 – within six years.

800. The psoriasis you had all over your body is down to a couple of spots on your elbows and knees.

801. Vacations seem to last much longer because you can experience more when you're not drunk by noon and passed out on a sun lounger all day.

802. Being able to reverse your fatty liver in three months, after your doctor predicted you had about ten years left to live.

803. Having intimate, sober, passionate sex that you can remember the next day.

804. The fatigue, depression and weight gain caused by your under-active thyroid is gradually resolving.

805. Touching your cheeks and thinking, "I can't believe this is my face; I can feel bones in there!"

806. Having the energy and time to step up and look after your aging parents.

807. Being able to drive home at night without having to call for a ride or crash on someone's couch.

808. You no longer tolerate anything that doesn't serve you well, including people, places and things.

809. Your body's ability to control its blood sugar levels has vastly improved.

810. Your life might be less exciting and dramatic, but you are calmer as well as more content and self-assured.

811. People ask for your advice because they know your judgement can be trusted.

812. The numbness and stiff joints you got in your hands every morning is going away.

813. The enamel on your teeth is no longer getting wrecked from all "The Exorcist"-style vomiting.

814. People who haven't seen you for a while are stunned because you look so much slimmer, younger and fitter.

815. When a police officer is driving behind you on your way home after a night out you are no longer struck by fear.

816. It has been a long time since you lost or broke your glasses or left them at the bar.

817. Seeing your home project ideas happen instead of just being vague ideas that never come to life.

818. You don't get colds or flu anymore because the immune cells in your upper and lower airways are better able to defend against infection. [15]

819. You develop the confidence and ability to walk away from all the other relationships in your life that aren't healthy for you.

820. No more getting the shakes at work and having to take shots in the restroom.

821. You are no longer on beta blockers and your blood pressure is within normal range.

822. Not feeling ashamed of yourself all the time.

823. Your dog snuggles you more and seems happier.

824. Being able to take medications without worrying how they will interreact with the booze.

825. Your house goes from being a hovel to a showpiece.

826. Not waking up having to pee several times a night.

---

[15] Alcohol and the Immune System
https://pmc.ncbi.nlm.nih.gov/articles/PMC4590612/

1001 REASONS TO STOP DRINKING

827. Being able to take your kids out for ice cream at 7:00 p.m. "just because."

828. Your cholesterol goes from over 300 down to 160.

829. You no longer suffer from constipation because you are so dehydrated from all the alcohol.

830. Flying to another country and being able to deal with immigration, collect your luggage and find a taxi without feeling overwhelmed.

831. Going from 50 to 80 premature ventricular contractions (heart palpitations) a day to just 5 to 15 within days of quitting.

832. No longer getting flare-ups from chronic gastritis.

833. Eating twice a day instead of twice a week.

834. Your alcoholic cardiomyopathy disappears, being the only heart disease that gets better if you stop drinking.

835. Not dying young like your parents and other members of your family.

836. After years of neglecting your yard, it's getting compliments from the neighbors.

837. Not having to power through hangovers and exhaust yourself to prove you can function.

838. Your doctor tells you to stop taking your blood pressure medications because your readings are not just normal but too low.

839. No more ER visits for stitches, concussions and broken bones.

840. You're no longer a raging, narcissistic, demanding asshole.

841. Your triglycerides go down from 500 to 70 within six months.

842. After neglecting your teeth for years, you now have a whiter smile, healthier gums and a reduced risk of dementia.

843. Showing up when your family and friends invite you over instead of canceling because you're too drunk or don't want to pay for the Uber rides.

844. Being able to adopt a rescue animal now you have the time, money and patience to look after it.

845. No more buttock-clenched races to the toilet before your ass explodes.

846. Not having to drink away the shame and humiliation of the things you did when you were drunk.

847. No longer having to watch a TV show more than once because you watched it half blacked out.

848. Your skin is glowing and smooth, your hair is thicker and your eyes are bright and clear.

849. Your bloodwork improves within a few weeks of not drinking after having been hospitalized with acute pancreatitis.

850. After nine months, the fat around your internal organs has greatly reduced and your bloated belly is shrinking.

851. Waking up to a clean fresh house instead of a stinking mess with empty bottles and food containers everywhere.

852. A potential cardiac event calculator puts your 10-year risk at 1.5%, which is down from 20% when you were drinking.

853. Going from a low-grade job as a barely functioning alcoholic to working as an executive at a major film studio, tripling your income and working with famous people.

854. No longer telling your kids, "We'll see," or "Maybe later" because you're too tired or hungover to do anything.

855. Not having to get to the bar before your friends so you can have a few drinks to stop the shakes and make yourself sociable.

856. You don't actively hate yourself anymore.

857. The red flaky eczema on your face you've spent a fortune on treatments trying to cure is gone.

858. Feeling normal as soon as you get to work at 8.30 a.m. instead of tired and useless until midday.

859. Your parents can relax and enjoy their retirement because you're no longer on the brink of being sent to prison or death.

860. Not having to replace all those lost credit cards and update your autopay settings every couple of months because you always remember to put them safely in your wallet.

861. Saving around $200 a week on Uber rides.

862. The people you despise at work are as awful as ever, but they don't ruin your day because their shit just rolls off you now.

863. Reduced medical bills and less time spent in the doctor's office.

864. Even though you're not dependent on alcohol you realize life is way more manageable without it.

865. Making eye contact with people, because your natural self-confidence has returned.

866. In just over a year your sober app says you've gained back over 2,000 hours that was previously spent drinking.

867. Summers are no longer the worst three months of the year because you're okay with wearing less clothes now you're in better shape.

868. Calmly reading your kids a story and tucking them into bed at night instead of rushing through it, eager to get back to your wine.

869. After a few months of cutting out alcohol and eating right an ultrasound shows your stage 4 fatty liver is down to stage 1.

870. Spending money you used to spend on alcohol on massages, manicures and getting your teeth fixed.

871. Your hand-eye coordination has vastly improved.

872. Going from tossing and turning with heartburn all night to getting eight hours of peaceful sleep.

873. Being able to trust that your decisions are sound and well thought out and not just a crapshoot between binges.

874. Finally having the confidence, money, time and energy to start your own company and making a success of it.

875. No more odd stabbing pains in your liver area wondering how much damage you've caused this time.

876. Being able to pay off your credit cards.

877. No more sweaty bed pillows that dry out and stink so bad the whole thing needs washing every week.

878. Saving over $10,000 in a year, plus more when you add all the reckless alcohol-associated spending.

879. Your makeup lasts longer because you aren't constantly sweating.

880. No longer having to take medications for anxiety and depression.

881. No more apologizing for offensive, dumb things you said but can't recall.

882. Being a far better parent now you're liberated from the "It's wine 30" mommy wine culture.

883. Saving on late night food deliveries that you leave forgotten outside the door, barely eat, or throw up later.

884. No more worrying if you're slurring, talking too loudly or repeating yourself.

885. No more anxiety-inducing nightmares and waking up feeling like you ran marathon.

886. Your credit score is progressing upwards.

887. Not having to hide from someone you know in the grocery store because you don't want them to see all the booze in your shopping cart.

888. Having a stronger clearer voice because your throat's not sore from all the puking and acid reflux.

889. Sending the most valuable bottles in your 1000 plus wine collection to auction, putting some of the proceeds into your kids' college fund, donating some and buying yourself a mountain bike.

890. The tingly feelings and numbness in your legs and feet are disappearing.

891. You can remember all the conversations you've had with everyone.

892. Feeling motivated to exercise when you discover how calm and positive you feel for hours afterwards.

893. Having confidence in who you are and the kind of people you want to spend time with.

894. You, your partner, your kids, your pets and your home are all happier.

895. Being able to join a Zoom call before midday on a Monday.

896. Your face is no longer bloated from booze (booze comes from the German word "bausen" meaning "bulge").

897. Demonstrating healthy habits and behaviors for your children.

898. Faced with challenging situations you are no longer flooded with waves of anxiety, just a slight ripple.

899. Better erections, more satisfying sex and higher libido because your testosterone levels have increased (applies to women too).

900. Being able to eat chips (crisps), crackers and hard vegetables because your throat is no longer in danger of tearing now your esophageal varices are fully healed.

901. No longer having to buy air freshener cans in bulk.

902. Getting in best shape of your life for an Ironman Challenge and discovering many other athletes are recovering addicts who have "scratched their need to go hard on something every day" with physical training.

903. Your criminal record isn't racking up new entries.

904. Going from stage 2 hypertension to normal blood pressure within a few months.

905. Significantly reduced hotel and restaurant bills.

906. Being able to exercise harder and longer without feeling like you're about to have a heart attack.

907. The aura migraines that often kept you in bed and miserable for 15 years have all but gone.

908. Leaving an abusive relationship because you are no longer numbing out with alcohol to tolerate it.

909. Your athlete's foot clears up within a few months.

910. Going from a lonely, overweight failure to a graduate with a PhD, wife, two kids and a job you love.

911. You are cleaner, better dressed and smell nice.

1001 REASONS TO STOP DRINKING

912. Your eye doctor says, "Your vision has actually improved."

913. Regaining custody of your children.

914. Quitting smoking, which always went along with drinking and saving close to $1,000 a month between the booze and cigarettes.

915. Your sciatica goes away after about five months.

916. Waking up feeling ready to take on the world instead of rotting in bed all day.

917. Seeing your thin, gray hair go back to being thick and black without using hair dye.

918. Waking up not hungover, going fishing, seeing your surroundings with new eyes and having the best day in a long time.

919. Choosing to be in a relationship with someone who wants to plan a life together instead of just a drinking buddy.

920. Going from feeling like an old man in your 30s to feeling like your life has just started.

921. Being asked to buy into the company you work for and being told that if you hadn't quit drinking, you wouldn't have been given the opportunity.

922. Going to the farmers' market early on a Saturday morning hangover free and able to enjoy the free cheese samples.

923. Your memory is starting to return because unlike Alzheimer's, much of the damage from alcohol-related dementia can be reversed if you stop drinking.

924. Gaining the respect of your peers, family, children, work colleagues and yourself.

925. Instead of numbing out, you cry when you're upset which gets some of the cortisol and adrenaline out of your system.

926. Wanting to go outside and walk the dog instead of treating it as a chore.

927. Your arthritis is less painful because you have less joint inflammation.

928. You now have a great relationship with your parents who you had nearly caused to divorce.

929. The chronic redness, flushing and irritation of rosacea on your face is starting to fade.

930. Going from an eviction notice, repo'd car and heart attack to having a beautiful wife, son, home, career and friends.

931. The nail fungus you had on your big toe for years is growing out.

932. Your general anxiety has decreased tenfold.

933. Keeping your promises and commitments, showing up for people and being fully engaged.

934. Your drunken arrogance is replaced with actual self-confidence.

935. Without the fatigue from drinking, you feel motivated to go to the gym.

936. Being able to drive anywhere at any time.

937. No more grey teeth and blackened tongue from red wine.

938. No longer having to Google your name after a night out to see if you embarrassed yourself because you're a celebrity and in the public eye.

939. Growing leg and armpit hair again, which is a sign your body is getting adequate nutrition.

940. You no longer have that tired, puffy "boozehound" look about you.

941. Feeling fit and confident enough to travel to and enter mountain trail ultra-running events.

942. Not waking up with a sore throat from your window-rattling snoring all night.

943. No more going to work on Monday with a killer hangover and not fully recovering until Wednesday.

944. The whites of your eyes are white again.

945. Real, two-way conversations and shared confidences instead of superficial banter and one-sided over disclosure.

946. Calmer relationships as a result of not bottling stuff up and letting rip when you're hammered.

947. No more PMS and regular menstrual cycles because your liver can actually do its job, which includes keeping your hormone levels balanced.

948. Learning a new language is easier because things "stick" better.

949. The grey matter in your brain's pre-frontal cortex starts to regrow.

950. No more acts of drunken largesse, like buying everyone drinks, giving people cash and gifts and paying for everything.

951. After around five weeks your Gamma GT level – an enzyme that surrounds the liver cells and leaks into the blood-stream if the liver is damaged – returns to normal.

952. Spending the weekend preparing for a motorcycling trip abroad having landed a better job that gives you more time off to do the things you love.

953. Losing the bags and dark circles under your eyes.

954. Not having to spend time hiding bottles of booze or decanting liquor into water bottles.

955. Always driving your car expertly with confidence, fully aware and awake.

956. Going from being bloated and fat with zero energy to looking and feeling like a new person within six months.

957. Appreciating new and exotic places and foods on vacation, instead of it being a blur of booze, burgers and hangovers like all the rest.

958. Sex is better now all your senses and body parts are revitalized.

959. You can watch a whole live concert instead of leaving to go for a drink or to the restroom every 30 minutes.

960. You no longer fear visiting the doctor's office or dread seeing the results of your blood tests.

961. Seeing and appreciating the beauty in the world instead of telling yourself life is boring and pointless.

962. Your partner no longer winces at your breath in the morning.

963. Your hair and fingernails grow faster and stronger.

964. No longer qualifying for a liver transplant because you're not sick enough to require a new organ.

965. No longer saying you need a vacation to recover from your vacation.

966. Checking through your bank and credit card statements is no longer the painful and horrifying ordeal it once was.

967. Graduating from college, getting your dream job and closing on your first home in your 40s, having pissed away your 20s and 30s.

968. After six months your nose is no longer red veined and swollen.

969. Permanently owning an iPhone, vacuum cleaner, TV and a laptop instead of pawning them to buy booze.

970. Having the time and focus to fix your gaming computer after two years of it gathering dust.

971. Folding the laundry that's in the dryer and putting it away instead of pulling things out of a heap.

972. Having the money to fly to another state to see your favorite singer perform two nights in a row.

973. Your kids no longer have to wake you up and ask you to do things before you start drinking.

974. Your beer gut has disappeared and you can see your feet for the first time in years.

975. Training to be a firefighter and getting straight A grades in your EMT class which you couldn't do as an undergrad because you were too drunk in class.

976. You're a better judge of someone's personality and attractiveness when you go on dates instead of seeing them through beer googles and taking them home.

977. You no longer have cardiac arrhythmias.

978. No longer craving the class A drugs that went along with the drinking.

979. Cleaning and flossing your teeth every morning instead of just swilling mouthwash.

980. Going from drinking every day and having the shakes, to getting sober and becoming a drug counselor.

981. At 46 your brain fog has gone and you're as sharp you were at 20.

982. Going from being unemployed with severe depression to having a job you enjoy, your own place and being an active and present parent.

983. People are sure you've had work done because your face looks younger and lifted.

984. Becoming a professional mountain biker and building bike parks for billionaires after going to prison for four years for an alcohol-related crime in your 20s.

985. Being able to answer the phone and talk coherently at any time of day or night.

986. No more having to contour your face with makeup to create cheekbones because you actually have them.

987. Feeling sharp, smart, unfazed and ready for anything life throws at you.

988. People are no longer able to say, "You wouldn't remember this from last night, but…"

989. You no longer tolerate demanding, rude, unstable people.

990. Instead of going to the bar after work you go to the gym, exercise, go home, cook, eat, shower and sleep like a baby.

991. You are winning your 12-year battle with anxiety and depression and rediscovering emotions like optimism and joy.

992. You face the things you were ignoring; remember the things you were trying to forget and deconstruct your problems until they make sense.

993. Going from daily cramps and diarrhea to normal bowel function within days.

994. Just being happy for the craziest little things like hearing a bird singing in a tree.

995. Waking up in safe, familiar surroundings with your keys, money, phone and credit cards still in your possession.

996. Having once been a functional alcoholic, you regain your health within a few months with the help of therapy and eating better.

997. Your cellulite starts to disappear after a couple of weeks.

998. Your mother's last memories of you on her deathbed at 2:00 a.m. are of you being fully present, articulate and sober.

999. 12 weeks after being hospitalized for pancreatitis and fatty liver that's on the verge of alcoholic hepatitis your bloodwork comes back within normal range.

1000. The episodic cluster headaches you've been having for the last 20 years have not come back.

1001. You have the time to learn who you are and realize that you are a whole and complete person, whether you're single, partnered, have kids or not.

PART 2

How, what and why people drink

Snapshots from Britain, Ireland, Romania, Moldova, Russia, Finland, Germany, South Africa, Kenya, India, South Korea, Japan, China, The Cook Islands, Australia and Greenland

Britain: The Star Wars tavern of Europe

I'm from the UK and the biggest distinction I've seen between this country and others is the drinking culture itself. In England – especially in the North – when a certain subsector of society goes to the pub with one mission: to get totally fucked up. And that inevitably leads to all kinds of problems, namely violence.

On an average night you can expect to see numerous fights, in pubs and on the streets, usually over nothing more than looking at someone the wrong way, inadvertently touching them on the way to the bar or accidentally spilling their drink.

I've seen pubs turn into war zones and women collapsed in gutters covered in vomit with their shoe heels broken off. I once saw a guy punched in the face and have his eyeball pop out.

Other than that, there's the usual national embarrassment of people pissing on the pavements, lying in the road,[16] flattening people's front gardens, vomiting in public areas, getting naked, chanting slogans at two in the morning, waving their genitalia around or terrorising everyone on public transport.

Some lads also seem to have a drop pants reflex which triggers after a few pints when they all have to show their arses.

On one occasion I had to get an early train for work and walked through Leeds city centre to the station at 4:00 a.m. The clubs were throwing everyone out and there were casualties everywhere. It was total carnage.

---

[16] Photo from The Daily Telegraph UK newspaper
https://www.telegraph.co.uk/multimedia/archive/03539/manchester_353936 4b.jpg

The police were out in force and people were singing, puking and fighting. I'll never forget seeing paramedics treat someone while a couple of scumbags snuck in and ransacked the ambulance.

Even in Las Vegas with tons of people drinking on The Strip you won't see the barbaric behaviour you get in the UK. Forget self-respect or dignity. It's like a non-stop American college frat boy hazing ritual.

And don't get me started on Brits abroad. The idiots and troublemakers in any foreign country are always British tourists. The joke in Spain is that the summer season hasn't started until a drunk Brit has fallen off a balcony.

When I left England after 20 years, I realised I'd spent most of my youth in a pub, met my wife in a pub and I even worked in the whisky industry. Yet I was considered a pretty modest drinker back home. I'd have a few beers after work once or twice a week, maybe a bit more at weekends and drink to the point of memory loss every so often. By UK standards I was pretty average.

After I moved to Germany, I got a new doctor and the first thing he did was order blood work. I was shocked to find my liver health was really bad. Getting it under control took six months of zero booze.

Because routine bloodwork and physicals aren't really a thing with the UK's National Health Service, I'm sure a huge portion of British adults are really damaging themselves without realising it.

Or maybe they do, but they're so miserable they just don't care. To be fair to the Brits they have seen their once great nation and standard of living crumble over the past twenty years.

As well as the shitty weather they suffer from wages that have barely risen in almost two decades, ever-increasing house prices, theft and knife crime, terrible traffic, potholes everywhere and the relentless influx of people who don't align with their culture all cramming themselves in on what feels like an even smaller island.

Perhaps this also explains why Britain's older generation are quietly annihilating themselves behind closed doors every night, putting away a bottle of wine or two to temporarily escape the dystopian nightmare of their once great country's decline.

One bright spot in this general dismal picture is that more young people are choosing not to drink.[17] They're much more focused on their economic future along with wellness, technology and social media.

Or perhaps growing up they saw their fat dad falling off a barstool and their trashed mother passed out on the kitchen floor and just decided to take a different path.

British women win an Olympic gold for binge drinking

At the age of 23 I've been put off drinking for life because of my mother's generation, a.k.a., Gen X. They all drink way more than the recommended number of units of alcohol a week because they grew up thinking the wine and cocktail culture was glamorous and cool.

None of them thinks they have a problem or wonders what they are doing to themselves. Their fridges are full of fancy craft gins, flavoured vodkas and Pino Grigio and they see nothing wrong with posting pictures of themselves with massive wine glasses in their hands on a weekday afternoon.

This old wine o' clock Bridget Jones culture"just makes me cringe. It's like they're pretending to be young and progressive even though most of them have grandkids and are on their second divorce.

Then there's the girls around my age who pre-game with Prosecco before heading out onto streets in minus degree temperatures dressed like strippers. These are the same ones who go on holiday to places

---

[17] Nearly 30% of young people in England do not drink, study finds
https://www.theguardian.com/society/2018/oct/10/young-people-drinking-alcohol-study-england

like Magaluf and Ibiza and get so fucked up they'll have sex under the table in a bar and compete to see who can shag the most guys.

They start off with their makeup plastered on, all decked out in the sluttiest gear with the intention of going out to get leathered. Then hours later they'll be crouching on a street corner puking their guts out or squatting with their knickers down to their ankles peeing in public and laughing at themselves.

Do females from other countries behave like this? No, because they don't get shit-faced like the Brits.

I am not being mean when I say this. British women are officially a global embarrassment. According to a recent survey[18] they are the biggest binge drinkers of the world. And I bet they are even further up the chart than the reports say because people who drink a fuck-ton always lie on questionnaires.

Put it this way, my mum and her friends are wasted even before they go out to drink! Once I had to take one of them to hospital after she fell off a table trying to dance. Another one peed herself in the back of my car and tried to hide it by sliding off the seat as she got out.

When they get together, they tell the same stories, scream and shout and get ridiculous. Then after a while they'll get all moody, can't walk straight and start picking fights. It's always the same.

That's what did it for me, seeing how being drunk affected their reasoning and demeanor and how their personalities changed. And all the walking dead hangovers the next day.

Officially, Gen X women in their late 40s and 50s are among the heaviest drinkers of all and I will never be like them. Call me uptight

---

[18] 'Wine o'clock' culture blamed for UK women being biggest boozers in world: Shock report reveals one in four get hammered each month
https://www.dailymail.co.uk/health/article-12720545/Wine-oclock-UK-women-biggest-boozers-world.html

I don't care, it's a "No" from me. And I'm not the only one that thinks like this.

My age group, Gen Z is drinking way less even than the millennials (who drink less than boomers) because we actually care about our health and don't want to look like absolute idiots.

Let's talk about the drunken Irish stereotype

For the American tourist arriving in Dublin to explore the pubs in its iconic Temple Bar area you might as well be visiting an Epcot-style Ireland experience. This popular initiation into "Oirish" culture requires you to knock back pints of Guinness in a stale aired standing room only pub with the requisite traditional band crammed in the corner.

It's full-on shamrock and leprechaun Irishness distilled to maximum strength where you get to take part in some kind of public improv stage show. And you'll need to rob a bank before you go because Temple Bar has the most rip-off pubs in the country!

So as an Irishman and resident of The Republic of Ireland – i.e. Southern Ireland – I'd like to introduce you to the real situation regarding the drinking culture here on this lush, windswept island facing directly into the Atlantic miles off the west coast of England.

If you didn't already know, us Paddys are quite a talkative lot. We like to congregate in tight spaces and drink copious quantities of beer or whiskey for sessions (also called "lashes" or "seshs") or "lashes" which can last many hours.

Unlike our British cousins who get loud and aggressive, the Irish are amusing drunks who tell stories, sing and dance and maintain a level of agreeableness mostly without vomiting, fighting or passing out. Except on St Patrick's Day.

Paddy's Day is a ritual of collective debauchery where we all unite to experience what it truly means to be Irish. It's the perfect storm of drinking to feel masculine, drown our sorrows and enjoy the "craic."

It's also the one day of the year where we shamelessly demonstrate to the world that their stereotypical ideas about us are true.[19]

People identify us as drinkers and partiers which to us is something of a validation and a national identity. Instead of shying from it we celebrate it! And rightly so. Because on top of being a great PR exercise for the country, Paddy's Day brings in over €70 million from tourists as well as boosting the profits of pubs all over the world.

Would you believe in America they spend $5 billion celebrating on our behalf. That's quite incredible don't you think? And have you seen Chicago? They even turn their river green!

But back to the real question. What are our drinking habits on a daily basis? Being at an age where I am young enough to have experienced a couple of decades of it myself without inflicting too much brain damage, I consider myself qualified to speak on behalf of my fellow Irishmen.

Yes, the answer is yes, we drink a lot. The latest figures are something like 400 pints of beer or ten litres per year of pure alcohol in various forms.[20]

But really is this a terrible amount considering what we have to deal with? First of all, there's the weather. Being outdoors 'til nine in the evening is only bearable for maybe three months of the year.

The rest of the time it's pishing down and freezing cold. So we either huddle up indoors and drink to stay warm, or run to the nearest pub with a cosy fireplace and huddle together to share stories and laugh.

---

[19] Irish Drunks | Season 5 Ep. 10 | FAMILY GUY
https://www.facebook.com/FamilyGuy/videos/521111912776774/
[20] New study shows average Irish person drinks equivalent of 400 pints yearly
https://www.joe.ie/news/400-pints-alcohol-study-797792

Pub culture is in our DNA and has always been a part of our history. There are around 7,000 pubs in our little country which is why almost everyone lives within walking distance of one. The pub in many ways replaces the large, comfortably furnished front room that is often missing from where we live.

Which brings me to reason number two for why we drink: our crappy, expensive, cold, damp living accommodation. Before I explain this situation, I must point out that due to our long and troubled history alcohol remains our main method for coping. Not just because it's the least shameful, but because growing up it was so ubiquitous it feels like the only choice.

Honestly to say there's a housing crisis in this country is an understatement. Too many people are chasing too few properties which means rental and house prices have gone through the roof. Dublin is the only capital city in the world where you will pay Ritz Carlton prices for a rundown studio apartment.

You can make a ton of money working for tech in Dublin, but housing will take it all away. To afford the cheapest house in Ireland you'd have to make at least €150,000, which puts you in the top 1% of earners.

Yet the government won't build affordable accommodation. Strangely enough many of our politicians are landlords and make a lot of money through property rentals. I wonder why there's no incentive for them to tackle the problem...?

Which brings me to reason number three for why we drink. The government. The apparent incompetence of the Irish government is something of an old tradition and an excuse for a lot of what goes on. It's extremely hard to believe that Ireland is the richest country in the EU because there's so much that needs fixing.

Our quality of life is terrible with poverty, homelessness, sub-standard housing and our public services and healthcare are a joke. Yet everything is ridiculously expensive. There have been many protests about the cost of living and rampant immigration but the government does nothing.

To the outside world everything looks fine. Dublin is a beautiful example of Irish heritage and offers world class hospitality. If you are a visitor you will surely have a grand time.

What you won't see is what's behind the scenes: the people who live here sitting in their tiny over-priced, apartment or grotty room in some old, rundown house while the stupendously rich tax dodgers and windbag politicians carry on without a care in the world.

For the ordinary person life in Ireland as a whole has no chance of getting better anytime soon. It's all for the rich and the greedy. Sorry, all this has pissed me off. I'm off to the local for a pint.

Romania's real horror story

Romania – the home of Dracula's Transylvania – is basically two countries: one is urban and dynamic and the other is rural, poor and stuck in the past, with people having toilets in their front yards and living on less than €6 a day. The vast majority of Romanians including me live in these rural villages surrounded by fairytale scenery with Disney-style castles everywhere.

You want to know why I drink? Unlike the Romanian people who grew up during the communist regime and learned to hide what they really think and say only the "good things" I am going to give it to you straight.

Other countries have nice roads, lots of good high street stores, on-time public transportation and good paychecks. You can fill your fridge with food, buy furniture and buy a car after working for a few months. In Romania it's the exact opposite.

We get taxes on top of taxes, have barely enough for food and hardly ever buy new stuff. There are virtually no good stores and a new car is something you plan to buy for a decade. A house is impossible without huge bank credit. So you are kind of fucked no matter what you want to do.

We joined the European Union and receive funds to make things better. The problem is they are mainly put into building personal fortunes. Our taxes and EU grants basically line the pockets of politicians, government officials and their buddies through arranged contracts and deals to fund vanity projects, for example, a €400 million church.

We still don't have a freaking highway from one side of the country to the other, but we have Ferraris, Lamborghinis and Teslas parked on the side of the road.

The sad thing is half the population doesn't care about the sleaze because they are either too old or have left to work in another country.

Many are young people like me who can't leave because they are too poor and/or uneducated and the rest are the politicians, government employees and people too rich to care. This is why we have historically elected politicians who have been sentenced for fraud, abuse of funds etc. who change the laws[21] to favour the corrupt.

A lot of us cope with our lives by binge drinking. Street drugs here are mostly non-existent, so anyone who would otherwise smoke weed, do cocaine or pop pills does alcohol. All this has led us to achieve first place on the list of countries with the highest alcohol consumption[22] and also to be known as the "drunkest country on earth."

Our usual choices are beer and wine and strong fruit-based liquors all of which are super cheap. Distilling your own alcohol is not only legal

---

[21] Protesters in Romania hold huge demonstration over government 'anti-corruption U-turn'
https://www.youtube.com/watch?v=CFysVucBFyE
[22] Our World in Data: In which countries do people drink the most alcohol?
https://ourworldindata.org/data-insights/in-which-countries-do-people-drink-the-most-alcohol

here but really common. The men make their own liquor which is basically rocket fuel and feels like it's burning holes in your stomach!

Historically, drinking in Romania is a code of manliness and how men bond so it's something that is done more or less without shame or concern for the harms that can come from it. So the alcohol industry targets young men with depictions of camaraderie, toughness and adventure.

For those of us with a drinking problem it doesn't help that having a small amount of alcohol in the morning to aid digestion has been the traditional Romanian way to start the day for centuries.

Even when I was a boy, I was given a sip before meals to increase my appetite and never grew up thinking of alcohol as being something bad.

Drinking and driving is not a problem as long as you don't cause an accident. Nobody will frown upon you for drinking or being drunk when you're in line at the local store at 7:00 a.m. to buy a cheap plastic bottle of the local rotgut. It's just a part of our culture.

The first sign that I had a serious problem hit me when I was 34 and began to feel sick if I stopped drinking. That was when I knew my health was under threat and I had to do something. Even though we have a drinking culture being an alcoholic is taboo, so getting help is difficult.

Private psychotherapy is quite a luxury, costing around €100 a session. I couldn't afford that so I joined the free online Alcoholics Anonymous meetings out of Bucharest via Zoom.

The weird thing is living here you never think you're an alcoholic because people like that are portrayed on TV as old guys drinking cheap booze living lonely, sad lives. Because of this young men like me don't think the dangers apply to them.

In Moldova "you're not a person if you don't drink"

For many years Moldova has held the record for drinking more alcohol per person than almost any other place in the world.[23] In case you were wondering where Moldova is, it's a country about the size of Maryland on the border of Ukraine.

We Moldovans drink, bleed and piss alcohol. Cirrhosis is our third leading cause of death after heart disease and cancer and one in four people here dies of an alcohol-related illness.

Almost everybody in Moldova makes their own wine. It's even used to pay people for small jobs being valued at around 50 cents a bottle.

It's a tradition passed down by our parents, grandparents and all their predecessors. I used to make 300 liters of it every year. We have converted our forests in wine yards mostly. Due to the rougher climate in the north people also make alcohol from things like apples, plums and sugar beets, which they drink mainly to keep warm.

Kids here are brought up with the idea that you are not a proper citizen unless you drink. Like all my friends I started at the age of 12. I believed alcohol was linked to masculinity and drinking more than the other boys meant you were the strongest. By the time Americans turn 21 most of us are already alcoholics!

I used to drink for relief from worry and to make myself indifferent to the chaos. All the government corruption and political instability here makes life very stressful. There is a lot of poverty, misery and hopelessness in Moldova and nothing for the young people to do.

I strongly believe the drinking culture here is encouraged as a way of keeping the population passive. People don't organize themselves or protest if they're drunk all the time.

---

[23] "You're Not a Person if You Don't Drink."
https://time.com/5654052/moldova-drinking-problem/

Because of the economic situation it's hard to find a job and you can't start a business unless you can afford to pay bribes. I tried running a restaurant but could not keep up with the extortion from the mafia. They would send people dressed up as officials to invent problems and charge me fines. There was no way to survive. This is why everyone is leaving to work in Italy.

When I found out I had pancreatitis at the age of 39 the choice to quit alcohol was made for me. The doctor told me a part of my body was rotting inside. To suddenly stop drinking like that was hard but necessary.

As an alcoholic I found it hard to get help. We are seen as a burden on society and morally depraved. I was lucky that Alcoholics Anonymous and their 12-Step program was around when I needed to get sober.

Once a week everyone crammed into a small room in a residential building in Chisinau. There were mothers with their daughters and fathers with their sons and single adults of all ages.

Being anonymous was very important because of the stigma around alcoholism. The prejudice against women drinkers is even worse. If their employer finds out they will definitely lose their job.

In the Soviet era back in the 1990s if you were diagnosed with an alcohol or drug addiction you were put on a national registry which ruined your chances of being employed. That register is still in place.

Family doctors will also tell employers if someone has a drinking problem which also stops people asking for help.

People were suspicious about AA because they wondered what the catch was. Trust in any kind of free service here is extremely low. These meetings no longer operate as far as I know, but we still have helplines, rehab centers and churches which provide space where people can meet to discuss their problems.

Everyone here has a family member who is addicted to alcohol. Most men don't live past 68. It's a tragedy because this country has so much to offer. We have beautiful countryside, great food, museums, gardens, honest, welcoming people and our claim to fame is we have the biggest wine cellar in the world![24]

Gen Z Russian here

Around 20 to 30 years ago Russia had a drinking problem, but this is mostly no longer true of today's younger generation. I'm a 22-year-old female medical student and like me, everyone I know either doesn't drink or drinks very little.

Today the drinking culture has changed[25] and the old stereotype of Russians drinking vodka like water is gone. If you drink vodka daily now you're seen as a lowlife alcoholic; you're weak and you will not survive the winter.

During Yeltsin's Russia people drank to escape reality and to protest against the anti-alcohol policies of the Communist Party. A binge drinking culture was formed and people would drink themselves to death or be reduced to human rubble by the age of 40.

Vodka is still very popular but sparkling wine and beer are starting to take over. The younger generation of today drinks mostly beer and has adopted a more casual, sociable way of drinking. We drink in groups and do not isolate ourselves just to get drunk.

A lot of students will drink vodka, beer and wine together in the pubs and bars which are Western style. We never drink alone. After we leave university most of us will stop drinking completely, or will choose things like low alcohol hard seltzers or only drink on holidays.

---

[24] The Biggest Wine Cellar in the World: Milestii Mici Winery
https://www.youtube.com/watch?v=PwCv7if2apQ
[25] Russian alcohol consumption down 43%, 2019 WHO report says
https://www.bbc.com/news/world-europe-49892339

Our focus on living a healthy life has meant that the under 30s are not obsessed with the old drinking culture. We are conscious of the link between alcohol and illness and do not want to look like a fool when we are drunk and get shamed on social media.

We also saw what happened to our parents and relatives during the collapse of the 1990s. Due to massive inflation there was hunger, unemployment and a fear of the unknown, all of which led to extremely heavy drinking. I heard that we even had a permanently drunk president who was tipsy when he spoke to the US president on TV, which is embarrassing.

There are still a few of the typical "Russian alcoholic" types but nowhere as many as before. Older members of my family drink in each other's houses not pubs. Drinking parties for teens and adults also happen at home and include a proper spread of food with lots of salty and fatty snacks after every sip or shot.

Another reason for the overall decline in drinking in Russia is that more people have cars, and drunk driving is considered very uncool. Our employers also have a zero-tolerance policy against being drunk, which instantly means a pink slip.

Finally, alcohol is expensive now due to ever-increasing taxes, which the government spends on fighting alcoholism.

Sadly, there is a feeling of instability since the Ukraine invasion. But Russian Gen Z will not turn to vodka as the solution for our sorrow. The turmoil of war and economic crisis is already enough. We want negotiations[26] but nobody talks about peace anymore.

---

[26] Propaganda Fails to Catch Up with Russia's Generation Z
https://www.wilsoncenter.org/blog-post/propaganda-fails-catch-russias-generation-z

Finland: "Binge drinking at home in our underpants!"

I'm an engineer based in Helsinki and have lived in quite a few countries around the world, including the UK. If I was to compare the Finnish drinking culture to Britain's, I'd say the main difference is sociability.

On the whole, Finnish people are quite serious, unsmiling and anti-social as a natural state. Being inward-looking, private people, we also tend prefer our own company. During Covid it was necessary to keep a social distance of 2 meters. We joked that this would be hard to maintain, because we never usually get this close to each other!

Alcohol gives us social courage. In Finland it's completely normal to say to someone, "Do you want to get drunk?" We don't go drinking. We go drunking! It's kind of understood that we don't do this during workdays but on weekends we get smashed.

Usually you start at someone's place and are pretty much shit-faced by the time you get to a bar at around 22 to 24. The next day we will talk with pride about how drunk we got. I think it's fair to say that binge drinking is totally normalised here.

In the smaller towns outside of the cities the weekend rule doesn't really apply. Drinking alone whenever you feel like it is pretty much the done thing. It's almost like it's not even supposed to be fun. Getting drunk makes the time pass quicker, which is understandable given our long, dark, freezing winters when the country turns into Mordor for five months of the year.

Inspired by this common practice we now have this thing called "pantsdrunk" or "binge drinking at home in our underpants." You just sit down, shut up and get wasted, preferably while online and alone. I guess it makes people feel like they're part of some virtual extended family.

Our Ministry of Foreign Affairs even had two emojis[27] designed to promote this cultural norm to the rest of the world. Yes, getting drunk in isolation is considered a good thing! If you don't drink to oblivion, you kind of get left out.

You may find it hard to believe, but Finland has been ranked no.1 on the United Nations' "World Happiness Report" for the past seven years. We are also a model country and an example to the world of how things should be run according to the World Economic Forum.

This is because Finland is a welfare state and the government looks after our basic needs throughout our lives and also provides free community services for the citizens. So I think by "happiness" what they really mean is safety, reliability, stability and social security. (Unless they are counting all the kids who come here, excited to see Father Christmas in Lapland!)

Nobody has to worry about paying for medical care or education and we receive allowances for things like accommodation and a pension, which is important in a country that has one of the highest unemployment rates in Europe, especially if you are a foreigner.

Our top happiness index ranking is also because we are brought up to have lowered expectations as per the Law of Jante, which is a cultural concept deeply ingrained in Scandinavian societies.[28] It essentially distills down to "You're not to think you are anything special. You're not to imagine yourself better than anyone else and you're not to think you are good at anything."

This has basically given us the Nordic lack of drive or "lagom" culture where mediocre is seen as better than excellent, which is pretty soul destroying when you think about it. It's like being pre-programed with low self-esteem, which is basically the root of depression.

---

[27] Forget hygge, let's all get päntsdrunk
https://www.bbc.com/bbcthree/article/8c1960fc-5a7f-4f4a-9e82-d9e774c4ee5a
[28] Law of Jante
https://en.wikipedia.org/wiki/Law_of_Jante

Finnish life is portrayed to the world as safe, cozy and modest. Everyone can pursue their personal dreams but only if they don't involve material wealth or being anything other than average. Because of such instilled beliefs if you see someone who is rich it is normal to ask "what's wrong with that person?"

The idealized depictions of our Nordic model do not give the full picture. It's certainly not all woodland walks, saunas, photogenic families and kaakao by the fireside. We still have serious social problems that nobody talks about because of our "shush shush" out of sight out of mind mentality.

The level of domestic abuse here is among the highest in Europe.[30] It is not unusual to see women picking up their kids from daycare wearing sunglasses or not being seen for days. Many Finns go to work until Friday, then hit "Alko" (our state-owned chain of liquor stores) on the way home and get hammered until Sunday, during which time they'll get mad at their wife/husband or kids.

Alcohol related crime committed by unemployed young men is also spiraling. Xenophobia is a serious problem and we are high on league tables for stress, depression and suicide with alcohol usually involved. We also have quite a lot of homeless alcoholics and our health services are starting to break down.

According to the government's own figures Finnish men consumed an average of 13 litres of pure alcohol a year[33] which realistically puts us second to Belarus in the World Health Organization's 2024 global rankings.[34] Yet for some reason we are placed at 16th.

---

[30] Report: One in three women in Finland experience relationship violence https://yle.fi/a/3-12204299

[33] Finish Institute for Health and Welfare: High risk alcohol use is still common although total consumption has decreased https://thl.fi/en/-/high-risk-alcohol-use-is-still-common-although-total-consumption-has-decreased

[34] Global Drinking Demographics https://alcohol.org/guides/global-drinking-demographics/

We most definitely are better off than some countries and I love my fellow Finlanders for their authenticity and earnestness, but there is no way we are close to being the happiest unless you count the effect of alcohol. There is a short video by VICE News that gives quite a good insight into this subject.[35]

The government does a good job with providing the basic necessities and good public facilities, but the statistics do not take the mental health of the country into account and the abject loneliness that is rife here.

A lot of people here say, "Finland is the happiest country in the world because all the sad people just kill themselves." Sadly, there's some truth in this.

Drinking is the German way of life

German alcoholic here. I have decided to live without alcohol and I am currently in rehab. As I sit here in my room, these are my considered thoughts on this subject. Drinking is a part of the German society. Even at sport clubs it is usual to drink some beer after the training or a match. In a lot of companies, a beer after work is expected.

It is socially acceptable to go to the market and drink a schoppen of wine at 10:00 a.m. on Saturday with your neighbours. At Christmas there are all the open-air markets with Glühwein (warm mulled wine) and every kind of schnapps you could imagine which is frequently given as gifts.

You can also legally drink here at the age of 14 with your parents' consent and buy beer at 16. Adults see drunk kids as being funny rather than concerning and think getting drunk is a rite of passage. Also, if

---

[35] Is Finland Really The Happiest Country In The World? https://www.youtube.com/watch?v=9FPU4F-Ajh8

you are male and you choose not to drink your manliness will be questioned.

When there is any sort of social gathering or holiday there will be beer and schnaps. Oktoberfest is an example. Every year six million people visit Oktoberfest and the tents serve alcohol on an industrial scale to 100,000 people at the same time for two weeks.[36]

People don't just sip a few glasses in these tents. They get smashed, vomit and pass out. It's pretty much a battle ground. But nobody really worries about it. They will just say "Oh that person has a problem but it's their business not ours." Normally the rest of the time we drink lots of beer but don't set out to get wasted.

The other thing here is alcohol is ridiculously cheap and you can buy it everywhere. It's mostly in the cashier area when you go to check out, so even if you didn't want it, you may buy it on impulse.

At the Lidl store you can buy a 500ml can of beer with 7.9% vol. for the equivalent of 70 cents which is less than sparkling water. The poorer you are, the easier they make it for you to become an alcoholic. My friend works in a grocery store and says the ratio of returns is about 10 glass alcohol bottles to every one glass water or soft drink bottle.

At least the government tries to help if you do get in trouble. When you commit a crime while you are drunk you can get a lower sentence. You will often get more empathy for losing your license for DUI than for suffering from depression.

The healthcare system is also here to help you if you want to stop drinking. I have been in a rehab for three months and it is all free. Without this system I would never be able to manage my situation. The hospital bills in other countries must really add to people's stress.

---

[36] Oktoberest YouTube shorts
https://www.youtube.com/shorts/_P8YdfQBlSY

There was a big outcry when weed was legalized here but no one cares about alcohol consumption. People don't realize you can develop liver failure after just a few years of binge drinking. It's quite fun at the beginning, but the more your organs deteriorate the more it becomes a psychological burden.

Having suffered with this myself I think all bottles of alcohol should have a proper liver warning, with a picture on it like cigarettes have for lung failure.

South Africa makes me drink

Here in South Africa, it's a competition between what will kill us the fastest, the government or the alcohol. People drink because the shit that's going on here would overwhelm them otherwise. Alcohol is a way of coping with depression because there are very few things to help with this besides religion.

To be a black man here there is a mentality where you don't talk about your feelings and use drinking to cope and can die too early because of it. A lot of rural families that live in homesteads have a history of deaths caused by alcohol[37]. They might have freak accidents, get poisoned by some illicit brew or get found dead in the roadside.

It is all due to being poor, having no real employment and mainly having no hope. Everything is expensive, even if you are working or middle class. It's fucked-up. People have become accustomed to poverty to the extent that they say they are fine, but deep down they are crying inside.

I have three family members in my township telling me they're down broke. I mean the kind of broke where you don't even have salt. Every time I go into a grocery store, I see price increases in essentials and I

---

[37] Wahu's 7 children were taken by the invisible monster that is alcoholism. https://www.facebook.com/watch/?mibextid=oFDknk&v=248261665008043&rdid=lAKYeaano1aHS9wp

have to use my credit card to pay part of the rent. You have to cut down on a lot of things and still can't get through the month.

I stayed in Cape Town after getting my university degree, but I often feel like drowning my worries because I cannot find proper well-paying work. Finding a good fulltime job here without money or social connections is very difficult so now I have an online business.

The people in power do not care or see our struggle. It's like the government is some other entity and not part of our lives. Everyone just grabs what they can for themselves.

Corruption is rampant because there are no consequences. We have politicians with zero skill or intelligence who do nothing to help their people. They know that once they get into power at any level they can do whatever they want and keep getting richer and all the masses will do is talk and get drunk.

All the government's lies and empty words, disappointments and crime has an impact on everyone's overall mental state. I'm probably never going to experience what it means to feel patriotic or good or proud about my country, because no matter who we vote for nothing changes.

This is a big reason why so many turn to alcohol and get addicted to it.. When the sale of alcohol was banned for two months during Covid to stop people gathering, there was looting across the country with people smashing down the doors of bottle stores.

There are gangs everywhere, half of the population is unemployed and nothing gets fixed. Driving into town dodging taxis and potholes, having to watch out for hijackers standing at the robots when they go red and all the urban decay is enough to drive anyone to drink!

The government must think a broken-down, babalas population is easier to control so they are giving Western liquor corporations the freedom to turn us into drinking zombies. But it is probably because they are just greedy and want to profit from all the tax on the alcohol sales.

Vast bottle shops are opening everywhere selling their products. To maximise their income, now the government wants our local brews to be banned for being too cheap and cutting into Big Alcohol's sales, which means less tax revenue for them.

The drink corporations are very aggressive and have taken over all spheres of social life. I have seen strawberry flavoured gin advertised like it's some kind of milkshake and sport has turned into alcohol sponsored events where people just drink and the sport is an afterthought. Just count the liquor ads during a televised rugby or cricket match!

What is the impact of kids growing up seeing all this being normalized? They are being programmed to be long term consumers. What you must realise is that nearly three quarters of Africans are under the age of 30, which is a huge potential market for these companies. Growing up it was cigarettes that were advertised everywhere. Now it's alcohol.

Young, single and drunk in Kenya

I'm 29 and used to build backend software systems mainly for enterprises here in Nairobi in Kenya. I was working long hours holed up in my room, coding all day for these companies and making over $3,500 a month.

The weekends were for "kupiga sherehe," let loose party time and weekdays were for work. A lot of heavy drinkers here don't think they have a problem because of this sherehe lifestyle image and I was one of them. I did it mainly to attract women.

Here the guys flex by popping bottles of expensive alcohol to prove they are living well to impress strangers in a club. Yet many of them don't have good bed sheets, car tires or even decent home furnishings. In Kenya there's this pressure to look rich even if you are not, unlike most other countries in Africa. Unfortunately, this can make you a target as I found out.

As well as the party life a lot of the music here now involves alcohol. This one, "Dax - Dear Alcohol"[38] is close to my heart. Notice the printed words at the beginning. It is interesting to me that he changed them for the latest version of this song, which is featured at the end of this book.

"Sip" by Joeboy and "People" by Libiancare are also relatable to me. They made me think I was not alone and didn't have a problem because everyone drinks to deal with the pressures of life. Getting drunk used to be looked down on. It wasn't normalised like it is today.

One night downtown my drink was spiked and I went unconscious. All the money that I had and my phone was stolen, but they left my documents so someone called my brother who took me to hospital. I was in a coma for 10 days in the ICU, with machines attached all over me. This should have made me stop drinking but it didn't.

It was two months after this I met my girlfriend at a nightclub. I noticed red flags soon after we started dating. She had a bad temper and I mean bad! She broke my laptop and grabbed the steering wheel while I was driving, swerving the car so we almost died.

Then she wanted to keep up with the Joneses as in, "My friend's hubby bought her a Range Rover. Other couples are going on vacations to Cape Town. We need to move to a bigger place." All this pressure pushed my drinking into a daily habit. Nothing could calm me down or lift me up like alcohol.

---

[38] Dax - "Dear Alcohol" (Official Music Video)
https://www.youtube.com/watch?v=k5ZtZEtDEGo

Then one day the binge drinking got me fired. I missed too many calls from being drunk or asleep. My girlfriend was crazy angry, so I drunkenly picked up some clothes, told her goodbye and drove off to stay at my mother's place. On the way I hit a post and dented my car.

Seeing my car looking like shit with all the other damage caused by driving drunk, my mother pushed me to get treatment before I killed someone or myself. It was the best decision of my life.

I went into a rehab centre where I attended classes and was given a lot of help from the counselling staff. My treatment plan included mental disorder and relapse awareness and also why alcohol is not the answer. They showed me I still had a life and a lot of potential. After three months of rehab my anxiety and insomnia were gone.

I had always been living on the edge, depressed and unable to sleep. Now my brain is calm and I'm a more relaxed human. My self-esteem is built up again and I understand myself. I have found the "I am Sober" app has been very helpful for me staying on track.

Alcoholism is a state where you are willing to stop but cannot. I learned there are many people like me, university graduates at the peak of their careers – the 25 to 35 age bracket – drinking to dangerous levels and the numbers are increasing. It is sad that one day they will probably go through the same thing as me.

When I think back to how I risked my life and other people's by driving drunk and all the meaningless sex, in addition to the hangovers, missed opportunities and wasted money I appreciate the gift of sobriety so much more.

Since quitting the sherehe lifestyle two years ago, I've travelled, had amazing experiences and got married to a beautiful woman. I've hiked mountains, ran marathons and triathlons and my body is transformed. Best of all, I'm about to become a father.

India leads the world for cirrhosis

I am shocked by what has happened to India. This country used to be staunchly opposed to the consumption of alcohol. Anyone who did drink was seen as a social outcast. Growing up, if my parents knew one of my friends drank, I was told to ditch them.

Now as a 48-year-old father with three young adult children of my own here in Punjab, the situation worries me a great deal. I am concerned that my kids will be tempted into this habit because many uncles of mine drank themselves to death before the age of 35 or finished up in a mental asylum.

It used to be that in the movies only the bad guys swigged from a glass of whiskey. This image has now been totally Bollywoodised. Now men who drink are seen as rebellious and badass. And women drinkers are portrayed as modern, sexually liberated feminists, whereas in the past they would have been looked down upon as embarrassing, loose party girls.

High end Western drink brands are seen as status symbols[42] among India's billionaires who have mostly been born into wealth and have used their money to create businesses in IT, real estate and investing.

They are known as India's new maharajas and live in luxury gated communities, flaunt their money and live lavish lifestyles,[43] oblivious to how they look against the backdrop of poverty and dilapidation all around them.

The less privileged, young middle-class people hold them in esteem and follow their example in their bid to achieve social status for themselves. They are aggressively business-minded and want to taste the same luxuries as the mega-rich, and that includes alcohol.

---

[42] "3,000 + Bottles at Asian Biggest Liqour Store"
www.youtube.com/watch?v=Ag14egbI1kI
[43] "Streets of Gold: Mumbai"
https://www.youtube.com/watch?v=dcNsk3wJaj0

Another problem that has arisen here is of young employees being encouraged to join their boss and drink with the team. If they are new to a company, they are made to feel like they have to hang out and party so that they can get promoted. Anyone who declines is either sidelined or shamed.

Then we have the Indian states where alcohol is banned. The people in these regions are so desperate they will drink anything with methanol in it, including hand sanitizer as well as hooch they make themselves. This has led to multiple mass deaths due to unregulated toxic country liquor[44] which accounts for at least half of all of the alcohol that is consumed in our country.

Obviously, these poor people do not drink to celebrate. They drink to cope with the crippling conditions in which they live, the result of decades of inaction by successive governments. Tax evasion, bribery and corruption are rife among the wealthy elite and our politicians.

Rather than spend money on giving people clean water, toilets and electricity our elected officials would prefer to put billions into a show-piece space program to impress the world.

Due to a combination of all these factors, India now has the world's highest rate of liver cirrhosis.[46] Crime, traffic accidents and domestic violence have all increased. And because whiskey is expensive many men will squander the family money, leaving their wives and children in poverty.

In Indian culture alcoholism is stigmatised as a mental health problem and it will get ignored or downplayed because it is associated with failure. For example, many Bollywood celebrities have drunk

---

[44] Indian politicians banned alcohol – now poisonous hooch is killing thousands | Telegraph dispatch
https://www.youtube.com/watch?v=8oybb_2gmZg

[46] Global burden of liver cirrhosis and other chronic liver diseases caused by specific etiologies from 1990 to 2019
https://bmcpublichealth.biomedcentral.com/articles/10.1186/s12889-024-17948-6#:~:text=At%20the%20national%20level%2C%20India

themselves to death, but the media stays silent on the details so their image remains untarnished. This is why nobody pays too much attention to alcohol's dark side.

More than half our population is under the age of 35, which means the youth market is a massive opportunity for the alcohol industry and our new generation of home-grown entrepreneurs. Many highly educated young people are opening bars as well as launching their own liquor, wine and beer brands.

India never had a drinking culture in the past. We live in a hot country unlike the Northern Europeans or the Russians. But unfortunately, the taboo that once surrounded alcohol has created enough curiosity for a generation to come. The forbidden fruit is always the sweetest

Career alcoholism in South Korea and Japan

We have an after-work drinking tradition here called "hoesik" (pronounced huway-shik). It is part of the work culture and everyone is obliged to take part. If you don't your career could be in jeopardy with loss of promotions because you are not considered a team player or loyal to the company. Your social skills are also rated by your boss based on this custom.

Many workers won't sleep and will drinking until 4:00 a.m. even though they have to be at work at 8:30 a.m. It is not unusual to hear stories about drunk surgeons operating on patients, teachers asleep on their desks and even inebriated police officers! There are few countries that glorify corporate communal drinking as much as Korea.

In fact, South Koreans drink more than four times as much liquor as Americans, mostly in the form of soju, a super cheap vodka-like spirit which is 20% to 50% alcohol. It's a huge thing in Korean social culture to go out with your coworkers and get drunk.[47] By the way, the closest translation to alcoholic is "awesome guy."

Drinking is both an equalizer and a revealer as you get to see everyone in a completely raw, unconstrained state. You get intoxicated, share ideas and opinions that you don't dare talk about normally, stumble around and even puke together. I've seen people stand up thinking they're fine and suddenly drop to the floor.

The theory is getting hammered together builds camaraderie, allows you to trust each other more, helps you come up with creative ideas and work better as a team. Your boss also gets the chance to show you they are human and can even be your friend.

The next day when you are all hungover and suffering together, an even stronger bond is created. It's all psychological and part of being an employee in this country. If you know how to drink and play golf you will make your way up the ladder pretty fast!

My old boss used to make everyone go drinking like this, but I always left early or said no, which really pissed her off. I explained I did my best work when I wasn't hungover and needed to rest so I could be super-efficient. I still sounded like I was a loyal team player so she couldn't argue. What I did not tell her was that I had a heart problem due to all the alcohol and did not want to die young.

After the Covid pandemic things started to change and younger workers have become more resistant to the pressures of enforced drinking.[48] Vomit on the floors of the subway trains has also become a major issue, with people slipping in it and injuring themselves. Plus, the deaths from accidents as a direct result of hoesik are now being classed as workplace related, which has made companies think twice about liability.

---

[47] Why Koreans love drinking
https://www.youtube.com/shorts/CR7mI0iGm30
[48] Young South Koreans Lament Return of Mandatory Social Gathering - Hoesik
https://www.youtube.com/watch?v=npoFkLbrqgQ

For a background to all this, Korea went from a being poor war-torn country to a rich tech and manufacturing hub in just a few decades. It was called "the miracle on the Han River." But this miracle meant a lot of hardship, with workers building high-rises, highways and factories overnight. The same thing happened in China. So now our leaders think overworking their people is the key to success.

We have one of the longest work weeks in the world at 52 hours and our insane president even tried to raise this to 69 hours which caused huge protests.

As well as being forced to sacrifice all our time, many of us are realising that no matter how hard we work we will never get ahead. We are taught to do well at school and university then you get success, but the reality is you get nothing much. When I see the effort, luck and generational wealth needed for people my age to succeed I just want to give up and say fuck it all.

In Japan the pressure is just as bad, maybe even worse as they are already very competitive with Korea. If you work for a really big company, your boss will make your team go to a "nomikai" (meeting to drink) at least once a week where you are expected to imbibe until the you're allowed to go home. It's pretty mandatory that you go, or else you run the risk of missing out on promotions and being ostracized.

The number of Japanese professionals in the business district with drinks in their hand at lunchtime is crazy. It is also typical for these salarymen in their smart suits to get black out drunk and pass out on central Tokyo's Shibuya streets or at the train station until morning, after being driven to extremes and working 60-hour weeks.[49]

In South Korea we put a lot of pressure on ourselves to succeed and to appear successful. Suffering from anxiety, stress and depression is seen as failure. You are perceived as being lazy, self-indulgent and

---

[49] https://fstoppers.com/spotlight/photo-series-businessmen-sleeping-street-spotlights-tokyos-disturbing-310440

weak. So virtually nobody gets help for alcoholism or anything much else because it's a taboo subject.

Drinking to show our loyalty in China

The saying among Chinese Communist Party government workers here is "The most seasoned Communist Party veteran is the one who can best hold his alcohol."

This sentiment is reflected across the entire country where drinking is culturally mandated. Officially the drinking age is 18 but it's not enforced. When I was a boy here in Shanghai my parents often sent me to buy beers and cigarettes from a mearby store and I started drinking at ten years old. It's very common for kids to drink with their family.

Now at the age of 24 it no longer holds any appeal for me. This is because in China, drinking is a symbolic social ritual and a work-enforced obligation that has little meaning or relevance to my life.

The venues where this formal rule-based drinking takes place are usually in private rooms of restaurants. At every family get together, wedding, celebration or event continuous toasting and the consumption of large amounts of liquor shows honor to the family, respect to your elders and allegiance to the Chinese way.

There have been many cases of people (especially bridesmaids) getting alcohol poisoning or dying as a result of the proxy drinker part of this custom, where you can request that someone else takes your shots.

At weddings, the best man's job is to get super smashed to "protect" the groom. Every table makes their own disgusting drink to challenge him, putting things like duck heads in the alcohol or mixing it with things like leftover soup or fish. [50]

---

[50] How to drink beer in China (at a wedding)
https://www.youtube.com/shorts/aZN7QKdivKU

In ancient China downing alcohol was used to test the obedience of soldiers. During military campaigns they would drink to show their solidarity and commitment to the cause. Because of this there is a lot of pressure on men to drink excessively to show how masculine they are. To refuse, or to barely drink is to lose the of your friends or business colleagues and to appear weak or suspect in some way.

There's a saying in China that professionals cannot trust their partners until they have been flat out drunk together. When doing business, getting inebriated is considered the best way to get acquainted with new employess, clients and suppliers. Even women are forced to participate in this ritual to earn the respect of their male peers, which has led to instances of sexual assault.

At these events, the host or businessman holds a bottle of liquor in one hand and a glass in another. Then he walks around the table and toasts each of his guests individually looking them in the eye and saying "ganbei" which is like "cheers."

After he's finished his tour of the table, another member of the group gets to his feet and repeats the same ritual until everyone has lost control of their faculties.

The degree of public humiliation and willingness to endure the pain of the hangover are used to gauge the level of someone's deference and to demonstrate the balance of power. The host is always standing and in control while everyone around him is destroyed. The unspoken rule is that everyone makes sure this is the end result.

The liquor that's mainly served at these gatherings is called baijiu (pronounced bye-jeeoo). This potent brew distilled from sorghum wheat has an ABV of around 55% and has been described as smelling like acetone and bubble gum and tasting like liquorice and medicine with a nose-burning, menthol effect.

Whereas getting drunk, passing out, being carried out by your armpits and even vomiting in front of people is socially normalized, alcoholism is severely frowned upon. It is considered a character defect and a moral failing that primarily affects those who are easily bamboozled, and weak. Alcohol dependent people in China are criticized and mercilessly mocked.

I have personally seen the incredulity and anger of the relatives of someone who knows they cannot control their drinking and refuses to partake for the sake of their health. Seeing them leave their glass, their elders will say, "You just have no self control! How can you not just take one sip? Unlike in other countries, in Chinese families troubles can actually start if you don't drink!

Predictably, fatty liver and cirrhosis are a major problem in China and are projected to worsen.[52] My father works in banking and is required to drink at least four days a week. It is definitely an unhealthy lifestyle.

When I ask him to refuse to take part in the custom he replies, "This is Chinese wine culture[53] you have to obey it!" He is talking about rice wine, not the wine made from grapes.

My father is sacrificing his life for a paycheck because heavy drinking is very bad for Chinese people. We cannot detoxify alcohol like other nationalities. Our faces flush and we get dizzy after a relatively small amount and are at far greater risk of liver diseases and cancer.

Despite China's long history as a drinking nation, there are signs that its old rituals are starting to be abandoned. The newer tech companies are rejecting the ganbei model as being incompatible with their work culture. Gen Z and the youngest millennials are also shunning the custom as we generally feel very pessimistic about our futures.

---

[52] Estimated projection of incidence and mortality of alcohol-related liver disease in China from 2022 to 2040: a modeling study
https://bmcmedicine.biomedcentral.com/articles/10.1186/s12916-023-02984-7

[53] https://www.ichineselearning.com/chinese-culture/chinese-wine-culture.html8

We call ourselves the last generation. Working, buying a property and building a family life is almost impossible today. After a childhood of intense study where nothing else matters but getting A grades, many of us graduating from university with master's degrees can't find jobs, or the ones that are available have low starting salaries.

Why work 72 hours a week for $700 a month to build the bank accounts of your corporate overlords who expect you to be on call 24/7 and will say you're lazy if you dare to whisper a complaint?

In other countries, people commonly use alcohol to numb out when they feel hopeless. Today many 20 to 40-year-olds in China are "lying flat" which basically means doing the bare minimum at their job or quitting completely. It's happening in a lot of other nations too.

Some of us have even gone down to the bai lan or "let it rot" level, where life consists of sleeping, eating, gaming and retreating back to bed to look at our phones. Drinking in general is expensive and the buzz isn't worth the discomfort, so we don't even do that. If we're not going own anything we'll do nothing.

It's like that stage of monopoly where one guy owns all the properties and collects all the rent. The only way out if you're on the losing end is to refuse to play the game.

Drinking ourselves to death in The Cook Islands

I will understand if you've never heard of the Cook Islands or don't know that the folks who live on them are known as Pacific Islanders. Try to imagine the volcanic islands of Hawaii, except on the other side of the world out in the South Pacific Ocean near New Zealand. That's us. Except we have 15 islands that make up our nation, the main and biggest one being Rarotonga.

Imagine the most beautiful, picture-perfect tropical islands you can, with huge white sandy beaches surrounded by miles of deep blue waters.[54] You'd think you'd be in heaven if you lived here, right?

Sadly, the beauty of our surroundings is not matched by the quality of our lives. According to recent global league tables we're pretty much at the top for being the fattest and most alcoholic nations of people on earth.[55]

So why are we eating and drinking ourselves into an early grave? I'll do my best to explain things as I lie in my hospital bed contemplating the entire situation. Two weeks ago, I was admitted with type 2 diabetes (we call it "sugar sickness" here) and lower extremity arterial disease caused by many years of over-eating and drinking.

My right leg is swollen and is very painful. So the doctor took a black marker pen and drew a line across my thigh just above where it had turned red. The line is to gauge the progress of the infection and show where to cut my leg off if it gets worse.

I have given myself a life-threatening "lifestyle disease" like the vast majority of the people who live here. These self-inflicted health problems are what finishes most of us off.

Today, when someone says they have cancer, it's like they're saying they caught the cold. Cancer, diabetes, heart attacks and high blood pressure are all very common throughout the islands.

Why is our small community in such poor physical and mental shape? You can trace it back to a few things. The first one is there is no taboo about being obese. We stuff our faces like we're hoarding calories for the future and eat too much processed food and food in general.

---

[54] The paradise of Aitutaki island - Cook islands - South Pacific
https://www.youtube.com/shorts/oDva0GHhSfI
[55] Alcohol consumption per capita
https://www.cia.gov/the-world-factbook/about/archives/2022/field/alcohol-consumption-per-capita/country-comparison

Our diet is mainly canned and packaged food like rice, noodles, Spam, potato chips and soda drinks imported from Australia and the United States. Because many of us are also genetically predisposed to storing fat everyone is overweight, and it's a problem for our children too.

The second reason is we have an entrenched drinking culture. For generations we have brewed "bush beer" from fermented fruit, sugar, malt, and hops which we traditionally drink in secret gatherings deep in the jungle. We also make papaya infused rum and coconut liqueur which the tourists also enjoy.

Our third issue is that we no longer have food security like we used to have. For thousands of years our people lived on fish, coconuts, fruits and root vegetables like taro. But despite having vast oceans and enough land to produce all the fish, vegetables and meat this country needs and giving us something to do, the government is not interested in self-sufficiency.

Instead, they removed the taxes on all the imported food which we can produce ourselves. Within a few months all our local egg and poultry farmers went bankrupt, except for one. So now we get egg shortages. To avoid running out of anything, we tend to sell much of the fresh things we take from the sea and grow ourselves to buy processed food, because it's cheap and longer lasting.

According to the government our economy is growing every year which creates the illusion that everyone is benefitting and must be happy. In fact, the islanders here are mostly poor, unemployed and disenchanted.

It is hard to feel motivated or positive about your life when you see the politicians vote themselves massive pay increases while everyone else is struggling. The incompetence and abuses of power by those in leadership roles with corruption, theft etc. has killed the spirit of our once proud nation. Many of us now refer to it as the Crook Islands.

Now we're dependent on tourism and overseas aid. A third of us in Rarotonga live under the national poverty line and can't afford to meet our basic needs for a decent life.

When you live in a place with few amenities, limited jobs and live off stipends and handouts you tend to smoke, eat a lot and sit around all day drinking home brewed beer and sweet rum. We've always had a tradition of communal drinking. I guess we've just taken it to the next level.

Booze is cheaper to buy here than water and can be found at any shop all around the island almost 24/7 any day of the week except Sunday. The drinking disengages people from society and stops them from challenging the status quo.

I was concerned to learn that when European colonizers dispossessed indigenous people of their land and culture, they always introduced alcohol or even paid the natives with it to ensure their docility and agreeableness, especially for the purposes of treaty making.

Today alcohol abuse has become a part of the cultural fabric of who we are as Cook Islanders. Men here still conform to the idea that we must be "the strong silent type." We use it to cope because mental problems are a taboo subject.

Sadly, the bottled-up stress combined with drinking often has terrible consequences for our women, teens and children. All of this probably explains our other top slot for having some of the highest suicide rates in the region. Plus, we have the loss of life due to drink driving which is another huge problem here and the no.1 issue our police deal with daily.

As I look at the black line drawn across my leg I realize it symbolizes how I have cut short my own life. I never considered how all my choices in the moment would affect the rest of my days.

You can have a painful, short, apathetic life or a long, active, socially involved one. It all depends on what you choose to eat and how much you drink. Alcohol just keeps you in a loop of bad decisions.

Hammered in Oz

Australia has a similar approach to drinking to the Brits (although I'd say they are definitely ahead of us in terms of the pints they put away). Every social activity in this country involves getting shit-faced. I don't even think people are shoving it down their necks with enthusiasm. It's basically just a race to inebriation.

Kids' party? Get hammered. Public holiday? Get hammered. Work do or family reunion? Get hammered. Mad Monday? Get magotted! Australia day? Get absolutely plastered! The more smashed you can get and the more idiotic you are the more it's applauded.

Added to this we have a culture where drinking is integrated with work, especially in the male-dominated occupations like trucking/transport, farm/rural labour, construction, roadworks and mining. Any man who can put away five litres of beer in 90 minutes is a "top bloke."

In most countries it's definitely not normal to be para with your boss at 1:00 a.m., but here if you don't partake you're basically losing social points at that job. And if you don't go the course you'll be classified as a Cadbury from the slogan "glass and a half" meaning that's how little you need to get drunk or a "two pot screamer." In Australia a pot is a half pint glass.

In recent years though, things have drastically changed. Since Covid in 2020 far fewer people are going out and the majority of Aussies are drinking cheaper booze at home due to having less disposable income.

Instead of being a necessity for social bonding, alcohol has become more of a legal and affordable part of self-guided therapy to cope with being priced out of life.[57]

Increasing healthcare costs, massive immigration, high taxation, high interest rates, stagnant wages, rocketing rents and sky-high house

---

[57] Why Living in Australia Is Impossible
https://www.youtube.com/watch?v=_TUVXfM1nqo

prices have turned everyone's worlds upside down. Working conditions in Australia have also gone belly up with just about every poor bastard being a casual employee with no job security to speak of.

We have a terrible housing crisis with a lack of affordable properties and young people having no hope of ever being able to get on the ladder. (They say the kids are drinking less these days. They can't bloody well afford it!) Meanwhile, most of our politicians own up to seven rental investment properties each, the greedy buggers!

I was chatting to the manager of my local bottle shop and he agrees that his regulars have definitely stepped it up since the pandemic.[58]

Even I'm downing copious amounts of cheap Australian Shiraz nightly, whereas before I was a pretty light drinker. When you can only afford goon boxes or bags and not bottles, you tend to drink more because you can't tell how much is in there.

The only thing that gets me through another stressful day is that big carton of wine waiting for me when I get home. It eases my mind and stops the spinning thoughts that tell me no matter how hard I work I will always be poor.

---

[58] Australian alcohol consumption is higher than it was pre-pandemic https://www.roymorgan.com/findings/9153-alcohol-consumption-march-2023

When Carlsberg came to Greenland

Greenland. What does that make you think of? Snowy mountains, glaciers and igloos with Mongolian-looking eskimos catching fish through holes in the ice? That's the stereotypical view of native Inuit life[59] in this remote polar region, but this culture now barely exists.

When the Danish people came here and built houses and roads in the 1970s all our traditional ways died out. For the purposes of civilization the Danish government decided it would be better for us to adopt their religion, speak their language, use money and abandon our heritage. Many Inuit children were even sent to Denmark to get "a proper upbringing" before being sent back to Greenland to orphanages.

Today, the Inuit community mainly lives in modern apartment blocks in one of the half dozen or so towns on Greenland's western coastline. The interior of this vast island – which is three times the size of France – is a mile thick of solid ice so you cannot build on it.

Apart from The Danish actor who played Jamie Lannister in "Game of Thrones"[60] who has a cottage in the south, a few famous Greenlandic footballers, artists and musicians[61] live here, but nobody you would really know.

Because of Greenland's size and tiny population of 57,000 (which includes around 5,000 Danish people), anywhere you live feels small and remote. None of the towns are linked by roads. So, despite the vast, surrounding majestic landscape, living here can feel isolated and weirdly claustrophobic.

For example, the capital city Nuuk where I live, has just 20,000 residents and would be classed as a small town in the US. It has one

---

[59] Innuit way of life in Greenland
https://www.youtube.com/shorts/jhuUE7WTgkU
[60] Nikolaj Coster-Waldauhttps:
www.imdb.com/name/nm0182666/
[61] Nanook – Ingerlaliinnaleqaagut
https://www.youtube.com/watch?v=Gp-fckkHG7M

movie theater, an airport with one gate for international flights and just four miles of paved road. If you want to travel to another settlement you must go by dog sled, boat or plane.

The harsh climate with year-round freezing temperatures and months of darkness also restricts a lot of what we can do. We have maybe four months when it's nice outside.

It's also very expensive to live here. Even worse than Norway. This is because Greenland can grow next to nothing except in greenhouses so virtually all our food (except fish, seal meat and reindeer) has to be imported. Fresh vegetables are a luxury.

Because we currently don't export a lot, we are pretty much financially dependent on Denmark who provides us with an allowance of $10,000 per person per year.

Denmark also funds our healthcare, police and schools and the Danish people who work in them. We pay them back with produce from our fisheries, oil and mines which produce minerals like diamonds, gold and platinum to name but a few. Tourism also brings in some extra money.

The reason I am painting this detailed picture is to help you understand why we have a major alcohol problem here. The erasure of our cultural identity coupled with our sadness about the past are the reasons for our inherent sense of pain and loss. We call it "the wound."

Our parents and grandparents obviously had a harder time of it. Half of the children that were relocated to Denmark ended up as alcoholics and/or killing themselves. Transitioning to the Danish way of life was – and still is – alien and bewildering for us and many native Inuits are prone to depression and alcoholism.

When the Danes brought their Carlsberg beer and liquor here it did a ton of damage. Families collapsed. Parents that drink forget about their kids completely. As the oldest son, it was left to me to bring up my siblings but luckily I was spared from abuse unlike others.

A lot of kids here are sexually attacked or beaten behind closed doors. You sometimes hear of a whole bunch of them dying from the same parents. During Covid in early 2020 the government had to ban the sale of alcohol in Nuuk because things got so bad.

Because of their traumatic home lives, the isolation and crushing boredom, young people killing themselves is very common here and even seen as normal.[62] In some towns you see the flag at half-mast outside the hospital at least once a week.

Another major issue for us is the use of Danish as the main language. By upper secondary school, all the lessons are in Danish, so the kids that can only speak Greenlandic eventually stop bothering to show up. The ones that can speak fluent Danish end up either going to the University of Greenland in Nuuk or traveling to Denmark to study for free. Once they experience the exciting life most of us only see on the internet they almost never come back.

Meanwhile the Greenlandic kids who don't fit into the system mostly just eat, sleep and get drunk at the weekends. Every month they gather at cash dispensers in the supermarket, get their welfare allowance and blow it on beer, drugs or drinking in the pub.

Last year I graduated from the university here in Nuuk and secured an interesting marketing job. I love my country and will never leave. The peace and beauty of the amazing landscape and the fact all my family is here are just two reasons of many.

Right now, only one in ten young people like me get to experience this path of higher education and local professional employment, but I'm hopeful things will change.

---

[62] Young people in Greenland call new suicide prevention measures necessary
https://www.courthousenews.com/young-people-in-greenland-call-new-suicide-prevention-measures-necessary/

PART 3

How self-destructive levels of drinking hurt the whole family

Recollections from adult children of alcoholic parents

He terrorized us all including the dog

After my parents' divorce me, my sister and brother lived at both our mom and dad's houses. Late on a Monday afternoon, dad would drive us to mom's house from school to get our stuff. One time he was super drunk and kept drifting off the road.

We all screamed at him to wake up, which he would for a few seconds, but then he'd start falling asleep again. I remember taking my seatbelt off because I wanted to punish him if I died and I just wanted it all to be over. I was tired of being scared.

We somehow got to mom's house and my sister told her what had happened. She told him he couldn't take us home because he was drunk. After that he screamed that everything in the house was his and started dragging a glass table outside.

Mom locked the door behind him when he was outside. He banged on the door swearing and yelling while we all huddled together crying in the living room. Mom said, "Don't worry, I know him, he would never hurt you guys. He wouldn't hurt anyone." So I had to tell her that he beat our dog when he was drunk.

There were a lot of incidents, but this is the one that sticks with me the most.

Dreading the afterlife

For the first two decades of my life, I never saw my father sober. He was either wasted, sleeping it off or hungover. My mum worked hard and was always taking my grandparents to see the doctor. I had to do everything – the cooking, cleaning, laundry, shopping, bringing my sister home from school, helping her with her homework and checking she had everything for athletics.

But nothing was as bad as hearing my father wake up, having to walk on eggshells and trying to keep him happy so as not to have plates or death threats thrown at me. I will never forget the fear and anxiety I felt in anticipation of being whacked for the slightest thing. He told me I was nothing and would never be anything in life.

During this time, he was also coming into our bedroom to give a six and a 10-year-old girl "massages." Mine were actual massages but my younger sister's were not. Dad assumed I couldn't see what was going on from my top bunk.

He continued to sexually assault my sister for years, even after she got her own room. When she told my mother what was really going on at around the age of 13, she sided with him and accused my sister of lying. I confronted her about the abuse again when I was in my 20s. At that point she cut both of us out of her life.

I have struggled with depression because of all this, and my sense of self-worth was so messed up I ended up in an abusive marriage, but I'm out of that now. My mental health isn't great, but it's better thanks to a lot of therapy with a brilliant counsellor. Even so, it's hard to sustain a romantic relationship or motivate myself to be in one now.

My childhood memories have transitioned into anger, bitterness and resentment and I've distanced myself from any family member who denies what happened. Now I'm dreading that there might be an afterlife because I never want to see my father again.

A different kind of home schooling

My earliest memories are of parties with tons of drunk adults hanging out at the house and an orange juice container in the fridge that already had vodka added to it.

I remember once barricading my door after my mom threw my dad out and he tried to break in. I also recall having to lie to the teachers and my friends' parents about why they couldn't sign something or take me to events.

After my dad totalled his car when he was wasted, he couldn't get a job because he had no license. All he did was drink and scream at me and my brother. His reactions were crazy because of the booze, but as a kid you don't make the connection and think it's something you've done.

He turned as mean as a junkyard dog. I never knew what version of him I was going to come home to or wake up to. It was either "I love you" or "You know you're a piece of shit, right?"

My parents taught me to evade interrogation from the school, the cops and other adults when I was about four. Dad taught me to lie about his drug use before I could count past 50 or write my name. Mom coached me on how to downplay my bruises and fake being okay like she would after my dad's drunken rampages which left us both battered.

I also learned how to bottle my feelings and to deceive the authorities. I'd been told that Child Protective Services would hurt me even worse than they did, so I played the game not realizing it was because I had to save their sorry asses.

Once when I was maybe 8-years-old, I remember being woken up in the middle of the night by screaming. My mom was yelling, "Give me the gun!!" over and over. I guess my dad finally gave the gun to her because after a while the screaming stopped. Later I realized my dad had been trying to kill himself, but I didn't figure it out until I was much older.

I remember always being hungry and having to eat lot of cereal and frozen pizza because that's all there was unless I got a MacDonalds with my lawn mowing money. I also remember not wanting my friends to come over because they'd see my mom trying to go out at 9:00 a.m. already shit-faced and mad at me because I'd hidden her car keys.

It's traumatic having an alcoholic parent. You end up feeling worthless as a person. I'm over 30 now and I'm just fucked trying to have any type of relationship, either romantic or platonic.

I've tried to date girls but my lack of any affection growing up has made it impossible because I can't trust or rely on anyone. If it wasn't for my dog, I would voluntarily exit this world.

Stuck with a crazy mother

Mom would work a full-time job then throw back two bottles of wine when she got home. This meant she forgot anything I told her: things about my life, my friends and school. Or more likely, she wasn't interested. Her drinking made her totally self-centered.

After my dad divorced her she would lock herself in the bathroom and sob for hours. Then she bought this bath set with shower gel, body spray and a mindfulness CD. That music still haunts me to this day. She'd cry while blaring out this soft music at full volume in the background. She thought it was loud enough to drown out the sound of her wailing but it wasn't.

By this time, she was easily downing three bottles of wine a night. Sometimes she'd come out of the bathroom and start making "dinner." A lot of times it was her famous drunken soup. She'd dump a bottle of ketchup, some vinegar, water and sugar in a pan and bring it to the boil.

When I couldn't finish it, she'd go crazy and start throwing things. Or better yet, beat me with whatever was in arm's reach like a broom, a chair or a frying pan. I'd run and hide under my bed or bury myself under some clothes. In her drunken state she never looked for me for very long.

When I was around the age of 14, she locked herself in the bathroom with a knife and threatened to kill herself. I stood outside the door begging her to come out. The next thing I know the door opens and she has cuts and blood on her arms. Then she starts chasing me and threatens to kill me! All I know is I got away somehow. But I will never forget the feeling of absolute terror thinking wtf is going on?

Sometimes I'd call my dad just to hear his voice on the answer machine. He never picked up because he thought it was my mom. I prayed for him to come and save me but he never did.

The rest of my memories are mostly of me being embarrassed with my mother shouting at me in front of strangers, slurring and swearing and being frightened she'd kill herself for real. Once she fell over in the street and cracked her head open and I had to scream for help.

After she got sober, she said something like "Well at least I didn't beat you up did I?" She won't acknowledge all the trauma she put me through and how I had to parent myself and her.

Unfortunately, as a kid you remember every detail. Now I'm left with social anxiety, general anxiety and probably PTSD but I have not been checked for it. I struggle with relationships and keep myself to myself as it's safer that way. I also ended up becoming an alcoholic myself for five years, but I'm sober now because I realize I've been punished enough.

My schizo stepdad

My stepdad would get drunk, break stuff, blackout then get mad at me and my stepbrother (his son), blame us for the damage and beat us.

There were no doors in the house because he got too drunk to open them, so he went around with a hammer one day and smashed them all out. Of course, he forgot what he'd done and me and my stepbrother were blamed. Mom never defended us, she just let us get battered. I guess she didn't want to upset him and take a beating herself.

He had this giant wooden paddle and used it to hit me while screaming that he'd told us many times not to wrestle inside the house. He only stopped when the paddle broke which he found hilarious. Then we'd have to hide the bruises so as not to attract attention. We couldn't ask for help because he would have gotten even madder.

The worst part was when he got really drunk he'd flip into his other character. He would say things like, "You're my number one son" and that I was his second chance at raising a son right. He'd say how proud he was of me and brag to his friends about how great and tough I was.

It was this constant questioning of whether he was going to be nice or hurt me that affected me the most. As a kid you don't understand all these weird behaviors are their problems and not yours. What you think, say or feel is totally irrelevant and makes no difference.

My mom left him when I was 13. They had been married for 12 years. She didn't leave because of the drinking or abuse. She left because she had "found God" and he wouldn't go to church with her.

I looked forward to going to school

My mom always kept a pitcher full of blue raspberry lemonade mixed with vodka in the fridge. I learned from a young age never to drink it. I also learned how to get her a beer on command and how to pour the perfect glass of wine with three ice cubes.

When I got home from school she'd be on her first glass of wine. Then later she would start crying and I'd be her therapist. She started telling me about her intimate problems with my dad when I was around the age of nine. I'd hold my breath whenever she talked because of the sickly-sweet wine smell.

My dad was always aggressive towards her when he was drinking too. Then there would be all these drunk yelling matches where they would misunderstand a totally innocuous statement and start screaming at each other.

Once I tried to get them to understand that they were freaking out over nothing, but that just ended up with them both taking it out on me. The next day they would always be back in love and talking about a getting a puppy or adopting a baby or some other nonsense.

Eventually they divorced and I went to live with my dad. My weekends weren't relaxing, they were horrible because I was trapped in the house and knew that by the afternoon he'd be drunk and passed out with the sports on TV. He couldn't drive me anywhere and I couldn't have friends over.

All of this has affected me greatly. I cannot drink wine because the smell of it makes me sick and gives me flashbacks, but I do drink far more liquor than I should. I never had a role model for safe alcohol consumption so I haven't really questioned my reliance on alcohol until now.

At the age of 27 I've decided to get help for my alcoholism. One of the main reasons I'm quitting is so my future children will have a level headed and sober parent, not horrible drunk ones like mine.

I learned how not to be like them

My grandma raised me even though my dad lived right across the street. When I was ten, I decided to live with my mom because it upset me when kids at school talked about their mom and dad and I couldn't. I was left alone a lot and cooked for myself, mostly noodles, and got myself ready for school.

When I was 11 my mom got pregnant again and I had to take care of my baby brother. I remember one night I couldn't get a hold of her when he wouldn't settle. I called every number I knew. Around midnight he finally stopped crying. We were asleep when she came back, so she had no idea how tough and scary everything was for me.

When I was 12, I met a boy who was 16. Then one night when I was around 14, my mom left me home alone and let him stay the night. Obviously, I lost my virginity and found out I was pregnant five months later. Mom forced me to get an abortion which I regret to this day.

I didn't smoke weed until I graduated high school and met the wrong people. Then I started drinking, doing pills and smoking PCP every day. I turned into my mom. The one person I said I would never be.

A few years later I got pregnant again and changed my life for my baby girl. I now work full time and I am going to school for nursing. I also have a son by the guy I lost my virginity to, who is now my husband. My daughter is not his but he treats her like she is.

It was hard getting to where I am now. I am 23 and getting much better. I can't be depressed or have trust issues because I have to do what I can for myself and my family.

There's an Indian guy called Sadguru who says that in life there are no problems and there are no opportunities, there are only situations and it's up to us to decide what we make of the situation.

My parents made horrible choices and I cannot change them. But what I can do is not hold a grudge and be the best parent I can, so my kids won't struggle like I did.

Nothing was good enough for my mom

As a kid I blamed myself for my mom's drinking, so I made up for it by trying to be perfect. I cleaned the house, cooked dinner, got good grades and even taught Sunday school. I never got into trouble and did whatever she asked me to do from the age of five.

All the while I put up with the humiliation of her being drunk in front of my friends, her never-ending complaints and took all of her insults without answering back. I hugged her when she cried and apologized for things I hadn't done. I reassured her that she was the best mother and I was lucky to have her in my life.

The more I tried to please her the more she seemed to loathe me. My mother couldn't love me no matter what I did, so I was convinced I must be useless and unworthy of affection. Because I was such a bad kid I needed to be punished, so I became a cutter.

As I was involved in sports, I had to be careful where I injured myself because I had to change in front of my teammates. So I cut the hell out of the bottom of my feet which caused intense pain, but I felt it was what I deserved.

Then suicide became the only way I could make her happy. How could I be expected to keep living when all I did was cause grief to those around me? I half-heartedly attempted to kill myself about half a dozen times from the age of 15.

Once I took about a hundred various prescription pills. All I did was make myself lose 20lbs over the course of a few days from vomiting. I was sick for about two weeks. When I ended up in the hospital having my stomach pumped after another failed attempt, my mother said, "You couldn't even do that right."

After this she took me to see a therapist who made me feel understood for the first time in my life. She gave me an appointment card for our next meeting which I put in my purse. When my mom asked for it in the car, I told her I'd like to hang onto it.

She flew into a rage and said, "Fine. You can frame it and hang it on your wall to remind you what a basket case you are." That was the best and worst moment of my life. I finally realized I had to look after myself and forget about her. I was 16.

Living on my own has helped. I've read a lot of books about adult children of alcoholics. I also journal and try to work on my self-esteem. I still have a tendency to take care of people and please them, but therapy has helped fix this to a great extent.

My mother has let her life slip by in a drunken haze, whereas I engage in it with a passion. She has no thirst for knowledge, whereas I love reading and graduated college with a 4.0. She hasn't exercised a day in her life, yet I qualified to run the Boston marathon this year. She feels entitled to what she wants and I work for what I want.

At 61 her alcoholism is as bad as ever, but she is no longer a mean drunk. When I was growing up, she'd call me worthless and stupid on a daily basis. She'd never dare do that now. She's nicer to me but is still very self-centered, so I rarely talk to her.

I'll never be a confident decision maker because I was told so often my opinion didn't matter. But overall, I'm happy, fulfilled, and mostly healed. After decades of feeling I was inherently bad, one of the biggest compliments I get is when someone who knows my mom says, "How did you turn out so good?"

Dad's drinking drove us all into depression

In the early 70s my father left the Punjab in India and settled in England. Like many immigrants he got a job driving buses and saved enough to buy a small house. Being Indian, whiskey was his drink of choice. A year or so later, he returned to India for an arranged marriage to my mother.

Back in England, despite his responsibilities he continued to drink and ramped it up when me and my brothers were born. There was endless shouting and horrible violence against my mother.

When we were all still in primary school he lost his job. After this, things got far worse. His self-loathing, bitterness and resentment of us all drove each of us into some form depression. My mother was isolated and miserable and the neglect was so obvious my brothers and I were close to being taken into care.

My dad had his first heart attack in his late 40s. Problems with his liver followed and his overall health got worse. He started buying second hand clothes and not washing so much or caring what anyone thought of him.

By this time, he'd spent all his and my mother's money on booze, gambling and women and had no fight left in him. He disintegrated into a shell of a human. Then one night he had a heart attack in his sleep, a so-called "millionaire's death." He was lucky. He just fell asleep and didn't wake up at the age of 64.

It wasn't so lucky for my mother who had stood by him for over 40 years and raised four boys on benefits. She had given her life to this selfish piece of crap. After he died we found out he had another son from one of his affairs and had been cheating with multiple women.

Looking back on all this I'd say an environment of zero parental support, domestic violence and alcoholism can destroy a child's self-confidence. I spent years hiding away, not wanting friends to come over, feeling desperate and worthless. Having a parent who puts drinking above their family is soul-destroying. The shame, trauma and pain stay with you.

If it wasn't for reading Anthony Robbins books as a teenager I would most likely have ended up like my dad, because children of heavy drinkers are four times more likely to become alcoholics themselves.

Thankfully there has been a lot of awareness about alcoholism among the UK's Indian Punjabi Sikh community over the past few years and the subject is not as taboo as it once was.[63]

---

[63] The unspoken UK Punjabi alcohol problem - BBC News
https://www.youtube.com/watch?v=Xf4wtlWOPnI

A professional perspective

I've worked in the mental health field for over 25 years. I don't think the problems of Adult Children of Alcoholics (ACA) are discussed nearly enough. The vast majority of these people have never heard of the term and aren't aware that because of their unstable upbringing and the cruelties they endured, they are vulnerable to using alcohol and other drugs to feel love, self-soothe and connect.

ACAs are often approval seekers, fear criticism and judge themselves harshly due to a learned set of beliefs from being raised by one or more negligent and/or abusive parents. They have difficulty figuring out and communicating their emotions and have a tendency to focus on and prioritize the needs and wants of others above their own.

As your relationship with your parents is the model for all your future relationships, these individuals grow up thinking it's their job to take care of other people. In intimate relationships such partners are referred to as co-dependents or empaths.

They tend to be attracted to emotionally distant people and often suffer from mental disorders like depression, anxiety and OCD. For them, intimacy has historically been associated with pain and rejection. Counseling, psychotherapeutic medications, education and support group participation can be helpful for this group.

By contrast, some abuse survivors adapt the opposite way, becoming selfish, impulsive, irresponsible, manipulative, dishonest and cruel. They see people as being either all good or all bad and develop an antisocial or narcissistic personality disorder, which can range from mild to severe, depending on the degree of harm they inflict on others.

In my experience these types of personality disorders are notoriously difficult to change or remedy as the individual not only believes there is nothing wrong with them, but is well served by their adaptive response to the emotional pain and other traumas they experienced as a child.

Russell Brand on childhood trauma

Cannabis isn't a gateway drug.
Alcohol isn't a gateway drug.
Nicotine isn't a gateway drug.
Caffeine isn't a gateway drug.

Trauma is the gateway. Childhood abuse is the gateway. Molestation is the gateway. Neglect is the gateway.

Drug abuse, violent behaviour, hypersexuality and self-harm are often the symptoms – not the cause – of much bigger issues. And it often stems from a childhood filled with trauma, absent parents and an abusive family.

Help for adult children of alcoholics

"Complex PTSD: From Surviving to Thriving: A Guide and Map for Recovering from Childhood Trauma" is written from by a trauma survivor Pete Walker. He explains how to heal abandonment depression and make sense of the behaviors survivors are forced to adopt.

"Adult Children of Alcoholics" by Janet Geringer Woititz, Ed.D. is one of the most well-known books on this subject and is useful for anyone who was brought up by an addict of any kind.

"Adult Children of Alcoholics & Dysfunctional Families" is a 12-Step-based support group which offers free meetings both in-person and online.

"Codependents Anonymous" is a 12-Step-based support group for codependents which offers free meetings both in-person and online.

Reddit also has a space for adult children of alcoholics: https://www.reddit.com/r/AdultChildren/

PART 4

Dealing with the alcohol addicted

Anecdotes and observations from emergency workers, hospitality and retail staff and service providers

Dispatches from the drunk tank

I'm a police officer here in the United States and I can confidently say that working at the drunk tank was better than any TV show. It was one of the most fun and also one of the most depressing jobs I ever had.

How it worked back then was a cop would pick up an incapacitated person and bring them in. We would then screen them to make sure they weren't violent and wouldn't run away. It wasn't a locked facility so we couldn't stop them from leaving. We had plenty of frequent flyers and some very sad cases.

One woman, who was about 35 and painfully thin, would pass out covered in her own urine, excrement and vomit at least twice a week. We would take her home if she could walk, but if she was too messed up we'd put her in the drunk tank until it was safe to let her out. Then she went to rehab, gained weight and we didn't see her again. That one was a surprising turnaround.

Another guy would come into town right after his welfare checks had been deposited. He was the nicest man when sober. Both his kids got full athletic scholarships, whereas most kids from where he was from were drug dealers at best. He would get hammered in an alleyway, get arrested, spend 8 to 10 hours in the drunk tank and go back out and do it all again. His record was three times in 48 hours. Apart from this, he was an otherwise functioning member of society.

Then we had the service workers like chefs and bartenders who had it rough working 12-hour double shifts on no sleep. A lot of them had spiralled into booze, pills and coke and would be brought in for jay walking or getting into fights. When they'd sober up, they would shake like a dog on the 4th of July because the withdrawals were so bad. We had to get these folks to hospital before they seized.

Then there was the Wernicke's encephalopathy crowd. They would forget who they were or keep reliving the past like Groundhog's Day.

We had one who would always sober up and think it was the 1980s and talk about Ronald Reagan.

The drunk tank program has since been torched due to fear of liability because law enforcement is legally responsible for the health of anyone in their custody. There were also the staffing problems due to garbage pay for very challenging work. The pandemic and defunding of the police were the final nails in the coffin.

Now we no longer prioritize calls for incapacitation, and if we do pick them up we just dump them on the ER. If they're too violent or drunk for jail it's off to the emergency department. Even drunk drivers are given the choice of jail or hospital.

Unfortunately, the emergency room is pretty much the only place you can assault a worker without recourse. It's also the only facility that can't turn anyone away. My heart goes out to the staff in these places.

Breaking bad news to the parents

I'm a policeman in the UK. I just attended a scene of a 34-year-old who was drinking a 70cl bottle of vodka a day. And by scene, I mean he died alone in his flat with empty bottles piled up under the sink.

His body stank like there was vodka seeping out of the pores of his skin and the whites of his eyes were yellow. Apparently, he had been a functional alcoholic and held down a job and probably thought he still had time to get help and go into recovery.

I had to get my hat and knock on his parents' door to tell them their son was gone. His mother screamed like only a mother who loses a child screams and her husband had to carry her back inside.

They huddled together on the couch like I'd just put a decade on their shoulders. The heartbreaking thing was they didn't even ask how he died. They knew.

The pub regular who turned green

When I worked in a pub as a bartender this bloke in his mid 50s would come in. I couldn't tell if he'd been drinking beforehand as he was never confrontational, angry or rude.

He'd usually stay for a pint of beer and go. If he recognised someone, he'd stay a bit longer. Everyone knew him as being quite a heavy drinker, so he had unfortunately gained the nickname Alcoholic Harry. Then I heard him and his wife were going through tough times and didn't see him for about two years.

One night he came into the pub. I'd never seen a human being that colour. He was green. I mean green like an actual lime. I knew drinking could make people turn bright yellow but I never knew it was possible for the body to turn that shade. It must have been liver failure. He was gaunt, trembling and his face looked like an old leather sofa.

He came up to the bar and asked for half a pint. I was hesitant to serve him given the state he was in, but poured him a beer anyway. He sat there sipping it looking down. Then I asked if he wanted me to call a taxi or his wife. He said no to everything, finished his half pint and left.

The next day I heard he'd left the pub gone to the corner shop, bought a bottle of vodka and died in his bed that same night.

The women who drink their calories

I'm a 35-year-old hair and makeup professional and I'm often called to work at my clients' homes before they go out to an event. These clients are very rich with far too much time on their hands and looking good is their full-time job.

They always have a glass in their hand while I'm trying to work and without fail, they'll be on their phone facetiming their friends at the same time. Sometimes it's like being a schoolteacher trying to control a misbehaving child, getting them to keep still and stop talking.

These women are like the loudest and most annoying of The Real Housewives. They will walk off, forget I'm there and come back 20 minutes later, often with white powder in their nostrils.

The funny thing is they all have that strange alcoholic body shape – skinny, with stick-like arms and legs and a midsection that's slightly barrel shaped despite them barely eating.

I've seen photos of them when they were younger. A couple were models and beauty queens and had naturally beautiful faces before all their surgeries. They are all married to extremely wealthy men who have access to anything they want, including younger women and there's nothing their wives can do about it.

One of my clients is married to a billionaire who's pushing 70, while she just turned 55. He spends his weekends in Las Vegas, while she drinks rosé from Brad Pitt's vineyard and shows off her new purses and jewelry on Instagram.

I have never known her to be sober, genuinely present or happy in all the years I've known her. She often tells me I'm her best friend.

I'm a police officer and even this one surprised me

Throughout my police career in Texas in the USA, I have dealt with numerous people who drink from the time they wake up until they go to bed. But one particular case stands out in my mind.

We got a call from a neighbor to report a chick who was fighting with her boyfriend. Because we ended up arresting her we needed a BAC (blood alcohol concentration) number. Over .25 means hospital. If it's under she goes straight to jail. She blew just shy of .40, and was more functional than I have ever been at .08!

To put this into perspective .10 is buzzed for most people. Up to .2 is slurred speech, trouble walking and feeling pretty good. .20 to .30 is sloppy, falling down drunk with a loss of motor control. At .30 to .40 you are pretty much unable to stand and are taking a trip to the hospital for alcohol poisoning.

We have a fairly accurate and calibrated preliminary breath tester. The hospital confirmed our result. Jail also tested and confirmed. I have never known anyone be able to stand up or hold a conversation above .35. But this chick could due to her huge alcohol tolerance built up from years of heavy-duty drinking.

A scary level of tolerance

Finnish policeman here. Drinking is a national sport here in Finland. So we routinely use breathalysers on drivers, whether it's an accident they're involved in, or we're just making a random check.

We once arrested this guy driving home from the bar. He was like an inch in the bike lane for too long, so we pulled him over. He was fully competent and cooperative to the point where when we breathalysed him we were like, "No fucking way! That's gotta be wrong."

His blood alcohol content was over .45! That's enough to kill a lot of people. But he acted completely sober. He had us totally fooled until the breathalyser.

He went to court and the judge read off the police notes which said he was competent, respectful and cooperative throughout. The judge looked at him and said, "Seems to me that you've developed some kind of superhuman tolerance to alcohol which is very frightening when you think about it."

Now I don't assume anything. Any slight indication of misjudgement we breathalyse them. They may well be an alcoholic who can act sober due to the massive tolerance they've built-up.

Who knows how many of them are out there still driving because nobody reported them to law enforcement or they were stopped and never breath tested because they seemed quite normal.

The morning drinker's commute

I work at a liquor store here in California. It is so fucking depressing working the morning shift. All the day drinkers form a line outside and wait for us to open. We refer to them as the morning club.

They shuffle in and count out the exact change with shaking hands for their nip bottles to dump in their morning coffees. Or they buy these miniatures as a way of rationing out their drinks at work so as to not get smashed. This is how they portion control themselves. The big bottles are purchased right after work.

I'll catch a whiff of mint from gum to cover the morning shots they've already had and cologne to cover the smell of their sweat. It's a funky, off-putting combination. Then they'll get back in their cars and drive off, technically three sheets to the wind despite being functional. Sometimes I feel like I am helping these people kill themselves.

I recently learned that when you see empty airplane sized shooters or pints on the side of the road, that's an alcoholic finishing their drink at the same spot every day on their commute to work.

They'll stop at the liquor store, get their commute liquor and finish it in the same amount of time each day. Then they throw the empty out of their car window and the bottles start piling up. Saddest shit ever.

As a store manager I see the decline

Liquor store manager here. I literally see how much and how often people drink. I can also tell when someone has a problem because there are different signs according to their age.

The under 30s come in frequently and are usually friendly but quiet and know not to come in visibly wasted. They have their money ready and are polite. They buy cheap beer or vodka or single items if their budget is blown. These folks aren't the party type despite their age and buy what they need to get drunk that night.

The 30 to 45 group are starting to appear unhealthy. They have bad skin, thinning hair, smell nasty and look older than they are. They buy a lot of liquor, beer and wine every second day or so in larger size formats. These folks will sometimes say they are having company over, using it for cooking or some other bullshit excuse.

If they're married, they'll pay in cash to avoid anything showing up on bank statements. I watch them come in, slowly disintegrating until they start looking sick all the time.

The 45 plus crowd are pretty much obvious. They have all the signs: a red nose, broken capillaries on their face and deep wrinkles. They also tend to have bad volume control on their voice. They buy whatever is on sale or cheap and shake so bad they can hardly get out the right change.

Some of them have that acrid smell that almost burns your nose like burnt rubber, which I'm guessing is from their livers starting to malfunction. I've had worried family members beg me not to sell alcohol to them, but I have to explain that they will just go elsewhere. Those are the times I feel pretty bad, but you have to harden yourself to it.

Then we have the hobos who will buy the cheapest gut-rot liquor or even cheaper Everclear which they dilute with water. I've seen them try and steal by stuffing bottles in their underpants and have to go and confront them which is always pretty awkward.

I feel I should add that I'm painting an image with broad generalizations based on hundreds of customers. But I'm mostly describing normal, good people with a functioning addiction.

I'm always curious when the regulars stop coming in, especially the handle guys. I have known a few to quit, but mostly I just hear they have died.

PART 5

Dealing with the fallout from alcohol abuse

Anecdotes and observations from nurses, doctors and other healthcare professionals

It's serious when your bloodwork looks like you've got cancer

Doc here. I work at a busy emergency department. In nearly 20 years of working in emergency rooms I don't think I've ever had a shift without an alcohol-related illness or injury.

Some of the sickest people I have ever seen are alcoholics with long-term complications that include ascites, pleural effusions (fluid in the lungs), hepatic encephalopathy (mental confusion), esophageal varices (bleeding in the GI tract) as well as lung and kidney dysfunction or failure.

We can manage most of these complications with meds and endoscopic procedures, but when things really start going downhill a liver transplant is required or the patient will die.

The reason all these symptoms occur is because alcohol – which we refer to as ethanol – causes fibrosis of the liver secondary to inflammation. When this happens, the blood pressure in the veins that enter the liver massively increases. Right up the line from the liver is the esophagus. The surge in blood pressure enlarges the veins in its lining which then have a tendency to bleed very badly.

I remember this one a guy in his 20s who came in complaining of dizziness and pain. He had difficulty walking and had no balance or coordination. He was sweaty, had a slight tremor and looked pallid. I checked his labs and was worried he had some kind of cancer because everything was wrong.

When I asked how he was feeling he said, "Oh okay, I guess. Just a little tired. I drank a bit more this week than usual and probably overdid it." Turns out he was totally unaware he was going through alcohol withdrawal because he hadn't stopped drinking long enough in recent memory to know what it felt like.

I pushed him for details and he admitted he'd drunk a gallon of tequila over the last three days and had only stopped because he was vomiting blood and pooping a mixture of bright red and almost black sticky stuff (which is digested blood). I sent him for an esophagography which confirmed an esophageal tear that required immediate intervention in the ICU.

All the alcohol-related liver cases are rough with long hospital stays, frequent readmissions and early relapse due to addictive behavior. Alcoholics are a very unpredictable and challenging bunch and a major source of burn out for ED staff.

Curious cases of alcohol tolerance

As a registered nurse I've had intelligent conversations with people with a BAC (meaning blood alcohol concentration) of over .45 which is normally not compatible with life.

Some of these individuals did not even appear drunk as they were not slurring or loud. They had most likely got away with serious traffic violations in the past because they seemed quite lucid and sober.

I once had an elderly lady getting checked in for alcohol withdrawal treatment by her son. On arrival she had a .45 BAC and was articulate and behaving reasonably. An hour later, within 15 minutes of her son leaving she had escaped from the psychiatry ward and found her way to the nearest bar to soothe her nerves with a drink!

The highest BAC I've seen was a 30-year-old female who was unresponsive for a while. We undressed her and put her in a gown and she didn't move a muscle. Her BAC was .56! Somehow she survived.

Another impressive one was a mid-40s female with a BAC of .55 who came in under her own steam wanting something to eat. Both of these ladies were petite, like 120 to 130lbs. Most people are slurring and obviously inebriated at up to .20. They are seizing or comatose at .30 and above. Staying alive at .45 or above is highly uncommon.

There was once a case report of a woman who was awake and lucid with a blood alcohol level of 1.10%! A blood alcohol level that high is truly mind-blowing. To put that in perspective, the DUI threshold for blood alcohol in the USA is .08%.

These career alcoholics or "frequent fliers" as we call them, come in with enough alcohol in their systems to kill a horse having built up so much tolerance over the years.

Admittedly, some of them do give it away by stinking to high heaven. Then we play "guess the alcohol level" when their blood samples are sent to the lab.

Just to be clear, you build up a tolerance to ethanol in the early stages of alcoholism. When you get to the late stages where your liver is diseased, your tolerance goes down due to the liver damage.
So please don't think drinking to reach tolerance is a good thing. It's just part of the journey towards terrible self-injury.

Frightening things about alcohol withdrawals

As a critical care nurse, I take care of more alcoholics than any other type of substance abuser. We treat them when they go into full withdrawal with agitation, sweating and uncontrollable shakes. This is when we have to tie them down to keep them safe and intubated.

We transfer them to the ICU because they need a level of sedation that would kill ten regular people. For example, a normal dose of the benzo Ativan is .5mg three times a day. I've given alcoholics 144mg of intravenous Ativan plus 360mg of benzo phenobarbital in a 12-hour shift without them ending up on a ventilator. Even a raging meth head doesn't need anywhere near that level of medication to calm down.

I've seen many individuals go through severe alcohol withdrawal and delirium tremens. Even the nicest people become growling, violent, drooling animals for five days, even with treatment. Without treatment it's seizures and possibly death.

My worst memory is of a guy in double-strength restraints on his legs and arms who almost stood up with the hospital bed attached to his back. Watching him thrash around like he was possessed by demons in a horror movie was truly terrifying.

Seriously, if a doctor asks you if you drink a lot before a procedure that requires sedation do not lie. Some drugs are less effective or have worse side effects in heavy drinkers. This is because they have different enzyme profiles, messed up brain receptors and other biochemical issues.

So always be honest about your alcohol intake or you may find an emergency procedure is not as pain free as it should be.

Unnatural bodily fluids

I work in a hospital lab and deal with urine and blood serum of patients with severe liver disease all the time. Urine colors range from neon yellow to brown as iced tea and the blood can be oily as hell.[64] Some of the other diagnostics can be pretty mind boggling too.

A couple of years ago, a patient was brought in after attempting to kill himself by drinking straight vodka and taking a handful of over-the-counter painkillers containing acetaminophen. This guy had AST and ALT values in the 15,000 range.

AST and ALT values tell us how much liver byproduct (i.e. dead liver cells) you have in your bloodstream. The higher the number, the more your liver has been destroyed. The normal range is around 10 to 50. Basically this guy's liver was torn almost completely apart and bits of it were flowing through his veins.

---

[64] https://en.wikipedia.org/wiki/Abnormal_urine_color

We had to verify the results by making sure the machines were calibrated properly. Everything checked out. This dude had essentially metabolized a lot of his liver. Amazingly he survived and was discharged a few weeks later after a lot of treatment.

Alcohol's terrible toll on young people

I'm an accident and emergency consultant and honorary clinical professor in the UK. I see the people coming in with every kind of addiction, but for me, alcohol is the worst.

It doesn't just kill people, it does so in the most prolonged, tortuous way, hollowing them out into emaciated, stumbling, shaking shells of their former selves.

At the end, they're bright yellow, mumbling zombies with vacant eyes, limbs that resemble twigs and a giant belly full of fluid. On top of all this, their brains have usually started to degenerate from all the toxins accumulating in their body.

Another unpredictable feature of their condition is oesophageal varices. If a swollen vein in their throat erupts, blood will shoot out of their mouth like a geyser and they can bleed out within minutes.[65]

These patients will then require a procedure called variceal banding using a gastroscope, which is a long flexible tube with a device attached to hold the surgical rubber bands that are used to tie the protruding veins.

Because there are so many manifestations of liver disease it's impossible to say which way it might go. One patient I saw was a real mess. His BAC was .49 when they pumped his stomach.

---

[65] Esophagus gastric varices
https://www.youtube.com/watch?v=1eBRkA8B-HU

He hadn't eaten for four weeks and because his body had started to digest itself, he'd developed lactic acidosis. This is when there's too much lactic acid in the blood from breaking down muscle and tissue to use as food. He was with us for over two weeks and actually survived.

Another one that has stuck in my mind was a man in his mid-30s who had developed diabetes and continued to drink. He got gangrene in a toe and lost it. As he kept drinking, he lost more toes. He finished up dying of sepsis as the gangrene progressed up his legs and there wasn't anything left to cut off to stop the advance.

A patient we're dealing with right now is a young mother in her mid-30s. She was brought in unconscious and jaundiced and has been intubated for weeks. All of her organs have failed, so we are putting her on dialysis once she's off life support so she can pass peacefully. and not end up drowning in her own fluids.

We have a massive drinking culture here in the UK with people drinking solely to get inebriated. Just because you're functional doesn't mean the damage isn't being done.

I routinely see people with cirrhosis who drink non-stop from Friday to Sunday. Yet no one seems to be talking about how many of these people are dying due to alcohol abuse. It's an ever-growing problem and the patients are getting younger and younger.

I once attended an autopsy of an alcoholic. After they sliced through about six inches of abdominal and chest fat, they cut into the rib cage to expose the organs. The fellow's liver was basically white with a few pink functioning areas. He was 41.

Now I show my recoverable patients scans of their liver in the hope of motivating them to reduce their alcohol intake and preferably stop it. Somehow, it's far more effective than just telling them they are one step closer to dying with every drink.

I have no idea if my interventions have any lasting effect. I hope that if I never see them again it means they listened.

Oesophageal varices are my worst nightmare

I'm a GI nurse in a gastroenterologist department at a major teaching hospital in the UK. I have seen many 40-year-olds and younger with end stage liver disease.

They come in with liver failure which causes ascites, which is a build-up of fluid in the abdomen. Gallons of it are drained off only to reaccumulate. Elsewhere their skin might be sweaty, itchy, sore and bruise and tear easily. The itching is bile salts leaving through the pores of the skin because they're also building up in their body.

The liver also produces clotting factors for your blood. When this process fails, you can start to bleed out of every orifice and even through your skin.

If you go into cardiac arrest we will do everything we can to keep you alive. Because we know this is going to be a bloody mess, we wear PPE from head to toe as it's going to be a literal blood bath.

I know that if we have to do chest compressions, blood will probably explode from your mouth. There's also a high probability that one of your oesophageal varices will burst and paintball the room and all of us red. I've seen blood on the ceiling, on the walls, pools of blood on the floor and we will slip and almost fall while trying to treat the patient.

Here in the UK, we tend to immediately administer vasoconstrictors, transfusions and omeprazole which usually gives us enough of a break in the bleeding to run a scope down and get the varices banded within about half an hour. The GI consultants in my hospital don't fuck about.

We do have the emergency Blakemore tube in our fridge but it has never had to be used on my shifts. We follow the protocol in the UK's guidelines on the management of variceal haemorrhage.[66]

---

[66] UK guidelines on the management of variceal haemorrhage in cirrhotic patients

If we are able to get any return of circulation, the survival rate is pretty high at this stage. But if you do die on a ventilator, the upside is that you will save your family from having to withdraw your care. Saying that, most of the time we get these patients back, sometimes for days, sometimes for months and there are even a few success stories who are still going to this day.

Unfortunately, I've seen young people in their 20s and 30s with advanced cirrhosis and the blood pressure of a 65-year-old who's been smoking their whole life. At this point they either get a transplant, or if they don't qualify, all that's left is palliative care or hospice.

If they are in a really bad state and we've run out of options I will call their relatives and explain that all we can do is make them comfortable and load them up with morphine until they pass away.

Liver failure is a terrible way to go. You'll be fine one minute, then one day your pee turns brown, your eyes and skin are yellow and you've got ascites. Or one of your oesophageal varices might burst and you'll bleed out alone at home or intubated and miserable in intensive care. I know because I've seen many of these patients and tried to save them.

Why being in a coma is not all it appears

As a physician in a busy emergency department, we do a lot of CT scans and can spot the heavy drinkers straight away. They have so much brain atrophy/disintegration that they are like elderly patients. We also have alcoholics come in with brain bleeds who need emergency surgery.

Afterwards they may seem like they are vegetables on ventilators, but the crazy thing is they still kind of know what's going on. We call this "covert consciousness." The part of their brain that enables them to

---

https://pmc.ncbi.nlm.nih.gov/articles/PMC4680175/

walk and talk no longer works, but the parts that register their environment do.

Say you get a ruptured blood vessel in your brain. It puts a ton of pressure on critical brain regions and wipes out the areas that make you appear conscious. At this point you don't look like you're aware of anything and can't hold two fingers up or blink on command. But if we put sensors on your head to check for electrical activity, the devices will pick up signals of a reaction even though you can't outwardly convert them into movement.

In cases like this the patient can recover, but it might take a year or more. During this time they will physically deteriorate and need feeding tubes for nutrition and tracheostomies so they can breathe.

It is always interesting to hear patients who have come out of a coma describe their very vivid nightmares because they are all related to their actual environment. For example, they will dream they're on a boat that's sinking. That's because their bed was moving automatically to prevent bedsores. Or they will talk about being held hostage or choked, which is probably from being intubated or restrained. Unfortunately, some of these patients can end up with PTSD that lasts for years.

Pancreatitis is a horrendous condition

Gastroenterologist here in Alicante, Spain. Sadly, we are one of the top countries in Europe for alcohol abuse. Half of our population drinks alcohol daily.[67] A cheap bottle of wine here is €1.5 which is $2.00 thereabouts and vodka can be around €6 per liter or less. It's a huge problem for us.

---

[67] The epidemiology of alcohol consumption in Spain
https://pubmed.ncbi.nlm.nih.gov/3045041/#:~:text=This%20paper%20is%20a%20comprehensive,public%20health%20and%20socioeconomic%20problem.

What I want to talk about here is an issue I see very often that has not really been talked about as being related to heavy alcohol consumption and that is pancreatitis. Also, duodenitis which affects the pancreatic head.

People think alcohol only affects the liver, but the pancreas is very vulnerable to destruction from alcohol and is often the first major organ to go.

What is the pancreas? It is a long, flat soft organ about 8" long with a bumpy surface that looks like corn on the cob. It is located on the upper left side of your abdomen and produces digestive juices that break down food proteins and hormones like insulin.

If it cannot function properly, it will start to dissolve/digest your body from the inside. Necrotizing pancreatitis from alcohol toxicity will kill you quickly and painfully if we do not treat it in time.

The most common symptoms of chronic pancreatitis are intense abdominal pain, typically below the ribs and through to the back, abdominal swelling and an increased heart rate.

The symptoms will be so severe you won't be able to eat or drink anything. Even a tiny sip of water will irritate the organ causing nausea due to unbearable pain, which mainly manifests in the back area. The only things that will help you at this point are meperidine, morphine or fentanyl.

I had one 29-year-old male screaming in agony and crawling on the floor almost delirious telling me to either knock him out or kill him. Due to protocol he had to have a suicide assessment after that.

Alcohol use disorder is hitting young people hard

ICU physician here. The official figures say one in five deaths of people aged between 20 and 49 are due to alcohol which includes accidents and disease.[68]

In my experience it's at least double that with all the suicides and domestic violence. I'd say 75% of assaults and about 50% of the trauma admissions we get in the ER involve alcohol. Then there are all the illnesses like cancer and heart problems which are not recognized as alcohol-associated.

In addition to this we had an escalation of alcoholism with the Covid lockdown situation which brought in the normalization of heavy day drinking. Everyone was stuck at home, bored, isolated and worried to death about their jobs with nothing to do but drink.

One such example was a patient who was admitted into intensive care two years into the pandemic with severe liver injury due to excessive alcohol consumption. She was just a social drinker before Covid; nothing more than one or two drinks at the weekend.

Then she started working from home. She'd get her work done before noon most days and out of boredom she'd drink a bottle of wine every afternoon. That one bottle turned into two.

A few months before her hospital admission she got laid off from her job and was hitting close to four bottles of wine a day. She came to us looking like a limp banana. Liver failure led to more organ failures. Then she started bleeding from everywhere due to lack of clotting proteins and platelets. After a month of full medical support, she succumbed to her illness at the age of 33.

---

[68] Estimated Deaths Attributable to Excessive Alcohol Use Among US Adults Aged 20 to 64 Years, 2015 to 2019
https://pmc.ncbi.nlm.nih.gov/articles/PMC9627409/

Another one of my patients was a 23-year-old male in need of a transplant. He was Homer Simpson color. His dad was also an alcoholic who had lost his job due to Covid in early 2021, so they both spent the pandemic drinking themselves to death together. This guy was so depressed he had no intention of quitting and died of cirrhosis.

It doesn't help that alcohol is so ingrained in our culture. There's this whole thing now with "wine moms" who get together and drink until school pick up, by which time they are probably in no fit state to drive.

College students must drink to fit in or find themselves socially sidelined, and every significant social event seems to revolve around booze. Heck I even had a 21-year-old patient recovering from her stem cell transplant who turned 21. Pharmacy sent her a Budweiser on her lunch tray!

The stereotypical picture of the alcoholic patient has definitely changed. The majority of them are now stay-at-home moms or work from home professionals, with many having young kids. And the number of severe alcohol withdrawal and end stage liver disease I'm seeing in 20 to 35-year-olds is astonishing. It's hard to see parents cope with the reality that their son or daughter won't see 40.

A no-holds barred description of liver failure

I've been a critical care nurse for 18 years, working in hospitals in the United States and the UK. Here are a few highlights of dying from advanced liver failure. The order may vary, but generally speaking you will experience all or some of the following. Warning – this reads like a Stephen King novel!

When you start developing liver failure, the first thing you'll notice is the whites of your eyes turning a weird yellow shade, like the color of concentrated pee. Your skin will then turn the same sickly orange/yellow color.

When the blood from your GI tract starts backing up because it can't physically make it through your liver, you will start to develop portal hypertension. The increased vascular pressure caused by this "blockage" will force the fluid component of your blood to leak out into your abdominal cavity and lungs causing a complication called ascites. Your belly will expand as if you are pregnant with twins.

You'll either be in the ER or the interventional radiology clinic weekly having a doctor stick a long needle into your abdomen to drain your abdominal fluid – a procedure called paracentesis – otherwise it will press on your lungs, causing you to feel chronically short of breath. Sometimes this has to be done daily. You'll also be given diuretics to prolong the time between paracentesis which will make you pee almost constantly.

Because you now have the immune system of an advanced AIDS patient, all the fluid accumulating inside of you will likely get infected and become septic. If this happens you'll be pumped full of the strongest antibiotics we've got and a tube will be inserted to drain off the foul-smelling liquid.

At some point you may be brought in by ambulance because you've gone crazy and can't form words or move your body because the ammonia your liver can't process anymore has reached your brain. This is called hepatic encephalopathy. You'll hallucinate, become agitated and combative and will most likely need to be placed in restraints.

You will be given – or more accurately force fed – mega doses of a sickly-sweet liquid laxative called lactulose that makes you shit out all the GI bacteria that convert nitrogen gas into ammonia. Outside of a liver transplant this is the only thing that will save your life and keep your brain going. Unfortunately, this stuff tastes terrible and you won't want to take it, so several nurses will have to hold you down to put a tube up your nose and down into your stomach.

On the subject of tubes, we'll also have to put a Foley catheter in for urine because you'll be too disoriented and weak to get out of bed and go to the bathroom. You will be hooked up to a lot of machines which will beep continuously 24/7.

In addition to all this, your legs will probably be swollen so badly from edema that you won't be able to lift them off the bed. Due to your compromised nutritional status, you will also get bedsores in places you never imagined: on your feet, shoulders, elbows and even the back of your head.

When your liver is too full of scar tissue to process blood efficiently it backs up into the veins of your neck which can rupture, causing you to vomit all your blood out.

At this point you may die with someone like me struggling to intubate you against the torrent of esophageal blood spewing from your mouth and nose. Minutes before this you may have been completely independent, continent and able to hold a conversation. Esophageal varices can take you out at any time.

All of this is putting a lot of strain on your heart which is trying to keep the blood moving to your tissues. But your blood is so thin and you're so anemic your heart is having a hard time keeping up. It starts getting saggier and weaker, resulting in a condition called cardiomyopathy.

As a result, the blood moving through your lungs just stays there, causing what's known as pulmonary edema. This is a medical emergency because now you feel like someone is sitting on your chest and you can barely breathe.

For reasons we don't fully understand, blood flow alteration through the portal system also causes kidney damage, so there's a good chance you'll end up on dialysis too.

Every few days your ammonia level will get too high and you'll forget who you are again. Or your sodium will plummet and you'll fall into a coma. Or your potassium will spike and now you're probably going to have a heart attack.

You'll be on oxygen because your lungs are so congested. Meanwhile your kidneys are failing and you're wasting away like a cancer patient because your stomach can't absorb the nutrients from your food. As well as being emaciated with sunken eyes and a dry mouth, you will go in and out of consciousness, be delirious and in pain usually for between one to four weeks.

The vast majority of patients who die from liver disease do so in hospital. By the way, the breath of a dying liver patient is just horrible. They call it fetor hepaticus.

In the end, a member of the medical team will be tasked with calling your next of kin to ask them if they know your DNR (Do Not Resuscitate) status. By this stage CPR would be futile and cruel because you will still die but with broken ribs. Being kept alive in a coma on life support will also be extremely expensive for your family.

I know a lot of people think, "Life's shit, I'll just drink myself to death," not realizing that their decision to commit suicide might take a moment, but their actual death might take one to two years. And incidentally, it will likely not even be your liver that gets you, or probably not even your heart as it struggles to pump blood. You are more likely to drown in your own fluids or bleed out.

Seriously, if you want to kill yourself with alcohol, liver failure is one of the slowest, messiest and most painful ways to go. I would not recommend it.

The one patient that made me stop drinking

I'm an ER doctor. I've had shootings, traumas and burns, but the worst cases for me are liver failure from alcoholic cirrhosis. It's so hard to take care of somebody you can't really help.

On being admitted it was assumed one female patient we had was pregnant. Instead, she had 10 liters of fluid in her belly and her eyes and entire body were the color of a goldenrod yellow crayon.

I listened to her tell me about her dogs and rubbed her feet while we waited for the equipment to get the fluid out of her abdomen. Her liver failure was so far advanced there was nothing we could do but try to keep her comfy.

Another upsetting case was a 31-year-old woman diagnosed with Korsakoff syndrome. She'd keep blacking out from drinking and confabulate a story about having been drugged and sexually assaulted. I did four sexual assault kits on this poor girl and other hospitals did even more. We wound up having to get a special waiver from the state because doing repeated kits was not good for her mental health.

Another one I try to help is a 26-year-old guy with recurrent pancreatitis. He comes in walking and talking with a BAC of .350 on a regular basis. He's had four attacks of acute pancreatitis this year with his heartrate going up to 120 and staying there. He sweats and is in a lot of pain but tries to be polite and thankful because he knows he'll be back.

Then there was the severely alcoholic mid-30s woman with esophageal varices that wouldn't stop popping due to portal vein hypertension. They'd fix one and then another one would go. We gave her over 30 units of blood. She was finally discharged with a follow up appointment for labs.

For some reason that one did it for me. I didn't drink for six months after that. Now I only have one or two drinks every few weeks.

I deal with every stage of alcohol use disorder

I've been an ER nurse off and on for 16 years. Every shift I take care of at least one intoxicated person. These are the kinds of alcohol associated admissions I deal with on a daily basis.

In terms of being actively inebriated we have our frequent-flyer drunks who are often homeless and have poorly managed mental illnesses. The best-case scenario is that they MTF (metabolize to freedom), fall asleep and snore in a hallway bed for hours, wake up, piss in the corner and quietly leave with a turkey sandwich.

If we're unlucky, they'll claim to be suicidal because they know it buys them hours in a warm bed with what they consider room service. Now I have to babysit them for the whole shift because social work can't assess them until they're sober, at which point I'm also managing their withdrawal.

Be assured that many attempts have been made to get them into rehab. It works on a handful but the vast majority will just relapse and start coming in again for their "emergency" shots of wine or Ativan. We know these folks well: their birthdates, tattoos and history. To them we're the only family they've got, which is sad.

Then we have the GI bleeds, pleural effusions, kidney failure and ascites in patients with cirrhosis. Next there are the liver cancer patients who acquired the disease after they stopped drinking. I also see withdrawal seizure cases regularly, plus lots of injuries like sprains, lacerations and fractures.

The alcohol-induced liver failure cases also come in multiple times a week. The pancreatitis people are next. After that we have the kidney damage patients and the ones with medical issues caused by forgetting to take their meds because they are too drunk.

Night shift sees young people and college students with alcohol poisoning on a fairly regular basis. These comatose 20-somethings are dragged in by their buddies who are themselves usually drenched in vomit and piss. The star of the show will eventually wake up, stumble around and will also need babysitting until they're dischargeable.

The cops will bring in the rowdily intoxicated. If we're lucky they will already be under arrest for doing something stupid and will only be with us briefly for medical clearance before going to jail. If not, we are left to deal with whatever drunken fuckery prompted them to be picked up in the first place. These folks usually end up in restraints.

A huge number of traumas and car accidents are also due to heavy drinkers. Some will board with us overnight because they're too inebriated to go home. In addition to this there are our "normal" ER patients who come in for other issues. It's always a surprise when they start withdrawing on day two or three of their hospital stay.

Cleaning up after Australia's booze problem

I'm an anaesthetist in Australia and have had two patients die in theatre from GI bleeds in the last two weeks. The second one looked like a bloated corpse that had been dredged from a river. She was just hosing blood from every single orifice. She was in her early 40s with teenage kids.

The one prior was a fella who had stopped drinking, but it was too late. The operating room looked like a fucking field hospital in Afghanistan by the time we'd finished. There was blood on the equipment, the walls, everywhere.

Then we had this one Aussie guy in his early 30s on an international flight from Europe. He went nuts half way through and tried to open the doors of the plane. He was brought into hospital red in the face with no idea why he was suddenly in Australia.

His wife and children couldn't understand why he'd got so ill on their international trip. The answer was he'd missed a few drinks during the 24-hour-flight and was going through withdrawals.

He needed heaps of medication to settle him and was trying to swipe imaginary bugs off his arms. His brain was atrophied like an 80-year-old. Found out later he'd get through about five litres of vodka per week. Unless you're a Russian pro wrestler that's too much.

The cost of drinking Down Under

I'm a paramedic here in Australia and have dealt with alcohol and its consequences and spend most of my time scraping drunk people off the pavement and getting covered in their vomit. Most times, the most serious cases die on scene and don't make it to the ED.

One of the worst I ever transported was a woman whose oesophageal varices had ruptured. She was spewing blood from her mouth like something from The Exorcist and we were struggling to control her airway. It was far more gruesome than most of the traumas I've dealt with.

Another sad case was this guy in his mid-40s who drank a liter of vodka almost every day. He had this lovely, friendly Labradoodle dog. This bloke would go on benders for days and the poor pup would hardly get fed and do her business on the floor.

When he didn't show up for work someone would call 000. We'd take him to the hospital and law officers would impound the dog. Then he'd sober up, go to AA a few times get his dog back and repeat the whole thing every few months. I've seen this situation many times with people with families, but for some reason this one hit home because of that poor dog.

Then there was the guy who had drunk 2.5 liters of vodka and an unknown quantity of beers in a single night. He could barely sit up and had to be stair chaired out. He could hardly answer any questions on scene, yet he was completely coherent by the time we got to the hospital 20 minutes later! Seriously, I'd be dead if I drank as much as that.

I remember when I was studying my paramedic degree, we reviewed research on the effect of alcohol consumption on the wider economy. The data is over a decade old now, but it cost the health system in Australia $12 billion per year and the wider economy about $30 billion.

To put that figure in perspective, we could have built almost 30 new hospitals or expanded our Navy Destroyer fleet of three by a factor of 10. I don't understand why the social and economic issues of alcohol get no attention. It's like society is rotting from the inside and everyone's turning a blind eye.

The brain damage no one talks about

I had a 55-year-old patient with Korsakoff's Syndrome which is permanent brain damage from alcohol abuse. I treated him until it became obvious he required fulltime care. Unfortunately, the memory care facilities kept kicking him out for attacking the other patients who were older and frailer than he was, being all of 270lbs and 6'3".

Despite not knowing what day of the week it was, this former computer engineer was still intermittently witty and clever. He couldn't cope with being parked in front of a TV all day next to old folks with dementia and Alzheimer's and got frustrated and kept lashing out.

On release he returned to alcohol and his brain damage become much worse. Six months or so later, he had some cognitive function, but was unable to care for himself. Unfortunately, he had also become so violent and dangerous it was recommended he have neurosurgery as a last resort.

One of his relatives told me he attended the marriage of his son recently and during the wedding ceremony he was grunting and shouting randomly the whole time. He passed three months later. I've known a few people die one way or another from alcohol abuse, but somehow this was more disturbing.

No – alcohol does not make you superhuman

I'm an emergency physician and spend most of my days off during the summer on my boat. Every year there's been someone killed by doing dumb shit that I'm forced to respond to.

Last summer we had a fatality. There was a boat full of 21-year-olds who dared a drunk 19-year-old to jump from one moving boat to another. The kid missed and went through the propellor and was bisected. The left half of his body was never found.

Back in the ER I also dealt with another guy who fell out of his boat while drunk. His right side from mid-thigh to the top of his pelvis looked like spiral cut ham. When we poked around to see how deep the laceration was, we could see right into his hip joint.

On the other hand, some drunken idiots can jump from a third story balcony using an umbrella as a parachute, land on a pile of rocks and walk away from it. Apparently, intoxicated people don't stiffen up and brace for impact. They tend to bounce like a soft, pliant ragdoll and acquire less injuries than if they were sober.

I believe this is why so many drunk drivers will walk away from horrifying accidents, sustaining only bruises and cuts while the unfortunate people they crash into do not.

But generally speaking, no you don't turn into Deadpool when you're intoxicated and inadvertently expose yourself to some kind of horrific, near-death event. You just don't notice the fractures, dislocations, burns, lacerations, missing teeth and concussions until – or more to the point *if* – you wake up.

We are all one bad day away from being a "frequent flier"

Accident and Emergency Department nurse here in the UK. Outside of active war zones there is nowhere on earth where tragedy occurs at the rate it does in A&E. It would psychologically cripple a normal person to experience the Charles Dickens novel type adversity we see on a daily basis.

A few years back I had a frequent flier whose only child had died while serving in Iraq. Two weeks later, his wife committed suicide. He'd been an alcoholic ever since and was currently homeless. He'd tried to quit alcohol numerous times and had been on a sober streak until the day he came in, about two months after his last visit.

During our conversation he told me that the A&E staff were the only family he had, despite the fact most of them were pissed off to see him. He knew how they felt but they were the only people who had been there for him and had prevented him from topping himself many times.

I can't blame him for becoming an alcoholic. I probably would have done the same thing in his situation. It's a reminder that although we stand at opposite ends of the patient-provider interaction, these poor sods could be us if the dominoes were to fall the wrong way.

Nobody grows up wanting to be an addict of any sort. For most people, alcohol doesn't start out as the problem; it started as the solution to incredible pain. A lot of people are just one bad day away from collapsing financially, medically and/or psychologically.

What I'm saying is everyone deserves compassionate care without judgement regardless. The reactions I get when I explain this to an apologetic, self-loathing substance abuse patient is heartbreaking. They literally hug me and cry.

Insights from a rehab center nurse

I work in drug and alcohol treatment but have also worked in ER as a nurse. Addiction is such a dark place. It's when people want to die but don't want to stop breathing. To quote Charlie Sheen from "Two and a Half Men," who says he drinks, "Because there are things inside of me I need to kill."

Virtually all the addicts I've encountered have suffered some kind of personal trauma, neglect or abuse or witnessed terrible horrors and do not have the psychological or emotional capacity to deal with it.

I've seen cops, athletes, teachers, doctors, lawyers, nurses, therapists and professionals from all walks of life come in to detox. I've had pregnant patients, people in wheelchairs and kids fresh out of high school. I even had an 80-year-old seek treatment for alcohol use disorder. They are typically humble, exhausted and open to help.

Having also worked in an emergency department, the intoxicated folks who are brought in seem to be taken over by a whole different type of demon. These so-called crippled alcoholics are fighting their battle alone and can't see their future any other way. Sometimes they have chronic illnesses that they're self-medicating and a lot of them use the ER because they don't have access to primary care.

You're often seeing someone at the lowest points in their life in the emergency room, but if a nurse or doc shows they care, it can give these people hope. It can lift them up and restore their dignity.

I know, you will be mostly wasting your time. But who knows, it could be the experience that finally convinces one of these suffering individuals to choose recovery.

A weird way to stop withdrawals

Male nurse here. I swear I'm not making this up. One night I'm working an overtime checking on a dude who had beaten up his wife. This guy was a life-long drunk and mean as hell. He tried kicking me and spat on me once. Just a horrible human being.

While he's strapped to the bed, I hear what sounds like water splashing onto the floor. Thinking he'd managed to knock something over next to his bed I go and take a look.

This dude is pissing straight into his mouth and drinking it! It was like one of those fairground games where you aim a stream of water into the clown's mouth to inflate the balloon on its head. What was even more impressive was this dude was in 4-point restraints.

Apparently, life-long alcoholics do this trick to stay drunk off their pee and stop withdrawals. I had no idea this was a thing until someone at the hospital told me that's why we keep prescription beer on hand.

Every drink buys you another ticket in the cancer lottery

As an oncologist I can't help but think about the scientific research[69] when I see anyone drinking. Even moderate amounts of alcohol increase your risk for liver, breast, head and neck, esophageal, colorectal and stomach cancers.

Surprisingly few people realize this and think they are all caused by genetics and chemicals in the environment. Lately I've even heard Covid vaccines and 5G mentioned, but never alcohol.

---

[69] Cancer risk based on alcohol consumption levels: a comprehensive systematic review and meta-analysis - Epub 2023 Oct 16
https://pubmed.ncbi.nlm.nih.gov/37905315/

What's particularly disturbing to me is the rising incidence of cancer among younger adults over the past 15 or so years. In particular, I'm seeing an increasing number of people under 50 with bowel and other cancers.

The problem is, the metabolic by-product of alcohol, a compound called acetaldehyde, causes DNA damage and cell mutations. It's one of the most toxic substances known to human cells.

Alcohol also increases the level of estrogen and insulin which prompt faster cell division, especially in breast tissue, which can lead to mutations and ultimately tumors. It also makes it harder for the body to absorb nutrients, disrupts hormone levels and destroys good gut bacteria, all of which add to your risk for malignancies.

One 37-year-old patient I treated recently told me he avoided doctors and didn't believe in colonoscopies. He came in with stage four colon cancer. About a month later I performed a six-hour surgery to remove parts of his intestines, liver, appendix, gallbladder and other affected organs. He'd been quite a big whiskey drinker for approaching 20 years.

After this he needed chemotherapy and I had to explain to him that if he continued to drink he would have worse side effects of dehydration, mouth sores and nausea as well as an increased risk for infection, bleeding and anemia, because alcohol and chemo affect the bone marrow. Chemo is also processed through the liver like alcohol so drinking is adding another layer of toxicity and inflammation that's best avoided.

Finally, of course, he would be increasing the risk of the colorectal cancer reoccurring or a new primary cancer developing. Despite telling all my patients this you'd be surprised how many keep drinking.

After I removed all his tumors, I sent him to the cancer dietitian, like I do with all my patients. As well as consuming unhealthy levels of alcohol most of them have spent decades eating lots of processed and fast food and not many of them are physically active on a regular basis.

They don't like it, but if they care about the quality and length of the remainder of their lives, they have to get used to the idea of eating more fish and vegetables, detaching themselves from their electronic devices and moving around a lot more. Of course, they must also say goodbye to the booze.

Another issue I am seeing is a huge increase in breast cancer in the under 50s. If there is one piece of advice I would give to women, it is to cut back or stop drinking and eat more fiber. It will really help to reduce your cancer risk.

Whether it's Everclear or a $100 bottle of Cabernet, all forms of alcohol are carcinogenic. I believe some countries are adding cancer warnings to the bottle labels. Hopefully it will become a global trend.

PART 6

Real-life anecdotes and observations from people who have experienced the consequences of heavy drinking

I spiraled during 2020

Before the Covid lockdowns I was a fit, social and overall happy human being. Then I was furloughed for six months and without work all I did was drink. Being unemployed with those ridiculous stimulus checks didn't help. Ridiculous as in I was making way more sitting at home than I was before, so of course I spent it all on booze.

Before the pandemic I never drank during the week. At the weekend I would have a few glasses of wine and I'd go to the gym 4 to 5 days a week. Then all the gyms shut down, the grocery stores had weird opening hours and the only things that stayed open in my area was a liquor store and a MacDonalds.

The liquor store only had a small parking lot and someone had to direct the traffic because of the volume of customers. I guess these places were kept open because they knew there would be too many people with withdrawals to deal with.

Then I discovered an alcohol delivery service and would order wine and a six pack every day. This turned into a few boxes of wine a week. I was drinking for breakfast and lunch and sleeping in the afternoon. The ritual of watching YouTube and getting wasted became my main activity.

Eventually my tolerance got to the point where it took more alcohol than I could physically stomach to get drunk. I also gained a bunch of weight and was in the worst shape of my life.

It really was a killer because I had previously cut down, lost weight, started training and gotten into a good head space. Incidentally, the more sedentary your lifestyle, the earlier you die. This is scientific fact.

The speed at which things escalated for me is a shocking reminder of how fast these things can happen to otherwise "normal" drinkers. To this day my head is still not 100% clear and I take pills for anxiety and panic attacks.

My therapist told me there's an unspoken epidemic of people who developed alcoholism during the lockdowns due to the lack of social interaction, domestic abuse/violence, financial uncertainty and the schools being closed.

I hope some psychiatric think tank takes the time to study the before and after effects of that whole event.

Senior health issues at 40

I have been drinking nearly every single day since I was 15 years old. I'm an accountant, and really good at my job, but have a lot of the common issues that alcoholics tend to have, like calling in sick on Mondays and being late for work etc. I'd usually drink after work, but at weekends I would drink from the time I got up until I went to sleep, hard liquor included.

Every year I ran to get into shape. I'd reduce the drinking, eat better and get more sleep. Until one year, I ran for a couple of weeks and got a strange pain in my groin, thigh and hip area. After that I started walking with a brutal limp.

I went to the chiropractor about 10 times. Then I went to a doctor who did X-rays and urinalysis to test my kidneys. Nobody could find anything wrong.

Finally, I went to an orthopedist who sent me for an MRI. This is where I got the news I'd been fearing for years. He said I had a dead spot caused by avascular necrosis on my femur that could possibly be drilled out, but more likely would need surgery.

Then he mentioned that this can be an issue associated with long-term drinking. As soon as he said that, my heart sank. You can't drink every day for 25 years and not pay the price, right?

I had a total hip replacement at 40 because of my alcohol consumption. This is the kind of procedure you get when you're approaching 70. I had nurses walk by to check me out like an exhibit because I was the youngest person to have that operation at their hospital.

My liver wasn't the problem

Me and my colleagues at the law firm would get our blood tested every year and our results always came back saying our livers were fine which shouldn't have been possible.

Then I ended up in an ICU after drinking two liters of wine and shots of tequila every day for approaching a couple of years. My liver was a non-issue but my pancreas was fucked.

It's not a measure of good health to have a tortured yet functioning liver while all the other organs around it are failing. Oh, and they will eventually fail. It's not a matter of if, but when.

I think was Ernest Hemingway who said, "We go bankrupt slowly then suddenly." Same thing with your health and drinking.

Why tf isn't there more awareness about cirrhosis?

I was a heavy drinker for four years. Sometimes it was a bottle of wine before bed and sometimes almost two. I must add that I am around 30lbs overweight and my diet has always been poor. I routinely saw my doctor and she always told me that my liver function was fine, my enzymes were fine and I was doing alright.

Then I found myself being unable to walk and feeling tired. I had the shakes and my feet felt like they were burning. I went to the ER after collapsing. My bilirubin was 6.5 mg/dl and my INR (blood clotting measurement) was 1.6. It was rough shit.

I quit drinking immediately and ran off to my doctor screaming about the results. She threw up her hands and sent me to an internal medicine guy. He ran bloodwork and everything came back as normal. I pressed him a little further and he agreed to send me off to a liver specialist.

The second I walked into his office he took one look at me and said, "You've got cirrhosis" just by seeing the palms of my hands, looking at my fingernails and gums and noticing some rashes.

He hooked me up to some kind of ultrasound machine that pulsed and sent waves into my liver. The results came back and they were bad. I had a biopsy two weeks later and it was confirmed. I had compensated cirrhosis, yet I had no major symptoms whatsoever. No yellow eyes, no crazy wet brain confusion, no massive belly or those bleeding things in the throat people get.

In my case even my moderate drinking plus being overweight was dangerous. My specialist explained the safe daily limits are more about harm reduction than anything else because alcohol is detrimental to every part of your body.

He said cirrhosis looks different in everybody with different levels of severity, different symptoms and different causes. He also casually mentioned that half of cirrhosis patients who die only find out they are seriously ill six months before that!

I have no idea what my prognosis is. I'm exercising, eating healthy and taking my medications, but living in this state of limbo is the hardest thing. The Internet has been scaring the bejeezus out of me as I've read about this thing and it's serious.

I feel as if I have been given a death sentence and I probably have. I wake up every morning in fear. I don't want to die.

Liver is fucked

36-year-old male here, binge drinking up to four times a week mainly beer and the odd whiskey. Blood tests were always fine except for a few times when the liver enzymes were slightly higher after a bender or holidays. They went down after a stint of cutting back.

MRIs had shown some fatty liver, but it wasn't treated seriously. Out of curiosity I asked my doctor for a Fibroscan (elastography in the UK). The result showed a liver stiffness of 25 KPa, which supposedly means my liver is fucked beyond repair.

Anything over 14 kPa is 90% likely cirrhosis. I have no symptoms whatsoever. The doctor says I have to repeat the test after two months of zero alcohol. He says it is unlikely my liver will ever fully heal. Even if I somehow survive, I will have this forever.

Diagnosed with cirrhosis at 24

I'm female and drank around 20 shots of vodka every day from the age of 20 to 23. I decided to get clean and completed 30 days of residential rehab. I was 85 days sober until I relapsed.

I immediately got readmitted and completed 34 days of a PHP (partial hospitalization program) before my therapist decided she was comfortable enough to send me home. I was sober for another year and relapsed again, so I started attending AA meetings and have not drank since.

Despite quitting on and off, I was recently diagnosed with stage 3 cirrhosis. My ALT was 182 and AST was 161. My doctor made it very clear that without a transplant I will be dead in the next two to three years. Within the last few weeks, I have got ascites pretty bad and look like I'm nine months pregnant.

The worst thing is, I knew I had liver issues to begin with due to genetics, yet I still caused further harm by drinking and pretty much destroyed my liver in just 3 years. I have a 6-year-old daughter and a 4-year-old-son and I'm devastated I won't be able to see them grow up.

I don't want to scare anyone but this is real life. People think you have to drink for decades to get to this level of sickness but that is simply not true. Youth does not protect you.

No matter what has happened in your life, poisoning yourself with alcohol is not worth it. It has ruined my life, my health and my relationships. My kids are truthfully the only thing that is getting me through this. If I didn't have them, I would have just given up.

Living with liver disease

I'm a 27-year-old male. Two years ago, I was in the hospital throwing up blood due to internal bleeding from varices. I had hepatic encephalopathy and a decompensated liver and was basically told there was no going back to healing.

I was taken into hospital with hepatic encephalitis, kidney damage, bilateral cellulitis and septicemia. I was in there for a month while they got me stabilized and drained the fluid out of me. I was on an albumin drip most of the time and was catheterized for the first week.

In the decompensated phase things go downhill fast. Usually at this stage the damage is irreversible but sometimes you get lucky. Thanks to a very clean diet and exercise (I was 400lbs and now I'm 220lbs) my liver has bounced back and I'm recompensated. That being said, I keep lactulose on hand in case the toxins start building up and I have a hepatic encephalopathy event.

Three years later I am still on medications and have an ultrasound, bloodwork every three months and imaging once a year. My doc is very optimistic about things despite saying he expects to have me as a patient for a long time.

He says although cirrhosis never goes away, the symptoms can be managed. Providing you listen to the medical professionals and do exactly what they say regarding diet (low sodium) and exercise it's not unheard of to live for decades.

I drank myself infertile

I went into liver failure at 26 years old. I woke up one morning and was yellow in my eyes and all over my chest and I couldn't think straight. I kept saying to myself this day would come if I didn't stop, but never thought it would be so soon. I realized I had just taken my last drink the previous night.

My friend arrived to drive me to hospital and I struggled getting into her car. I spent hours in the emergency department where they medicated me for withdrawals and performed a series of tests including ultrasounds and a full MRI.

A doctor said "Wow, a young woman like you shouldn't be having liver problems like this." I spent an entire week there, having been diagnosed with stage 4 liver disease.

I am now 28, still sober and healthier without the toxins of alcohol. But due to the irreversible effects of cirrhosis I'm on 10 medications, several of which I take more than once a day. I suffer from memory loss, osteopenia and infertility, so I'll never have a baby. I also have paralyzing night terrors and hot flashes and no longer own a vehicle because I had to report my hepatic encephalopathy to the DMV.

I'll be honest, I used heroin for a while and ended up addicted. Quitting that was easy compared to quitting booze. I can go weeks without thinking about heroin, but I can't go more than an hour without thinking of alcohol. It's one helluva drug.

I mostly killed my liver but totally ruined my life

At 27 I was burning through jobs, friends, and relationships after drinking every day for about 10 years. Then one day I had delirium tremens when my alcohol level got too low and was taken to the hospital. They said if I hadn't gone in I wouldn't have made it through the night. My bloodwork showed high levels of liver enzymes which only leak out of dead liver cells. I was told my results were more typical for an autopsy.

I spent a week in an ICU and was sober for another three months in a residential setting. I stayed sober after that, changed my diet, consumed a set amount of fluid and no more than 1000mg of sodium per day. It was miserable, but I stuck with the recovery program and aftercare and got active in AA.

Now I have about 20% liver function and I'm considered too healthy to be on a transplant list, but not healthy enough to do much of anything else. Saying that, there's no point regretting anything at this point or worrying about when I'll die. No one knows how long they've got.

My liver transplant story

My rotting liver was poisoning my body. It was so bad I got E.coli from myself! After six weeks in the hospital the doctors said I had between two months to a year left to live and started doing tests to see if I met the transplant list requirements – lung, heart test, MRIs, etc.

Turns out I was officially the most urgent case in the state at the age of 34. But I still wasn't on the list because the doctors had to decide if I was worthy of a new liver. This included looking at my behavior, what I had done to try and get better and how long it had been since I had drunk any alcohol. Thankfully they didn't apply the six-month rule. I was sent home and 12 days later I got a call saying I was on the transplant list. I went to the hospital signed the paperwork.

Unbelievably, three days later the hospital called to say there was a liver for me and surgery was scheduled for the next day.

I got a whole liver transplant not a partial and was extremely lucky. A biopsy of my liver showed it was dead like a war zone with virtually nothing left alive. The surgeon said it looked like a lump of smoked brisket.

Altogether, from finding out I had cirrhosis to the transplant was 57 days, which is amazing I know. For the first two weeks I laid in bed and took anti-rejection drugs twice a day plus around 12 different pills. For around six weeks they were not sure if the liver was going start working and it took a long time for my bilirubin to be normal.

Many donor organs to fail because there's rarely a perfect match, so I will be immunosuppressants for the rest of my life. This means I'm also more prone to infections.

Life is still barely livable with tons of side effects made worse by the added guilt of pretending to be grateful that I'm alive. Since the surgery there have been hospitalizations for a respiratory infection and a stomach virus and I have been in rejection twice.

I knew there would be bumps in the road, but I wasn't expecting so many. My doctor told me this is pretty common and the first year is usually quite rocky. People overestimate what medical science is capable of in this situation. One in ten don't make it.

PART 7

Medical conditions associated with uncontrolled drinking

Nervous System Side Effects
Black outs and memory loss
Gradual brain damage
Wernicke–Korsakoff Syndrome
Hepatic Encephalopathy
Dementia
Peripheral neuropathy

Blood
Macrocytosis (abnormally large red blood cells)
Anemia
Leukopenia
Thrombocytopenia
High triglyceride levels
High LDL (bad) cholesterol levels.
Folate deficiency syndrome

Liver
Infiltration of fat
Enlargement (hepatomegaly)
Alcoholic hepatitis
Cirrhosis
Cancer

Skin
Dilated blood vessels and broken veins
Reddening of the palms of the hands
Psoriasis
Rosacea
Seborrheic dermatitis
Acne
Enlarged pores
Cancer

Gastrointestinal (GI) System
Acid reflux
Gastric erosion
Tearing or rupture of the esophagus
Internal bleeding due to inflammation of the GI tract
Gastritis
Type 2 diabetes
Pancreatitis
Cancers of the mouth, voice box and lips
Esophageal cancer
Gallbladder and bile duct cancer
Pancreatic cancer
Colon and rectal cancer

Lungs
Recurrent chest infections
Acute Respiratory Distress Syndrome
Chronic bronchitis
Pneumonia
Tuberculosis

Mental health problems
Depression
Anxiety
Paranoia
Irritability, anger and violent behavior
Suicidal thoughts and tendencies

Skeletal
Osteoporosis
Fracture of the femur

Heart and Circulatory System
High/low blood pressure
Brain hemorrhage
Portal hypertension

Congestion in the heart and lungs
Abnormal heart rhythm
Heart muscle damage
Enlarged heart
Heart disease
Heart failure
Stroke

Sexual/Reproductive Problems

Male:
Loss of sex drive
Shrinkage of the penis and testicles
Reduced sperm production and poor-quality sperm
Prostate cancer

Female:
Female menstrual irregularity and infertility
Shrinkage of breasts and external genitalia
Breast cancer

Fetal Development Problems
Fetal alcohol syndrome
Birth defects: heart, kidney or skeletal problems
Fetal brain damage

General
Alcohol poisoning
Malnutrition
Reduced ability to fight infection
Reduced wound healing
Chronic fatigue
Chronic pain
Muscle damage
Gout
Obesity

PART 8

More hellish experiences

Withdrawals, delirium tremens, alcohol poisoning and tolerance

A warning to the seriously alcohol dependent

For alcohol dependent drinkers who for example, wake up, vomit and have to drink to stop the shakes, or anyone who has drunk straight liquor non-stop for a couple of weeks, abruptly quitting can cause an adrenergic firestorm – basically a massive neurological aftershock – known as delirium tremens.

Essentially alcohol (and benzos like Xanax) act like brakes on the brain. When you are constantly pressing the brake pedal with alcohol, your brain eventually stops hitting the brakes itself. Then when you stop drinking your brain turns into a runaway truck, going faster and faster downhill with no brakes of its own.

You lose control physically and mentally and enter into a living nightmare of central nervous system hyperactivity. Your blood pressure, heart rate, temperature regulation and organ function all escalate off the charts.

We are not talking about the kind of withdrawals where you spend a few days in bed crawling to the bathroom and being unable to eat, sweating, dry heaving and having worse tremors than usual.

Delirium tremens (the DTs) is a terrifying near-death experience where your brain takes you on a tour of hell with no guarantee of coming back. This torture trip is starts between day two and day three from your last drink, with the worst of it usually being over within a week.

According to some survivors, if you're lucky you will wake up thrashing and convulsing while restrained to a hospital bed attached to a Valium IV. If not, then hopefully you will be one of the lucky ones that makes it out alive without medical assistance.

In time leading up to the full-blown DT experience you may feel disorientated, full of dread, restless, agitated and bad tempered. You will be unable to sleep and have vivid nightmares if you do. Sweating, severe nausea and shaking are also signs of worse things to come.

On your first day without alcohol you might even wake up and think the withdrawal process is over. Despite feeling exhausted and unable to eat you go about your day with racing, confused thoughts zapping through your head.

By the second day you are crippled by a rising sense of fear and dread. But even with extreme anxiety, inability to focus and the occasional loss of balance, you may convince yourself you can do things like work or drive. This is the calm before the storm. You are about to start your descent into purgatory.

Reports from those who have survived delirium tremens feature themes and characters which are remarkably consistent from one account to the next. Here's a very short summary of the kinds of things that can happen during this extended period of extreme psychosis.

It might start with you hearing the sound of a radio station and music in the distance. Or you may hear faint police sirens, loud whispering, voices outside your door or your name being called in a menacing way.

You might see smoke start to billow out of a book you're trying to read. A tall, shadowy silhouette of a man hovers over you. You are sure there are people in your house. You can walk up to them, examine their faces and even get close enough to smell them.

Then these things and entities start physically touching you, pulling your hair or grabbing, punching, cutting and biting you. These tactile hallucinations feel so real that you check for blood. There's no question in your mind that all this is happening. You notice every detail about what you are seeing, hearing and feeling.

Evil-looking beings taunt you about your past mistakes and say they won't stop tormenting you until you die of sleep deprivation or kill yourself. These gruesome entities mock and imitate you, target your deepest inner fears and threaten to destroy everything you care about.

Snakes, crawling insects, bats, rotting corpses, dark ghostly shapes, phantom cats, things with glowing eyes, aliens, demons, disfigured faces and other grotesque sights are moving around, making sounds and casting shadows. They appear to clearly exist.

You dare not close your eyes because you are frightened of what you can't see and terrified to open them because of what you can. You are panic-stricken, breathless and paralyzed with fear. It's an unparalleled state of turmoil and terror. There isn't a room in which you feel safe.

There is no sleep. You are trapped in a complex, yet coherent narrative that demands your full and constant attention. The hallucinations are so powerful and convincing that you perceive no difference between them and reality. This is what makes delirium tremens so dangerous.

You may try escaping from, chasing after or attacking these apparitions, potentially injuring or killing yourself or being shot by the police in real-life. That is, if you haven't already died of a heart failure, stroke or a tonic clonic seizure. Because now the adrenergic storm in your brain has turned into a category 5 hurricane.

The people who die from delirium tremens generally die of strokes and heart attacks which are either physiological in origin, the result of sheer terror, or a combination of both.

Another common side effect of severe withdrawals are tonic clonic seizures caused by a sudden surge of electrical activity in the brain due to a deluge of glutamate and other excitatory brain chemicals.

After falling unconscious, your arms, legs and torso will go rigid and your limbs start jerk as if you're being electrocuted. At this point you can lose control of your bodily functions, foam at the mouth, bite your tongue or stop breathing.

If you are admitted to hospital in time, you will probably spend up to two weeks in recovery. By the end of it you will probably have to learn how to walk and eat again and may have to use a walker for a while.

Most people who have been through delirium tremens remember everything they did and said during their ordeal. Some are convinced their hallucinations were demonic in origin and believe alcohol creates a portal to another realm or fourth dimension like a Ouija board.

Whatever their take on it, everyone is left emotionally shattered and unable to trust their senses or perceptions. They also gain a whole new perspective on what alcohol can do to a person and the horrors it can unleash. Most drinkers who go through delirium tremens vow never to drink again and some convert to Christianity.

Those who do resume their habit are far more vulnerable to going through this process again. Only the next time the experience will be even more horrendous and their risk of death far greater.

For a firsthand account of what delirium tremens is really like, watch the "Bat Country Alcoholism & Sobriety" videos on YouTube.

Why delirium tremens needs medical assistance

The brain doesn't want you to be constantly drunk and overly-relaxed because it goes against its survival instinct. So, as you are drinking it tries to bring things into balance by shutting down the production of its own calming brain chemicals and the receptors they bind to them, while ramping up the production of the brain chemicals that make you awake and alert.

Now, if you suddenly stop drinking your non-drunk brain doesn't have the ability to make enough brain chemicals to calm you down or functioning receptors to respond to them. What it does have is a massive overload of "fight or flight" chemicals which force the brain to be hyperactive for an extended period. In severe cases, seizures can occur, which are basically your brain short-circuiting due to an overload of activity.

Delirium tremens is not like withdrawals, with days of anxiety, panic attacks, vomiting and being unable to keep even water down. This is a very serious condition which is characterized by severe confusion, a rapid and/or irregular heart rate, high temperature, sweating, hallucinations and seizures.

If someone has these symptoms after taking a break from alcohol they should be taken to hospital immediately due to the risk of heart attack or stroke. Treatment typically includes sedation, IV fluids and electrolytes and oxygen therapy.

Getting off alcohol: a safer approach

Of all the drugs on earth, only a few can kill you if you suddenly stop taking them. These are alcohol, benzos (like Xanax, Valium and Librium) and opioids like fentanyl (where sudden withdrawal can cause death from persistent vomiting and diarrhea).

So, it must be stated again, if you are a heavy drinker you must never quit cold turkey. And if you are trying to help someone with a drinking problem you should never cut them off by doings things like locking them in a room, pouring their alcohol down the sink or watering their drinks down. You may think you are being cruel to be kind, but they could go into acute withdrawal and possibly die as a result.

Similarly, if someone has a benzo addiction, never confiscate their drugs as they could have a grand mal seizure which can be fatal as they are very difficult to treat.

There is a test that is used to determine whether someone needs medication for withdrawal and admission to the ICU. The Clinical Institute Withdrawal Assessment for Alcohol lists 10 signs and symptoms that assess how dangerous a person's situation is. This scale is used in clinical settings like detox and psychiatry units as well as general medical wards.

Each person is graded on a scale of 1 to 7 for nausea and vomiting, tremors, sweating, anxiety, agitation, tactile disturbance (crawling skin, itching, burning etc.), auditory disturbances (hearing things, intolerant to noise), visual disturbances (seeing things, being unable to withstand bright lights etc.) headache and confusion.

A score of 15 or more indicates severe withdrawal and impending delirium tremens. In other words, you are in a dire state and need urgent medical help.

If your drinking has got to the point where you are unable to control it and you have not been eating for days you will need to go to the hospital for a medical detox. After that, you will need to find a local mental health or substance abuse clinic to continue your treatment and join a recovery group.

If you want to stop drinking but are scared your withdrawal symptoms will be unbearable, you can ask your doctor to refer you to an in-patient hospital or detox center. Another option is to check yourself into a detox or rehab facility that's covered by your insurance or Medicaid.

If money's no object, there are premium physician-guided services where they send a nurse to your home to monitor you 24/7 and give you medications to get you through the withdrawals from alcohol in relative comfort.

To help you through the process and to prevent seizures, your doctor can also prescribe a short course of benzodiazepines such as Ativan. But be careful these meds don't become a permanent crutch as the comedown from benzos can be just as brutal as alcohol.

Due to cost and the inability to take a lot of time off work most people taper down at home on their own. The key is to plan ahead and make sure someone knows what you are doing and can check on you. Two practical guides for safely tapering are sipandsuffer.com and hams.cc/taper.

Without medication, you will likely experience shaking, agitation, nausea, mild hallucinations, confusion, a pounding heart and breathlessness as well as dry heaving and diarrhea. The inevitable hormone and neurotransmitter crash will also result in anxiety and depression.

As with all dopamine-inducing drugs, the equation is always "the higher the high, the lower the low."

It's wise to pack a hospital bag in advance and have someone who can check on you and drive you to the emergency room if your symptoms worsen. (Again, refer to The Clinical Institute Withdrawal Assessment for Alcohol to get an idea of how serious the situation is.)

During the tapering process it's important to drink lots of water, get plenty of rest and try and eat. If you can't get any solid food down, try soups, nutrition drinks or make protein powder smoothies. If you can eat, stick to simple food like vegetables, rice and proteins such as chicken and fish. Bananas and applesauce are also safe options for a shell-shocked stomach.

After drying out it is usual to feel extremely low and numb, a state known as anhedonia, which means a reduced ability to experience pleasure or joy. This is due to your mind and body having to deal with the lack of dopamine and all the other neurotransmitters alcohol your brain was used to being flooded with. Having ramped down its own production of happy, calming chemicals, your brain will need time to reset itself.

Alcohol also wires the brain for instant gratification which adds another layer of frustration and anxiety to the situation. That's why you can expect to have that feeling of "white knuckling it" in the first couple of weeks.

Any kind of activity that increases your heart rate or tests your muscles will give you temporary relief from anhedonia. In the longer term, physical activity will also help boost dopamine production as well as creating new brain cells and new pathways to help you feel pleasure.

It's generally reported that it takes between three and six-month mark for your brain cells to fully regenerate and fire at full strength. Even after a month of not drinking the brain starts showing visible signs that it's repairing itself.

Improved memory and better information processing should be noticeable at three-month stages, with full recovery taking anything from a few months to a few years depending on your drinking history.

Being sober is extra hard if you have been self-medicating with alcohol because of a mood disorder or emotional problems. A counselor, therapist or psychiatrist will help you identify the reasons why you drink and/or prescribe medication for underlying psychological issues like chronic depression.

Alcohol poisoning: the danger of sleeping it off

If someone drinks to the point of losing consciousness do not assume they will sleep it off. There have been many times when someone has helped a severely intoxicated friend get to bed only to find them dead in the morning. Or they go to wake them up on the couch and find them bluish colored, having passed away in their sleep.

Signs of alcohol poisoning are:

Confusion and/or seizures
Unconsciousness to the point of being unresponsive and being unable to stay awake for more than a couple of minutes
Slow breathing (less than 8 breaths per minute or more than 10 seconds between breaths)
Deep noisy breathing
Cold, clammy, pale or bluish skin or slightly blue or gray lips
A weak rapid pulse
Vomiting while passed out

If the person has any of the symptoms listed above and you know they have drunk a dangerous amount call the emergency services and prepare to give CPR. Do not try to make the someone who is semi-conscious or passed out vomit as they could choke and stop breathing which can lead to brain damage, coma or death. In fact, you should actively prevent them from choking by putting them in the recovery position:

1. Raise their closest arm to you above their head. Bend the knee of their leg that is furthest away from you.

2. Roll them towards you carefully. Their head should now be on its side and facing you.

3. Tilt their chin upwards slightly to maintain an airway and put their nearest hand under their cheek. You can also use a cushion or a pillow. Then cover them with a blanket or jacket to keep them warm.

If they are semiconscious don't give them anything to eat or drink as this can trigger vomiting and choking, plus they could breathe vomit into their lungs, a condition called aspirational pneumonia, which can be fatal if left untreated. Do not give them a cold shower either, as that could send them into shock. Keep checking their breathing and do not leave them alone.

Alcoholic ketoacidosis

Alcoholic ketoacidosis is most likely to occur in someone who drinks large amounts of alcohol every day and rarely eats and ends up with an overload of ketones in their blood. Ketones are made in the liver from the breakdown of fats which it is forced to use as fuel when the body isn't getting enough food.

Symptoms include fever, headache, nausea and vomiting, loss of appetite, abdominal pain, irrational anger and confusion. They may also have an acetone or nail polish remover type smell, although some people give off a sweet odor like radiator coolant or formaldehyde.

Urgent medical treatment is needed because this is a life-threatening condition which requires IV saline for rehydration as well as dextrose, vitamin C, magnesium, and thiamine.

Why a few weeks of abstinence can be fatal if you relapse

In 2007 I went to the UK to see Amy Winehouse perform live at Glastonbury. She arrived an hour late, stumbled and lurched around the stage swigging from a bottle of wine and told the jeering crowd to fuck off. When she tried to sing, she could barely hold a note. It was obvious she was completely trashed.

By the following year, according to one of Amy Winehouse's many doctors, she managed to quit heroin, cocaine and marijuana but still struggled to stop drinking. Multiple periods of abstinence were followed by booze binges where she admitted, she could "easily drink a bottle of toffee vodka every night."

In 2011, following another one of these dry spells, Amy probably thought she could handle a liter of vodka as she had before. Unfortunately, all those sober intervals had made her more sensitive to alcohol's effects and a lethal level of drinking was easier to reach.

According to Professor David Nutt, a world leading expert in psycho-pharmacology and psychiatrist for over 40 years, Amy Winehouse died because she had lost tolerance to alcohol. What's more, he says, she would not have died – even with a BAC of .416 – if she hadn't stopped drinking.

It's similar to what happens when heroin and fentanyl addicts are released after spending a long time in prison or rehab. A lot of them die soon after because they can no longer handle anything like the drug dose they took before they detoxed.

When you repeatedly use a drug, your body adjusts. Your liver metabolizes it more efficiently by producing more enzymes to break it down and remove it faster from your system. Your brain also turns down the reactivity of the receptors to that substance to decrease its effect. In other words, the body becomes tolerant.

Think of tolerance as a seawall that is gradually built higher to cope with the increasing height of the incoming waves to safely prevent a deluge wiping out whatever's behind it. When you dismantle that seawall, the first average-sized wave will come crashing in and destroy everything in its path.

Similarly, without tolerance, a lesser amount of alcohol will hit the brain with catastrophic results. Without the metabolic defenses to deal with it, alcohol floods the bloodstream which causes the brain to shut down and stop activating basic functions like breathing and the beating of the heart.

Interestingly, tolerance could also be called mithridatism. This refers to the idea of gradually consuming poison to develop immunity to it. The term comes from Mithridates the Great who ruled over an area of the world that's now known as modern-day Turkey.

He built up immunity to poison by regularly drinking large but non-lethal amounts of it every day because he was scared of being assassinated like his father who was poisoned at one of his own banquets. Ironically, when Mithridates tried to poison himself to avoid being slaughtered by his enemies he failed because of his tolerance to the substance, so his bodyguard had to kill him with a sword.

In addition to this, there is another phenomenon called "kindling"[71] where repeated weeks to months-long breaks from alcohol leads to worsening withdrawal symptoms.

In other words, the more times you quit drinking, the more serious the adverse events become, including permanent brain damage. Plus, with every withdrawal period of not drinking and relapse, the addiction process intensifies. The cravings get stronger and recovery is more difficult.

---

[71] Kindling (sedative–hypnotic withdrawal)
https://en.wikipedia.org/wiki/Kindling_(sedative%E2%80%93hypnotic_withdrawal)

This is why anyone who has become seriously alcohol dependent needs medical supervision, group therapy and ideally, long term individual psychological support to avoid relapsing.

According to her mother Janis Winehouse, "Amy was ashamed of being an alcoholic and determined to beat her addiction. She didn't want to die. She didn't have a death wish… There was so much she still wanted to achieve.

Amy was incredibly strong, both physically and mentally, but alcohol addiction seemed to creep up on her and took her by surprise. On the afternoon before her death, she didn't seem drunk or tipsy. She was completely normal and coherent."

PART 9

A closer look at the liver

What it is, what it likes, what it doesn't and what to do when it's damaged

Your body's filter, factory and power plant

The best way to describe what your liver does is to think of it as the sponge component of a fish tank filter. In the rest of this analogy the tank is your body, the water is your blood, the water pump is your heart and the fish comprise all your other tissue and organs.

The pump pulls the water out, sends it through the filter which removes the dirt and sends clean water back out into the tank. When the filter doesn't work, crap builds up in the tank and ammonia levels start going up. The fish start gasping for air, bleeding from their gills and gradually die from ammonia poisoning. (In humans, ammonia build-up hurts the brain the most.)

This is a broad and simplified description of what the liver does. Because as well as filtering all your blood each day, it performs nearly 500 other functions to keep you alive. It destroys old red blood cells, stores and releases vitamins, produces hormones, stores glycogen for energy and regulates blood clotting. So, it's also something of a factory and a power plant.

But its main job is to keep your blood clean in order to safeguard the health of your brain, heart, lungs and kidneys – in that order.

Unlike the components of a fish tank filter, we are not able to pull our livers out and run them under the faucet when they get gunked up. So, the human liver is connected to an additional waste disposal system whose main operating parts include the kidneys, bladder and large intestine or bowel.

The liver converts ammonia to a less toxic substance called urea which is sent via the blood to your kidneys where it is processed for disposal in your urine. It also produces a substance called bile, which your intestines use to process everything you eat, drink or otherwise consume.

Bile, which is stored in your gallbladder, plus pancreatic enzymes break down your food. This mush then travels from your small intestine to your large intestine where it is dehydrated and excreted as feces.

Once again, to make things clear, the liver doesn't directly deal with the stuff you eat and drink, your intestines do. The liver's main job is to process whatever ends up in your bloodstream. This is why up to two liters of blood flow through your liver every minute.

Basically, anything that is absorbed by your gut goes into the blood surrounding it. All this nutrient and toxin-filled blood then heads straight to your liver via the portal vein. After that it travels down the millions of little blood vessels in your liver which branch off, getting smaller and smaller.

All these vessel walls provide a huge amount of surface area for toxins like alcohol to be absorbed into the liver's cells and to be broken down by enzymes. At the same time, anything good for your body like vitamins, is processed and released back into your bloodstream.

This amazing multi-purpose organ is located on the right side of your abdomen under your rib cage and weighs just over three pounds which is about the same weight as your brain. Another thing it has in common with the brain is that both of these organs lack pain receptors.

Any discomfort, or aches are caused by the membrane around them called the fascia becoming inflamed. Fascias contain six times more nerve endings than muscles, so they have pretty sensitive pain perception.

Finally, the liver is the only organ in your body that can regenerate lost mass completely, even when only 24% of functioning tissue remains. Anything less than that and you are in trouble.

In patients with liver disease a surgeon can remove the diseased part of the liver and the rest will regrow to its previous size and regain most of its function, all within as little as three months.

In evolutionary terms the liver evolved this way because it expects to be damaged. Even in a clean-living person, liver cells only have a lifespan of between 200 and 300 days. So, on average your liver is always around three years old, whether you're 20 or 80.

Incidentally, the oldest 1% of red blood cells are thrown out every day and replaced with new ones. This means that after around four months everyone has completely new blood!

The various stages of liver disease

Generally speaking, the liver is made up of two different types of cells: functional liver cells and structural cells. The functional cells deal with everything in the blood that needs processing. The structural cells build the connective tissue that gives the liver its shape and form.

When the liver is injured on an ongoing basis, i.e., by toxic chemicals like drugs and alcohol, the liver is forced to repair itself with scar tissue.[72] This tougher material forms a kind of tight, dense matrix or three-dimensional mesh throughout the entire organ. This abnormal formation is called fibrosis.

The remaining functional liver cells inside this mesh continue to regenerate to replace the ever-increasing number that are being killed off. But with limited space, eventually they erupt through the gaps in the scar tissue creating what look like little nodules or blisters all over the surface. This blobby appearance is the classic look of cirrhosis.

The fibrotic mesh constricts the parts of the liver that are still working and eventually cuts off their blood supply. When the functioning cells are unable to receive oxygen and nutrients, liver regeneration is almost impossible.

Toxic metabolic by-products start accumulating in the blood and pressure builds up in the veins when your liver is mainly comprised of scar tissue and becomes a blockage in your body's circulatory system.

---

[72] Can you survive with liver cirrhosis?
https://www.youtube.com/shorts/DrdH04QZijo

The liver is capable of optimizing any remaining potential it has for recovery. Even with as little as 10% liver function, people have been known to pull through and have a good prognosis after 10 months without alcohol. So, it's worth doing everything you can to stop the disease from progressing, even if you think your outlook is hopeless.

Some people live active normal lives for many years with a diseased liver under the care of their hepatologist or gastrointestinal (GI) doctor. But if you ignore their advice about abstaining from alcohol and keeping your sodium intake down for example, your prospects will obviously not be so good.

As an idea of the various stages of disease, physicians grade the different levels of cirrhosis based on following:

Class A – the early stage of liver scarring, when the liver is working normally and there are probably no symptoms.
Class B – mild to moderate liver damage, with symptoms such as jaundice, ascites (fluid build-up) and encephalopathy (confusion).
Class C – severe liver damage to the point where the liver has stopped working.

Stages A and B are most likely to be reversible. Even recovery from class C liver damage is possible, especially in younger patients.

When a cirrhotic liver fails completely and has no remaining function, liver dialysis may be used in the short term. Dialysis filters out toxins like ammonia, but it can't produce blood clotting proteins, store and release nutrients, break down fats and convert them to energy or do all the other complex tasks the liver does.

To replicate all these functions, you would need a whole warehouse full of specialized machines. Liver dialysis is a temporary measure to buy some time while you are on the transplant list or exploring other treatment options.

Immunotherapy[73] is a new approach which is in its early stages, but has proven very effective in trials: reducing fibrosis, helping with tissue repair and inflammation. Immune cells called macrophages are taken from the patient's blood and the enzymes in the macrophages help dissolve the scar tissue.

Resolution Therapeutics Ltd in the UK began recruiting patients in October 2024 for a 3-year study to test the viability of immunotherapy for advanced liver disease.

Stem cell therapy is another innovation that is improving the lives of people with cirrhosis. For example, mesenchymal stem cells can improve liver function, reduce fibrosis and regenerate damaged tissue.

This treatment is available within the US, mainly in California, but there are centers across the country. Other stem cell therapy centers can be found in Switzerland, Germany, Mexico, Grand Cayman, Panama, Colombia, Thailand, Bangkok, India and Israel.

When the liver has completely failed, a transplant is currently the only realistic answer for most. There are two ways this can be done : with liver tissue from a living donor or a deceased donor organ.

A living donor – usually a close relative of the patient – volunteers to have part of their liver removed. Within around six to nine months, the donor's remaining liver should have fully regenerated and the partial liver in the recipient will also have grown to its correct size. The advantage of this is that the transplant can take place before the patient is very ill and their hospital stay is shorter.

Living donors are also usually in better health than deceased donors at the time of surgery. However, the procedure does come with a 1% risk of disability or death. It's estimated that 40% of donors have

---

[73] New 2023 study shows macrophage cell therapy holds promise to treat people with liver cirrhosis
https://britishlivertrust.org.uk/new-study-shows-macrophage-cell-therapy-holds-promise-to-treat-people-with-liver-cirrhosis/

complications after such a large part of their liver is removed, but in virtually all cases these issues resolve within three months.[74]

In Europe and America livers are mostly transplanted from dead people. The deceased donor organ is matched to a person's blood type and body size in the same part of the country the person died. This means the wait time can stretch from months to years. Other aspects that are taken into consideration are the patient's Model for End-Stage Liver Disease (MELD), with the sickest patients going to the top of the list.

Generally speaking, liver transplants from 80-year-old donors can work just as well as younger organs because liver cells are only three years old on average. But because older livers lose their capacity to regenerate at the same rate as they did when they were younger, transplant recipients have to be strict with their diet and never touch alcohol again.

At least one complication occurs in 70% of recipients of this kind of organ, but overall, the results are very good, with the vast majority of people living for five years or more.

Things that would prevent you being eligible for any type of liver transplant include being over the age of 65, having certain serious mental or physical illnesses, being severely obese and/or continuing to drink alcohol, smoke or use recreational drugs. The use of marijuana or any of its active ingredients will also make you ineligible for a transplant in countries and states where it is still illegal.

Liver disease is very unpredictable. There are many instances where people have been told their liver is rock hard and they have weeks to live. But instead of giving up and waiting to die these individuals changed their diet and started taking supplements (cleared by their doctor) and ended up defying their dire prognosis.

---

[74] Complications of Living Donor Hepatic Lobectomy—A Comprehensive Report
https://www.amjtransplant.org/article/S1600-6135(22)27438-3/fulltext

There are many examples of people with MELD numbers as high as 30 who have drastically altered their lifestyle and are taken off the transplant list a few weeks later. Then their doctor will tell them to just keep doing what they are doing to stay healthy. Genetics and age play a huge role in each individual's prospects for recovery.

What to do if you're worried about your liver

If you binge drink on a regular basis, it's worth going to the doctor and being honest about your alcohol intake and having some tests done to see how your body is holding up.

Your doctor can order a comprehensive metabolic panel of blood tests, including liver function. (In the US, blood tests are often cheaper when bought online from discount lab sites that work with blood draw facilities, depending on the level of health insurance you have.)

If the results show markers of possible liver damage your doctor will most likely recommend a non-invasive form of ultrasound called elastography, commercially known as FibroScan. This device measures the stiffness of the liver of the liver and reveals any masses, blockages and imperfections.

If you can't find a health center in your state that does free FibroScans, they are normally covered by health insurance. In the UK they are available on the NHS and via traveling mobile units.

If your results show evidence of liver disease, a biopsy will clarify the stage it's at with a greater degree of accuracy. This procedure takes around 15 minutes and should be minimally painful.

A radiologist uses ultrasound to locate the place from which the sample needs to be taken and the area is injected it with local anesthetic. A fine biopsy needle is then inserted through the skin and muscle and guided into the liver using ultrasound and tissue samples are extracted.

The Enhanced Liver Fibrosis (ELF) blood test is used to measure three liver fibrosis biomarkers and is another way of gauging the level of damage. If fibrosis is detected, a CT scan with dye, or contrast enhanced CT scan may then be performed to determine the health of the vascular structures and amount of blood flow through the liver.

As with any health condition the earlier you are diagnosed the better your chances for recovery, so don't treat your health like your bank account and avoid checking it because you're scared of what you might see. Liver disease is something that can get very serious very fast with relatively few obvious symptoms at the start.

Things that are bad for your liver in addition to alcohol

Being overweight is one of the most common causes of fatty liver which can lead to inflammation and scarring. When you think about a fatty liver, foie gras (which literally means "fat liver" in French) may come to mind.

This abnormally bloated organ is produced when geese are force-fed liquidized corn and oil which is poured down their necks through a tube up to four times a day. This induces an extremely painful disease known as hepatic lipidosis, where the birds' livers are overloaded with fat and expand up to ten times their normal size.

To produce a human foie gras all that is required is a diet high in sugar, carbs and fat along with almost no exercise. Alcohol expedites the process.

A human liver-fattening diet is full of seed oils, trans fats (listed as "partially hydrogenated"), refined carbohydrates, sugar and high fructose corn syrup. These ingredients are typically found in things like cheeseburgers, fries, pizza, cakes, pastries, ice cream drinks, fruit juice and soda.

For example, an Oreos and Reese's Peanut Butter shake from Sonic has 1,720 calories and Double Down Fries from Shake Shack has 1,910 calories. To add blubber to your liver quickly and cheaply, visit any popular fast-food outlet, ask for extra cheese on your burger and order a frozen milkshake with your meal!

Acetaminophen (paracetamol) is the go-to hangover remedy but has a dangerous side to it, particularly for drinkers. That's because one of its break-down products can damage your liver cells. This chemical is neutralized with a chemical the liver produces called glutathione, but if you take too many pills the liver can't keep up.

Alcohol's by-produce acetaldehyde is also neutralized by glutathione. So if you're already low on glutathione from drinking and then take acetaminophen your liver will take a direct hit from its toxic by-product. This is why you should never take more than eight 500mg tablets within 24-hours or take them after three or more alcoholic drinks.

Acetaminophen toxicity is the leading cause of liver failure in Western countries, accounting for 50% of all reported cases of drug-induced liver damage and around 20% of liver transplant cases.[75] Overdoses are easy to treat if you catch them in time. The problem is that in the early stage they are usually asymptomatic and by the time you start feeling ill it's already too late.

Acetaminophen is sold under the brand names Tylenol, Panadol, Calpol, Excedrin and Hedex. If you suffer from chronic pain, ask your doctor about injectables because they avoid the liver's first-pass metabolism which is when the damage occurs.

Non-steroidal anti-inflammatory drugs (NSAIDS) such as ibuprofen (Advil, Nurofen and Motrin), diclofenac (Voltaren), aspirin (Disprin), naproxen (Aleve) are also known to cause liver and kidney

---

[75] Acute liver failure including acetaminophen overdose
https://pmc.ncbi.nlm.nih.gov/articles/PMC2504411/

damage when taken at high doses or when combined with alcohol. Surgeons also report that because these drugs dissolve in your GI tract they can literally burn a hole through your stomach causing perforated gastric ulcers if you take too many, or use them while drinking.

Antibiotics such as azithromycin and nitrofurantoin are another class of drugs that can cause liver damage.[76] As well as producing harmful metabolites when they are broken down, they destroy the gut's good bacteria. The liver, gut, and immune system all work together, so if the gut microbiome is out of whack the liver is vulnerable to inflammation and damage.

Immune suppressant drugs like methotrexate, leflunomide or azathioprine, which are prescribed for conditions like arthritis, can damage the liver within days or after long-term use.[77] If you are on these drugs regular blood testing is needed to make sure your liver enzyme levels are not affected.

Remdesivir, an antiviral used for the treatment of AIDS and coronavirus disease is toxic to human liver cells. The FDA has warned about the incidence of elevated liver enzymes and liver injury in patients treated with this drug.[78]

Anabolic steroids or synthetic testosterone used by bodybuilders and athletes to increase muscle mass and performance can cause liver damage and cardiovascular disease. Liver tumors and liver cancer

---

[76] Unusual effects of common antibiotics
https://www.ccjm.org/content/86/4/277
[77] [Hepatotoxicity induced by new immunosuppressants]
https://pubmed.ncbi.nlm.nih.gov/19889479/
[78] Hepatic manifestations of COVID-19 and effect of remdesivir on liver function in patients with COVID-19 illness
https://pmc.ncbi.nlm.nih.gov/articles/PMC8224190.

have been reported in people who have taken high doses over a long time.[79]

Chemotherapy drugs pass through the liver and can damage liver cells in various ways. They can increase the liver's fat content, destroy its bile ducts, cause blockages and create liver-toxic metabolites.[80]

Up to 85% of patients undergoing chemo develop fatty liver disease which can progress to the inflammatory stage with markers of liver damage being seen in blood tests. Silymarin extracted from milk thistle has been found to be helpful in preventing these side effects.[81]

Cigarettes contain toxins that can cause permanent liver scarring. Smoking also leaves nicotine deposits in the intestine which can trigger a build-up of fat in your liver and start the inflammation cascade.[82]

PFAS (polyfluoroalkyl substances) are manmade chemicals that can cause metabolic changes that lead to fatty liver disease and higher levels of liver enzymes.[83] PFAS are found in cleaning products, microwave popcorn, non-stick pans, greaseproof paper, stain and water-resistant coatings, mattress pads, shampoo and makeup.

---

[79] LiverTox: Clinical and Research Information on Drug-Induced Liver Injury
https://www.ncbi.nlm.nih.gov/books/NBK548931/
[80] Management of hepatotoxicity of chemotherapy and targeted agents
https://pmc.ncbi.nlm.nih.gov/articles/PMC8332851
[81] Silymarin and Cancer: A Dual Strategy in Both in Chemoprevention and Chemosensitivity
https://pmc.ncbi.nlm.nih.gov/articles/PMC7248929/
[82] New insights into why smoking causes fatty liver disease
https://ccr.cancer.gov/news/article/new-insights-into-why-smoking-causes-fatty-liver-disease
[83] Study links synthetic chemicals to liver damage 2022
https://www.nih.gov/news-events/nih-research-matters/study-links-synthetic-chemicals-liver-damage#

Basically, these things are everywhere – even in tap and rainwater. If you want to avoid PFAS completely you would have to move to Antarctica. A few ways to reduce exposure to these chemicals is to invest in a water filtering system, donate plasma (PFAS bind to red blood cells) eat probiotic foods and take folate supplements.

Stress and anger can cause hypoxic (oxygen-deprived) liver injury due to the release of hormones like glucocorticoids which restrict blood flow to the liver.[84] The subsequent lack of oxygenated blood can cause some of the liver cells die leading to fibrosis.

Sleep apnea is another source of liver injury related to the lack of oxygen; this time caused by repeatedly stopping breathing. Other aspects of sleep apnea include rapidly gasping for breath, periods of quiet choking and long, loud snores. Untreated sleep apnea is also linked to fatty liver disease, elevated liver enzymes and fibrosis.[85]

You can check the liver toxicity of prescription, over-the-counter medications and herbal and dietary supplements at livertox@nihgov.

---

[84] Brain-gut-liver axis: Chronic psychological stress promotes liver injury and fibrosis *via* gut in rats
https://www.frontiersin.org/journals/cellular-and-infection-microbiology/articles/10.3389/fcimb.2022.1040749/full

[85] Significant Nonalcoholic Fatty Liver Disease, Fibrosis Risk Found in Patients with Obstructive Sleep Apnea
https://www.ajmc.com/view/significant-nonalcoholic-fatty-liver-disease-fibrosis-risk-found-in-patients-with-obstructive-sleep-apnea

Things that are good for your liver

While commonly recognized liver supplements like milk thistle will do you no harm, most doctors agree that switching to a modified Mediterranean-style diet,[86] cutting carbs, sugar and processed food and being active on a daily basis are the best things you can do for your liver long term.

That said, there are many cases where people with fibrosis and cirrhosis have pulled themselves back from the cliff by eating the right food and including specific vitamins and other supplements.[87]

With supplements you get what you pay for because it's expensive to create compounds that your body can actually absorb. So buy the best you can afford that have been independently verified for quality.

Powder filled vitamin capsules have a higher level of bioavailability compared to hard pills due to a combination of the surface area of their contents and fast-dissolving outer shell. Gel caps and liquid drops are also very good.

Gummy vitamins typically contain less vitamins than capsules or pills, plus most manufacturers use ingredients like sugars, gelatin, corn starch, artificial flavors and dyes to make them look and taste like candy. Their shelf-life is also shorter, which means they will lose their potency faster.

Although extremely rare, death has occurred from taking extremely large doses of supplements – especially those that act like hormones – and/or herbal remedies on a daily basis. It is therefore very important to stick to the recommended dosage and check with your doctor before deciding which supplements you want to add to your routine.

---

[86] The Best Diet to Reverse Fatty Liver: The Modified Mediterranean Diet
https://www.fattyliverdiary.com/whats-the-best-fatty-liver-diet/
[87] Cirrhosis Nutrition Therapy
https://www.med.umich.edu/1libr/Hepatology/CirrhosisNutritionTherapy

This especially applies if you are pregnant or breast feeding or being treated for a condition like diabetes, alcoholic hepatitis or cirrhosis, as they may alter the effectiveness of your medications or interact with them to cause unwanted side effects.

A high-quality multivitamin supplement is something worth investing in. As well as making up for any alcohol-related shortfalls in vitamins B1, B2, B6, B12, folate and zinc, vitamins C and E are good for flushing fats from the liver, while Vitamin D can help treat liver damage and calm inflammation.

Vitamin D3 (cholecalciferol) is a powerful immune system and tissue remodeling system steroid hormone our bodies generate from exposure to sunlight, and is good for rebuilding functioning liver cells as well as being anti-fibrotic.[88] It works best when taken in combination with vitamin K2.

Magnesium is lost on a massive scale when drinking alcohol and is eliminated through the urine. Alcohol withdrawal and delirium tremens both involve extreme magnesium deficiency. Low magnesium levels also make liver disease worse by increasing scar tissue formation. A supplement can help offset these issues.[89]

Berberine is nicknamed the jaundice berry for its beneficial effects on the liver. A review of 12 studies found that taking berberine led to reductions in body weight, belly fat and liver inflammation.[90]

---

[88] Vitamin D3 supplementation alleviates chemically-induced cirrhosis-associated hepatocarcinogenesis
https://www.sciencedirect.com/science/article/pii/S0960076021002156
[89] Magnesium and liver disease
https://pmc.ncbi.nlm.nih.gov/articles/PMC6861788/
[90] The effect of berberine supplementation on obesity parameters, inflammation and liver function enzymes: A systematic review and meta-analysis of randomized controlled trials
https://pubmed.ncbi.nlm.nih.gov/32690176/

Bromelain, an enzyme found in all parts of the pineapple, lowers cholesterol and triglyceride levels, protects against thrombosis, helps reduce the accumulation of fat in the liver and remove plaques.[91] It is also known to assist in restoring the liver's enzymatic balance, is anti-inflammatory and helps slow and prevent liver fibrosis by targeting the liver's stellate cells which cause scar tissue to form.[92]

R-alpha lipoic acid is a strong antioxidant which works positively against the adverse effects of fibrosis.[93] People have been known to heal their cirrhotic livers within a year using this supplement in combination with selenium and milk thistle. As it can lower blood sugar levels, people with diabetes should take alpha lipoic acid under medical supervision.

Tauroursodeoxycholic acid (TUDCA) is a bile acid derivative that can help treat liver damage (including fibrosis), and has been shown to reduce inflammation, protect against liver cell death and improve liver function. Another claimed benefit is its ability to interrupt protein misfolding in the brain.

Dihydromyricetin (DHM) is derived from fruit from the Japanese raisin tree and has been used in China for liver ailments and hangovers for over 500 years. It helps the body to metabolize alcohol faster by triggering the liver to make more ethanol-neutralizing enzymes, reduces fat accumulation in the liver tissue and reduces inflammation in the liver by dampening down immune cell activity.[94]

---

[91] Bromelain Confers Protection against the Non-Alcoholic Fatty Liver Disease in Male C57bl/6 Mice
https://pubmed.ncbi.nlm.nih.gov/32443556/
[92] Bromelain mitigates liver fibrosis via targeting hepatic stellate cells in vitro and in vivo
https://www.sciencedirect.com/science/article/abs/pii/S0040816623001064
[93] α-Lipoic acid modulates liver fibrosis: A cross talk between TGF-β1, autophagy, and apoptosis
https://journals.sagepub.com/doi/full/10.1177/0960327119891212
[94] Noted hangover remedy has added benefit of protecting the liver
https://today.usc.edu/hangover-remedy-dhm-liver-protection-usc-study/

N-acetylcysteine (NAC) is used to treat liver conditions including alcohol and acetaminophen (paracetamol) induced liver failure, fatty liver, inflammation and fibrosis.

SAM-e a prescription drug in some countries and a supplement in others, is a methyl donor which has been shown to improve liver disease survival rates and delay the need for a liver transplant. Other studies show that SAM-e also helps normalize levels of liver enzymes.[95]

Dandelion tea stimulates bile production, lowers cholesterol and reduces liver fat accumulation and is known to be beneficial for liver health. 1 to 3 cups of tea per day is typically consumed.[96]

Omega 3 reduces the risk of developing all kinds of liver diseases and is used as prescription drug to treat high levels of triglycerides and for lowering liver fat. Oily types of fish such as salmon, tuna and mackerel are high in omega 3 fatty acids.

The Brown Formula by Wei Laboratories is a herbal remedy that helps facilitate the liver damage repair process as well as promoting healthy blood lipid (cholesterol and triglyceride) and sugar levels.

IMPORTANT: You must ask your doctor before taking any supplements or herbal formulas on a regular basis, especially if you are on any medications as unwanted interactions can occur.

---

[95] S-adenosylmethionine metabolism and liver disease
https://pmc.ncbi.nlm.nih.gov/articles/PMC4027041/
[96] Protective Effects of Taraxacum officinale L. (Dandelion) Root Extract in Experimental Acute on Chronic Liver Failure
https://pubmed.ncbi.nlm.nih.gov/33804908/

Olive oil might seem like a counterintuitive choice for reducing liver fat but the evidence shows that it reduces stored fat deposits.[97] The suggested amount of four tablespoons a day can be drizzled over anything you eat or used to make salad dressings or dips.

Choline-rich foods, especially eggs, beef, chicken breasts, liver, fish, milk, nuts, quinoa, broccoli and cottage cheese are vital for liver health. As well as helping to break down fats and remove them from your liver, choline helps form and repair cell walls. Most people do not realize that very low levels of choline can lead to liver damage outside of excess alcohol consumption.

Flavonoid-rich foods especially decaf coffee, green or black tea (4 cups a day max), apples, pineapple, berries, blueberries, oranges, grapefruit, fresh parsley, peppers, avocados, broccoli, sweet potato, red cabbage, sprouts, spinach, kale, onions, garlic and walnuts were shown to reduce the risk of fatty liver disease by 19% in one 10-year study.[98] These foods are potent liver fat removers, cholesterol reducers and general health promoters, with noticeable improvements being seen within three months of consumption.

Fruit should be eaten its whole, original form as the amount of fructose in its juice alone is beyond the capacity of the liver to handle and the excess is converted into fat. Diluted lemon or lime juice is an exception to the rule.[99] A squeeze of either added to warm water can help release fat from the liver and reduce inflammation.

---

[97] Effects of olive oil on hepatic steatosis and liver enzymes: A systematic review
https://www.sciencedirect.com/science/article/pii/S1756464623004152
[98] "A flavonoid-rich diet is associated with lower risk and improved imaging biomarkers of nonalcoholic fatty liver disease: a prospective cohort study."
https://pubmed.ncbi.nlm.nih.gov/39341459/
[99] Limonin Alleviates Non-alcoholic Fatty Liver Disease by Reducing Lipid Accumulation, Suppressing Inflammation and Oxidative Stress
https://pmc.ncbi.nlm.nih.gov/articles/PMC8762292/

A Mediterranean diet that includes oily fish, choline and flavonoid-rich foods plus olive oil – traditionally eaten in Spain, Italy and Greece – is recommended by most doctors, dieticians and liver specialists. It is based on minimally processed foods: vegetables, whole grains, beans, nuts, seeds, fresh herbs, extra virgin olive oil and fruit plus fish and poultry and moderate amounts of red meat, cheese and yoghurt.

Walnuts contain high levels of glutathione, omega-3 fatty acids, antioxidants and fiber, with studies showing they are effective at removing liver fat.[100] The suggested daily amount is 10 a day.

Probiotics are beneficial for people with cirrhosis, act to reverse hepatic encephalopathy, improve liver function and regulate the balance of bacteria in the gut according to a meta-analysis of studies.[101] The best way to get probiotics is through fermented foods and drinks like kombucha, yogurt, kefir, tzatziki, kimchi, sauerkraut, sourdough bread and some cheeses.

Chicory and chicory coffee have been shown to be beneficial for the treatment of acute liver injury as well as fatty liver disease by reducing inflammation, stimulating the growth of good gut bacteria and promoting the secretion of the bile. When roasted and dried, chicory is used as a substitute for, or additive to coffee as it has a similar flavor.

Coffee drinkers are less likely to get fatty liver disease or cirrhosis. Coffee also acts as a natural Ozempic by simulating the release of the appetite-suppressing hormone GLP 1. The best effects are seen drinking between 1 and 3 cups of fresh brewed caffeinated or decaf coffee a day.[102]

---

[100] Walnuts ameliorated hepatic inflammation and toxicity induced by thermally oxidised high-fat diet in mice
https://www.sciencedirect.com/science/article/pii/S1756464624000823
[101] Probiotics Emerge as Promising Intervention in Cirrhosis
https://www.mdedge.com/gihepnews/article/268986/liver-disease/probiotics-emerge-promising-intervention-cirrhosis
[102] Can Coffee Help Your Liver?

Water can help reduce the risk of developing fatty liver disease and stopping it from getting worse. A dehydrated liver is less efficient at doing its job. Aim to drink between 1.5 and 2.5 liters of water a day in some form, including plain water. The best way to judge your hydration is to look at your urine color. If it's pale-yellow, you're good to go. If it's darker you should drink more.

Exercise in any form can help reduce liver fat, improve heart and blood vessel health and enhance blood flow. This can all help make it more efficient at metabolizing and delivering glucose to your body's tissues as well as regulating blood sugar levels.[103]

---

https://www.webmd.com/hepatitis/coffee-help-liver
[103] Exercise and the Regulation of Hepatic Metabolism https://pmc.ncbi.nlm.nih.gov/articles/PMC4826571.

PART 10

Real life recovery stories

Battling the Army's booze culture

The US Army isn't a place for the sober. The drinking culture in the military is like it got stuck in the 80's when every other TV ad was some slick, sexy booze commercial full of beautiful people. Because of this there's a kind of functional alcoholism that's specific to the US Army. It's accepted and even expected that soldiers go out and get totally shit-faced every weekend.

For many, the Army is a soul-crushing, life-sucking place and alcohol is one of the few coping mechanisms that hasn't been banned. Most of my fellow soldiers – men and women – self-medicate and do incredible chemical violence to their bodies to cope with stress, anxiety, PTSD and depression. Rather than confess to having a problem and go to Behavioral Health, it's more acceptable to just get blackout drunk.

What you have to understand about the Army is that it dictates your entire life. You miss family events such as the birth of a child because you can't get off CQ (Charge of Quarters) which means staying awake all night to handle emergencies, or to do some BS 10 level task like sitting in the motor pool moving empty boxes from one truck to another. Civilians think you're lying and flaking on them.

But you know what's there at 10:00 p.m. when you finally get back to your living quarters? Alcohol. You don't have to schedule it. You don't have to go anywhere. You don't need to cooperate with other people and you aren't disappointing your friends and family when the Army ruins your plans. Alcohol is there when nobody else is. Booze is a comfort item that makes soldiering tolerable.

At the height of my drinking career, I was grinding a pint of whiskey every night. I told myself all the Army lies: I don't have a problem because I don't drink when I'm deployed… I don't come to work drunk… I drink slowly… Almost everyone I know does this.

After my divorce – another standard issue thing for career soldiers – I decided to do the opposite of what seemed normal. I quit drinking for a long time. I've had a few beers since then, but I've become someone who drinks rarely rather than regularly.

Moderation is impossible for me

I have stayed sober for six years. It gets easier at the 90-day mark, even easier at the 180-day and so on. The cravings and temptation start going away as your brain repairs and heals.

Early on, I thought there was no way I could keep fighting the urge to drink 24/7. The days were long, boring and miserable. It was also uncomfortable to feel real emotions for the first time in years after numbing them out.

I didn't become an addict overnight so I wasn't going to get back to being normal overnight, so I did 90 AA meetings in 90 days and could've done more. It occupied my time and it kept me on track having support from people who had made it through, as well as people at the beginning of their journey who were a mess like me. I still go to those meetings because I find the human connection fills the empty hole that I used to fill with booze.

We didn't come out of the womb drinking, smoking cigarettes, popping pills or snorting drugs. These are learned behaviors and the brain can be reprogrammed to function as it did pre-addiction.

Unfortunately, I can't moderate or drink responsibly or socially. I'm all in or I'm all out, and because of that I'm all out.

Alcohol's under the radar effects

I was diagnosed with polycystic ovary syndrome (PCOS) and pre diabetes. My blood pressure and bad cholesterol were both high. I also had high blood sugar, joint and tendon pain, sinus and ear issues, itchy skin, hives, mental fog, sleep problems, thyroid problems and low energy and my once glowing skin went to looking like I'd spent every day in a freeze dryer. Turns out all of these symptoms were caused by alcohol.

I had no idea how bad it could affect the body. I knew it could cause cirrhosis, but I thought that was just for the addicts who drank hard liquor in the mornings. Apparently, my "normal" drinking was enough to wreck my hormone balance and everything else. My liver was too busy processing alcohol so it couldn't prioritize the main functions it had to do.

I quit drinking and all of the issues I had that led to my PCOS diagnosis and everything else resolved. My blood pressure went down the very first day. I went from four hours of sleep to nine. I'm off my depression meds and my thyroid is balanced so I don't need meds for that either.

My hair has stopped falling out and my lips are no longer cracked from being dehydrated. Also, my allergies are much better now that my liver isn't focused strictly on alcohol and can filter out the histamines.
People don't realize how many health problems are caused by a stressed-out liver.

I shamed myself sober

I was sitting in my attorney's office during evidence discovery before I'd spent half of the $15,000 my DUI ended up costing me, when it hit me and I was so ashamed. How did I think it was okay to drive when I was absolutely fucking hammered? I couldn't look my attorney in the eyes.

I feel the same self-disgust and shame daily. Every time my ignition interlock beeps for a random retest while I'm driving down the highway and I'm blowing into something the size of a fucking brick for the world to see. And when I have to pay $12 to have someone watch me piss into a cup for a drug test every month.

And you know what? I fucking deserve it. I fucked around and found out what happens. I could have killed somebody. I could have wrecked my car. I could have lost my job or destroyed my liver to the point of no return. Instead, a concerned person called me in to 911 and got my ass in line. My drinking days are over.

I hauled myself out of alcoholic hell

I've ruined every relationship I've ever had, woken up viciously hungover every day and started drinking in the morning before work. When I stopped, I had to be in hospital because of the seizures and hallucinations from withdrawal. Even after all of that, my crazy addicted mind told me I could figure out a way to drink like a normal person.

Blackout drinking led to multiple violent and painful sexual assaults while unconscious, as well as jail which fucking sucked. I've been homeless, slept outdoors and been hungry and sick. When I saw a lady who couldn't talk due to a stroke from meth, suck dick for left over onion rings behind a dumpster in Las Vegas I saw my future.

It took me two years and five rehabs, but I got sober. Today I live my dream life. I'm a home owner, business owner, wife and mother. I couldn't be more grateful for the gifts that come with quitting alcohol.

My humiliating rock bottom

I got diagnosed with pancreatitis and diabetes. It was the worst pain I've ever been in. I almost died and they put me into a drug induced coma. I guess I was conscious but I only remember two days out of the week I spent in the ICU.

But even after that, I kept drinking. My blood sugar was running at about 500 every day. I was blacking out every night and waking up and dry heaving for 20 minutes. I had bruises, scrapes, burns, busted lips, black eyes, all from falling.

Rock bottom for me was waking up with a different pair of underwear on than when I went to bed. I had pissed myself standing at the toilet and collapsed in the bathroom. My dad had to get me out, change my underwear and put me to bed. I was 34. I had to stop with the booze, not only for my physical health but my mental well-being.

Every day is a struggle, but it was the best decision I've ever made. Whatever you think your problems are now, they will continue to progress and get worse when alcohol dominates your life. The most embarrassing thing you've done while drunk to date will pale into insignificance compared to the stuff you've yet to do.

I was sick of fake drunk me

Missing work from hangovers, having high blood pressure and pre diabetic symptoms and generally feeling like shit all the time wasn't what made me stop drinking. What made me stop was waking up and remembering how insincere and obnoxious I am when I'm drunk.

As an example, I went to a wedding recently and there was an open bar with free cocktails beer and wine. Most people were drinking alcohol all night and for a change I wasn't so I had the chance to play amateur sociologist. I could hear myself as I listened to them getting more ridiculous with every glass.

"We should hang out more! I'll email you next week! Yes, sure you can borrow my power washer I'll bring it over soon! We should all hang out sometime! My brother's company is hiring, I'll send him your resumé tomorrow! We need to play golf next week!"

Every word was complete crap never to be followed up on or likely even remembered. This was me. But as well as all the false promises, fake concern and over the top flattery, I would interrupt people constantly and be rude and crass. With that drink in my hand, I was powerless to stop it.

I never had a rock bottom moment like lots of people, but it feels like I've been at rock bottom for years. Never having to experience that cringing embarrassment ever again drives me to stay sober.

I drank until my heart stopped working

Vodka with a mixer is all I have ever drunk. I kept ramping it up and knew something was bound to happen. I was waking up every three or four hours at night, soaked in sweat and tremoring so badly that I'd drink out of a plastic bottle of premixed vodka and Powerade to calm down.

One morning I woke up and felt weak. I could barely walk or stand up. I was shaking and had massive anxiety. It felt like my heart was about to jump out my chest and I was so short of breath I thought this is it. I'm going to die at the age of 37.

I told my wife to take me to the hospital and needed a wheelchair to get in. After having every test and scan under the sun I was diagnosed with heart failure.

It's been six weeks now and I'm stable. My life has drastically changed. There are only specific things I can eat. I can't have anything with sugar or salt and I have to watch my cholesterol. I can only drink a set amount of liquids a day and obviously I'm never touching alcohol again. I wish I'd quit a long time ago. Living with a chronic heart condition is not fun.

Recovery isn't linear

Prior to going to see the doctor I had a dull aching pain in the side of my abdomen. My blood tests showed I was on the way to liver disease with all the fat that had accumulated in there. I had to get serious about getting sober so I got myself into therapy.

My therapist told me to be prepared, because when people quit for good it's after an average of nine to twelve relapses! And she was right. I slipped up every couple of weeks and got mad at myself. But after thinking about it, I saw that a relapse shouldn't mean resetting your sober counter back to zero and feeling like a total failure. Recovery will include the occasional stumble for the vast majority of people.

Now I think about the progress I've made rather than get down on myself for wiping out all my "good" days. I told my doctor about the difficulties I was having and he said as long as I kept drinking less than I did before and increasing the sober days in between I would be okay.

Another encouraging thing he mentioned was that once you stop drinking, it only takes about a month for signs your liver is healing to appear in your bloodwork, and at around two months your enzyme levels should be fairly normal. It's amazing how quickly your liver will forgive you for all the abuse.

Healing a diseased liver is possible

I was told I had a 50% chance of mortality after being released from hospital three years ago. My odds of survival were dismal before I "miraculously" went from late-stage cirrhosis to stage 2 fibrosis to stage 1 fibrosis over the space of a few years. When I was first diagnosed my FibroScan score was 24. Now it's 7 which is normal.

I reversed my death sentence after complete liver failure by eating only whole foods, lots of baked vegetables (broccoli, asparagus, fennel, sweet potato), wild caught fish, like salmon, organically raised chicken, eggs, oatmeal, some fruit, water, fresh brewed coffee and unsweetened tea – basically a modified Mediterranean diet. Plus, I took supplements in addition to all my meds, which my hepatologist said was okay.

I did not touch juice, cereal, fries, artificial or real sugar, candy, fast food, white wheat flour-based carbs (sorry, that does mean bread, cakes and pastries) or anything with garbage like high fructose corn syrup, seed oils, MSG, emulsifiers, additives and colors. On the advice of my doctor, red meat was limited to none and I bought an air fryer.

I also did lots of walking – around two miles a day – took supplements like milk thistle, curcumin vitamin E and niacin and drank more water Not only did I reverse my liver disease; I also reversed my fatness and risk of type 2 diabetes!

Today I have no symptoms of cirrhosis, no edema, no further paracentesis and I'm on zero medication. My hepatologist commented that out of all the patients he has seen in his career, very few have achieved what I have. (I have heard of several others who have cut their liver enzymes in half in six months doing the same kind of thing.)

I know cirrhosis presents very differently from person to person and not all cirrhosis is reversible. Some people will have scarring that will not go away no matter what diet or medications they take. But in my case, a total lifestyle shift worked to rebuild what was left.

The liver is an amazing organ that has the power to regenerate which is literally why it can take so much abuse. Apparently, all mine needed was a permanent break from alcohol, exercise and the right kind of nutrients to heal.

I was drinking to stay in a bad relationship

My ex used to mock me for drinking too much. He was a drinker too and liked to make out he had better control of it than me. His tolerance was higher than mine and he could slam tequilas without sounding different, although he went from nice to nasty pretty fast. At that point I would just drink to pass out. It was drink, sleep, suffer, repeat.

I put on 10lbs, my face was bloated, I always felt tired and irritable and every year my blood pressure and cholesterol numbers got higher. I remember my dad saying once when we joined them on vacation in Italy, "I bet you can't go a day without a drink." He was right. This situation went on for six years.

After we broke up, I started losing weight. Turns out, when the ex was no longer around, I didn't feel the need to zone out with alcohol, so the pounds fell off. Now I can see that the drinking was all due to an attempt to make things work, even though I was walking on eggshells half the time and feeling depressed and exhausted the rest. I had been so focused on someone else's wellbeing I had sacrificed my own.

Since then, I have read up on abusive relationships and have learned that you should focus on what you want to achieve in life and not waste it on some situation or person that takes all your energy and time.

I found this quote by someone on Quora pretty motivating and accurate: "Addicts decide who they want to be with, which determines where they will be, which influences what they do in life. Non-addicts decide what they want to do in life, which determines where they will be, which influences who they are with."

In other words, you should choose the people in your life very carefully. As Dr Phil advises, it's better to be single, sane and healthy than sick and crazy with someone else.

Prison was my rehab

I have spent most of my life hotel hopping and working random jobs on construction sites. I do not miss drinking from 6:00 a.m. passing out at 8:00 p.m. and waking up at three in the morning searching for any drops left in one of many empty bottles of cheap vodka, then pacing around the house sweating and sipping dollar store mouthwash.

I'd pray for the sun to hurry up and come out because the darkness would drive me insane. At 6:00 a.m. I'd begin vomiting so I'd search for coins to buy another fifth of vodka. During daylight hours I would try and make money doing manual labor so I had enough for another bottle and a $6 pizza.

Then I'd be elated, not because I had food and a place to go back to, but because I had enough liquor to last through the night which meant not having to try to sleep going through withdrawals. The whole cycle would start over when the second bottle was empty at 6:00 a.m. This was my life for 20 years. It was 20 years of pain and misery.

Then I got arrested for falling asleep in a truck I stole. I got violent and was tased three times. My first few months were spent at the intake prison. After that I went to a level two unit for 30 months. It was 50% workcamp and 50% treatment and a rehab program which forced me to deal with the stuff that got me there.

Being locked up for a couple of years forced me into getting sober whether I liked it or not. Personally I want to thank the judge. He gave me a lot of time to think about things and reevaluate my life. Now I'm sober, have a place to live and work fulltime as a painter. Everything is possible as long as you don't give up on yourself.

I could help other people but not myself

I'm a therapist and I'm an alcoholic. It's a very lonely and scary place to be. Nobody talks much about alcoholism affecting counselors because of the stigma around it and because we are meant to be the in control, responsible ones.

Despite being hungover and full of shame I always found a way to give everything I'd got to my clients and would see the progress in their lives. But it really bothered me that I couldn't help myself. After work I'd escape into alcohol, which had become a real problem after Covid. I'm good at what I do and have a waitlist, but drinking had me beat.

Medication assisted treatment was a total game changer for me. I've been on naltrexone for a while now and it has completely stopped any cravings for alcohol. It makes it taste gross, cuts out the feel-good chemicals and I just feel nauseous.

Attending SMART Recovery meetings was good too, because of the way the focus is on science and clinical evidence and the approach is more flexible and unique to the individual. I also found the online forum r/stopdrinking very supportive.

Working with my own therapist has also helped by relieving me of the hypocrisy, shame and secrecy of it as well as helping me recognize how emotionally drained I was. Apparently, alcohol use disorder is rampant in our field. I guess it's hard to ask for help when you're supposed to be the helper.

I believe I am now a better therapist and clinical supervisor compared to how I was pre-recovery. My empathy and ability to understand how easily addiction can happen to someone and how hard it is to stop have allowed me to connect to my clients in a different way.

Getting sober gave me a job, a family and a life

I lost a great management job due to drinking and applied for similar positions left and right. But showing up to interviews hung over, still drunk or smelling of alcohol it was no surprise that nobody wanted to hire me. I wouldn't even have hired myself.

With nothing to do all day I was drinking a couple of 1.5-liter bottles of cheap wine a day, sometimes more on the weekend and eating maybe once a week. I was 5ft 8in and 110lbs. I lived in despair and sorrow. All I wanted to think and feel was nothing.

I made it a year and a half before I had a withdrawal seizure and was told I was lucky to survive. That's when I chose to go to an inpatient treatment rehab center.

Even with insurance it was expensive, but it was worth every penny because it allows you to focus on yourself 100% full-time which is rare for many. I did 30 days inpatient and four months of outpatient treatment along with AA meetings.

People think that AA is religious but to me it is more spiritual. I didn't see the religious aspect of it at all. The meetings I go to are sometimes laugh out loud funny, thoughtful or somber at times.

The 12-Steps is about admitting you have a problem and need help as well as making amends for past harms. You also have a sponsor who is like a non-judgmental friend who you can call or text any time. It's amazing how much peace of mind that gives you.

Fast forward to now. I have a challenging job making as much as I was before I lost my previous well-paid job. I have a wonderful husband who I met on a recovery website and a three-year-old daughter. I know I would have none of these things if I hadn't chosen to make the hard journey into recovery.

Escaping the matrix

Drinking starts off as a pleasure. Then it's routine and then it's earlier and earlier every day and then it's basically non-stop. You are sabotaging yourself and pretty much hate yourself for it, which makes you drink more.

I had to make a drastic and massive overhaul of my entire life. Some people might call it monk mode or an existential crash-diet. I gave up everything mind-altering including coffee, cigarettes, drugs, video games, news media and even my ADHD medication, which is controversial I know.

If it made me angry, got my blood pressure up or kept me awake at night I got it out of my life. People too. Anyone I had to psyche myself up to deal with, or left me feeling stressed and exhausted were out. It was like a huge mental, physical and spiritual detox.

I started cooking my own meals (vegetables, meat or fish and rice with no sauces), exercising (walking 5 to 10km each day outside in nature), doing house projects, meditating and reading.

My life dramatically changed in just two months. I feel and look 15 years younger; my mind is sharper and I have zero depression, anxiety or cravings. I truly think I have escaped the matrix.

Most people who have a drink problem stop of their own accord. Some can moderate and just have a social drink or two. Others choose abstinence because it's just simpler to manage.

PART 11

The practicalities of quitting alcohol: battling the "fuck-its"

As I mentioned in the introduction, I compiled this book to stop myself drinking once and for all. It took quite some time to whittle everything down into a list of hard hitting, relatable information that my own fickle attention span could tolerate. At the end of it, alcohol no longer had a grip over me. Success! Job done! Or so I thought…

Within days I realized that making the decision to quit alcohol was just one relatively small – albeit major – step along my new life's journey. But how would I manage from here? What would I do instead? How would I cope without my trusted wingman, entertainment manager, off-switch disabler and partner in crime?

Drinking softens the sharp edges of the world and temporarily frees you from yourself. Without it, social situations were either cringingly awkward, deadly dull or plain exhausting. In the absence of pre-gaming, the bar scene looked depressing, with people mostly staring up at the TV or down at their phones between gulps of booze.

Going out clubbing was another study in human behavior, which was typically a set pattern of tipsy banter, loudening aggression followed by the inevitable loss of bodily functions, morals, money and possessions.

My friends were unhappy about the loss of their drinking buddy and suspicious of my new, mostly observant stance. They lectured me on how drinking was the norm in European cultures and had been for centuries and how the Romans drank wine all day. Well yes, I thought that too until I did a bit of research and found that just like every other drug on the planet, the strength of alcohol has been ramped up to ridiculous levels.

In the old days, beer used to have an alcohol content in the 2% to 3% ABV range and wine was 8% to 10%, because that's the maximum amount you naturally get from turning sugar into alcohol. A lot of cultures like the Romans and Greeks would never drink their wine full-strength because it was considered uncivilized, so up to 75% of it was water. They basically drank to hydrate not to get loaded.

Now we have genetically modified yeasts capable of fermentation rates as high as 16%, which is currently the upper limit. So, while mankind may have been drinking beer and wine for thousands of years, it's only recently that these brews have become super strong.

Spirits like whiskey used to be made by heating up a liquid and distilling out the alcohol to create liquors that would take the skin off the roof of your mouth unless they were left to mellow in caskets for years.

Now there are things like diffusers, which are machines as big as basketball courts, that churn this stuff out faster and purer than the old-fashioned methods. That's why a lot of today's mass-produced vodkas and tequilas taste like high end brands.

I was also told that people who don't drink are annoying and come across as superior and boring. The word "boring" came up a lot. Yes, I got it. I was boring.

There is no doubt the moments of silliness and spontaneity that happen when alcohol takes the edge off things are great fun. But my court jester antics and buffoonery came at a high price. Getting drunk for me invariably triggered a cascade of events over which I had no control. "Moderation management" wasn't an option for me. A couple of my group managed to cut back by following this program,[104] but their

---

[104]"Does moderation work and for whom?" https://recoveryoptions.us/is-moderate-drinking-a-realistic-option-for-you/

brains weren't wired to be compulsive about drinking like mine. Once I picked up a drink I was on an unstoppable wild water rapid ride down to the bottom of the bottle.

My friends didn't know that after a night out I'd go home and chug wine until I blacked out or stuff my face with delivery pizza and throw up over the side of the bed in my sleep. They didn't know that being the funny, crazy one meant my cholesterol and triglycerides were code red and my blood pressure was vessel-poppingly high.

I had never told them about the two DUIs that had cost me the price of a decent car, or about all my visits to the ER for alcohol-related injuries. No, I did not trip over the dog, slip on the bathroom floor, drop a weight on my foot at the gym or any other such nonsense. I'd been wasted and done stupid shit because the more I drank the more I drank.

But now with all these reasons not to drink vaguely swirling around my subconscious, a profound change had occurred. The desire to piss away my life had all but gone. I realized I was not the cool hedonist I thought I was. I was just an drunken, out of control asshole.

I'd also developed a newfound respect for my liver and felt quite protective towards it. My brain also deserved some recognition for its years of loyal service. Both had been on the frontline of the self-assault, taking hit after invisible hit, with the alcohol punching microscopic holes into them for years.

But as neither of them had pain receptors, these stoic organs had battled on, weathering all the assaults without complaint. Except for the short-term memory loss and the occasional dull ache under my ribs, so far there had been no major, lasting issues.

But now I was familiar with the common themes that feature in all heavy drinker's lives. I'd done a shit-ton of research and could see where I was headed. No, no one is unique or immune to alcohol's effects. Nobody has hollow legs or a Teflon liver. Alcohol hurts everyone the same. It's just the timeline that varies, with women beating men to the finish line for cirrhosis.

Everywhere you look, alcohol is associated with success, sophistication and the good life. Whether it's in cocktail glasses on silver trays, trickling out of ice sculptures or spurting out of champagne bottles, the message is clear: you can't enjoy life without it.

Movie stars have liquor brands, whiskey buffs trade bourbons, bearded men bond over craft beer and finding a good cheap local wine is the highlight of every British expat's life.

Except now I was like the boy who'd seen the emperor without his clothes. I could never unsee the reality of what booze really was. I couldn't be fooled by its celebrity endorsements, sparkling commercial image or casual presence on a rustic dining table under a shady gazebo in the Tuscan hills. For me, alcohol in all its forms was disaster in disguise.

Unlike the "white knucklers" who cling to sobriety no matter what, quitting booze was not a linear progression for me. It was the old two steps forward one step back, hesitant, uneven pace. Because every few days a cunning little voice in my head would say, "Fuck it! You can handle a drink."

Sometimes I could, sometimes I couldn't. It was impossible to predict whether I'd take myself for a quick ride around the block or blast myself into oblivion. But knowing it wasn't forbidden or an object of guilt made it easier not to obsess about it and end up getting wasted.

Those evil little fuck-its hid like a virus, ready to get me when I was at my weakest or stressed, or ironically at my strongest and thought I could exercise restraint.

The first three months were hard, in a way that's similar to getting out of an abusive, roller coaster type relationship with someone you are addicted to. Nobody can understand why you can't just leave.

Because along with inflicting mental and physical pain, alcohol had also been my solace, excitement and means of escape. So, I romanticized the "good times," minimized the suffering and rationalized that things weren't all bad. In effect, I was trauma-bonded to a cruel deceiver who had no interest in my welfare, but occasionally made me feel happy and loved. So relapsing was inevitable in many ways.

I got a sober app on my phone which counted my alcohol-free days and all the money I saved on booze. But if I slipped up with just one drink it was back to the dreaded "day one."

There are some sobriety experts who believe that even the smallest failure should incite the deepest level of shame and that nothing less than total abstinence is the holy grail. This seemed unnecessarily harsh and demoralizing, so I changed the rules so that I would only do a reset if I had an exceptionally bad hangover or threw up.

Education, self-tolerance and forgiveness were key factors in my eventual ability break free from this curse of a drug. I stopped beating myself up for every lapse of control and eased away at my own pace.

Brief drinking episodes do not automatically mean escalating alcohol abuse will follow according to the research.[105] The vast majority of people attempting to quit will become stable enough to leave their destructive drinking days behind them, despite hopping on and off the wagon multiple times.

Eventually my relapses spaced themselves out longer and longer, going from days to weeks then months. Every so often, a fuck-it would cross my mind and reason with me that a couple of beers wouldn't kill me or a little wine sample at the grocery store wouldn't hurt. It would say I wasn't being sociable by having no alcohol in the house and

---

[105] "How Many Recovery Attempts Does it Take to Successfully Resolve an Alcohol or Drug Problem? Estimates and Correlates from a National Study of Recovering U.S. Adults"
https://pubmed.ncbi.nlm.nih.gov/31090945/

should keep some in stock for visitors. That little voice had a whole repertoire of bullshit ready to spring on me.

After a few "experiments" to remind myself what I was missing, I stopped kidding myself that boozing made my life better. I knew that even the smallest amount would set off a shitshow of regret.

I'd fast forward to the next day's headache, vague embarrassment about things I couldn't remember and two-day long slump and I'd open a can of seltzer. Not quite the exciting prospect the impulse-driven part of my brain wanted, but because it couldn't be trusted anymore, my intelligent brain had been promoted to chief decision maker.

Another scary thing I learned is that you don't have to be addicted to alcohol to develop liver disease. A bottle of wine or a few pints most evenings can lead to build-up of fat and inflammation. So I booked myself a free FibroScan* at a nearby research center which operated on the basis that you'd be referred to one of their gastroenterologists if there was a problem.

A technician in a white coat used a hand-held device to shoot pulses of energy between my ribs. There was a small thud every time he activated the probe which calculates the liver's stiffness and fat content. He used two probes, one that analyzed the outer layer and one that went deeper into the tissue. The whole thing lasted for around ten minutes.

I waited in a separate room until the young guy came back with a clipboard with the results. To my amazement all the sporadic binges over the years and a bout of hepatitis A hadn't caused any lasting damage. The numbers said I was two points away from official fatty liver, but there were no signs of cirrhosis.

He then explained the stages of liver damage and interestingly described cirrhosis as being a mass of stretch marks caused by the liver expanding when it's filling up fat. These stretch marks – which are essentially made of scar tissue – form in the liver's deepest layers as well as the outside of the organ.

I celebrated my liver's almost good health with a cup of coffee at a nearby breakfast place and reflected on how I was going to get its score down. The booze was on its way out obviously, but I wasn't quite there with totally quitting. There was something about the word "sobriety" I just didn't like for some reason. It sounded a bit sanctimonious and not me somehow.

Then I realized after a few weeks of quitting booze that I now had another problem. Sugar.

Chocolate and ice cream had become the new highlights of my day, which made sense as sugar and alcohol both activate the same reward pathways in the brain. The sugar gave me energy and something to look forward to and was my reward for staying sober. A pint of ice cream in exchange for a pint of beer seemed like a fair trade off to me.

This all changed when I learned that sugar also fills the liver with fat. Even worse was sugar in the form of high fructose corn syrup (HFCS) which is just as bad as alcohol.[106]

When it's broken down, this evil stuff creates uric acid which is toxic like acetaldehyde and inflames the liver. Plus, it triggers the brain's reward centers to make you crave it. Why tf do they invent these things?

By the way, the fructose in man-made HFCS is not the same as the fructose in fruit which is only good provided you eat the whole thing and don't just drink the juice. The juice is a concentrated form of fructose which again, is mainly metabolized by the liver.

Oh, and now they think this high fructose corn syrup crap – which a lot of other countries have banned by the way – is behind the explosion in colon cancer in young people in the United States, including teenagers and kids.

---

[106] "6 Reasons Why High-Fructose Corn Syrup Is Bad for You" https://www.healthline.com/nutrition/why-high-fructose-corn-syrup-is-bad

This is because HFCS carpet bombs the good bacteria in your guts, the barrier that defends you against viruses and infection. So, these invaders get in there and cause inflammation which damages the cells. Cancer cells are essentially these same slightly mutated cells multiplying uncontrollably, being fed by this artificial liquid sugar concoction.

So out went the soda, candy and junk food and I started checking the labels to see where this gut-wrecking, fatty liver causing substance was hiding. You'd be surprised. High fructose corn syrup is in everything you can think of including microwave meals, salad dressing, peanut butter and even deli-counter meat.

Grocery shopping was turning into a minefield of potential disease hazards. There was nothing for it. I had to learn to cook.

With guidance from YouTube, I started making soups from scratch, baked all kinds of vegetables as a starting point for meals and crunched on raw nuts and chopped apples instead of chips.

Proteins were mostly in the form of eggs (which actually reduce cell damage in the liver), chicken, canned tuna and grilled steak. Eating right became a new obsession and took my mind off the alcohol my brain still kept thinking it needed.

This major dietary shift had the dual effect of balancing out my blood sugar levels and getting me off the metabolic crash and crave rollercoaster. When I was eating crap my blood sugar had been surging from high to low all day because of all the glucose from the carbs.

When you overload your body with sugar or glucose your blood sugar levels rocket upwards. This sudden increase forces your body to pump out insulin to bring them down. And because it usually overcompensates, now your blood sugar levels crash.

The same thing happens with booze, which is why just about all heavy drinkers have bipolar blood sugar levels. When they're low you get anxiety and crave carbs, sugar and alcohol and the whole exhausting cycle starts up again.

I began filling my body with good things and walked past the grocery store's freezer cabinets full of boxed meals without a sidewards glance. Cooking turned out to be one of the most rewarding efforts I had ever made for myself. The effects were almost immediate.

Nutrients! Finally, my poor, starved yet overweight body was getting the vitamins, minerals and amino acids it had been craving all these years.

Instead of wasting its limited vitamin stores detoxing alcohol, my tissue and bone cells were rediscovering how it feels to be bathed in the elixir of life. My long-suffering liver finally got some time off to make repairs, while the dead zones in my frontal lobes started to fire up again.

Another improvement happened when I bought one of those insulated mugs with a straw in the lid. I'd fill it with ice, water and a bit of lemon juice and keep it on hand all day. Who knew hydration would have such an effect? I could see, think and process information more clearly. All these years I had been mistaking waves of thirst for ripples of anxiety and making things worse by my "all I need is a drink" delusion.

For the first time in forever, I discovered how it feels not to be constantly hungry, parched or drained of energy. And because I wasn't cranking myself up with candy and caffeine all day, I wasn't hyped up and desperate to unwind with booze every evening.

Relieved of its duty of fighting booze-initiated fires, my battle-weary brain finally started to relax. All two hundred billion of its neurons were getting a well-earned break from being drunk or hungover.

No longer able to blame alcohol for every random ailment, I noticed my belly expanded massively every time I ate pizza or bread in general. Turns out I had an allergy to gluten which is another common issue with people who are prone to addiction-style drinking.

I wondered what else had my long-suffering belly been putting up with all these years. So I went online and found an allergy testing center, sent off ten half inch bits of hair and got them tested for reactivity to a thousand types of foods.

The results arrived in my inbox about a week later. Chickpeas, hummus and shrimp were all listed as inflammatory and off the menu for me. I was also code red level deficient in B1(thiamine) despite taking a multivitamin every day. So, I upgraded to a more expensive, higher quality brand.

With my new alcohol, almost sugar-free gut-approved regime, my dopamine receptors started to flicker back online. And without the alcohol in the way, the tryptophan that comes from food was able to get my belly's serotonin factory running properly again.

After years of cattle-prodding my brain into cranking out neurotransmitters it was great to be reacquainted with my true, unjacked up self. Fueled by self-generated happy chemicals I discovered to my surprise that my natural state was not one of chronic dread and inertia. Mental stability, confidence and vigor had been there all along.

Alcohol had been stopping my neurons from doing their job of regulating my response to stress and wiping out my meager vitamin stores, leaving me physically and emotionally drained. Yet another strike for booze.

It took a while, but I eventually got to experience proper sleep with actual dreams I could remember. Plus, my natural waking time turned out to be 6:00 a.m., which meant the dogs got a walk before breakfast.

Then another nice thing happened. Although I'm not obsessed with my appearance, I couldn't help but notice that things were improving on that front too. My face was thinner; I had clearer eyes, my hair seemed to be growing in darker and that tired, defeated look about me had gone.

Spurred on by these ego boosting transformations I joined the gym and hired a trainer to make sure I stuck with it. Six months later I was wearing tighter clothes on purpose.

Exercise was an upward, self-propelling spiral of improvement, with one little change or vague curiosity turning into a new habit. You don't need a ton of money, specialized equipment or a complex gameplan. Any kind of regular physical activity will do.

A lot of people say they are bored when they don't drink alcohol. I agree, life is quieter and slower at the beginning, but new preoccupations and interests will start catching your attention when you feel better about yourself.

For me it was fitness and learning about food. The Reddit forums r/dryalcoholics and r/stopdrinking also helped enormously. These vast arenas of shared experience are full of people who know what you are going through and their advice and knowledge is inspirational as well as life-saving for many. I can't say enough good things about these online support groups.

Other things I did, which I had no interest in or energy to do before included organizing my house on a room-by-room basis, which kept my mind occupied. Then I sorted out my finances and started the side business I'd been planning but had never found the time to focus on.

Waking up early also meant I was showing up for work an hour in advance. While my coworkers were dragging themselves in at 9:30 a.m. I had replied to my emails and was on calls setting up appointments. This resulted in a promotion to a more senior role and a pay rise, which never would have happened in my old drinking days.

The fuck-its are always going to dormant, just lurking in the shadows of the instinct-driven animal part of my brain. I know they are still there just waiting to surprise me or talk me into doing something stupid.

Historically, I know when they will strike and their little voice will tell me I should drink: when I'm bored, on a date, on vacation, at events and celebrations, feeling super happy, super sad or just walking past a buy one, get one free beer deal at the grocery store. Or for absolutely no reason at all. It's not an easy coexistence but being aware of them helps.

The start of a downward spiral can also happen as a result of other situations or triggers. For example, I won't subject myself to people who stress me out, reality TV shows that feature mainly screaming, drunk people, or going on dates unless I've FaceTimed them first and know I won't be putting myself through some kind of ordeal.

I used to live on burgers, chips, diet soda and energy drinks, but now I've got some knowledge about nutrition, I know that as well as sugar, other crave-factor substances like monosodium glutamate disguised as "natural flavors" will jangle my brain's neurons and make me a hyped-up, booze-craving monster.

Now I buy the raw materials to make the kind of food that keeps my brain on an even keel. It's more work and takes longer but that's okay. Every day I exercise, every time I eat right or order a soda water at the bar I know the fuck-its will have a harder time getting to me.

Saying goodbye to alcohol really was like leaving a crappy relationship. Some days I look back and reminisce about the good times. But then I remember all the pain, drama, despair and destruction that went with it and I'm just glad I got away.

PART 12

Things people have done, some by choice and some by accident, to stay off the booze

Sometimes extreme addiction calls for an extreme solution in the form of an unforgettable shock to the system, radical treatment plan or complete life overhaul. Here are some real-life examples of the choices, legally mandated programs and unforeseen circumstances that have helped long-term excessive drinkers reboot their lives.

Going to rehab

They say once you hit the brakes on your drinking all the undealt-with shit you'd put on the backseat flies forward and hits you on the head. Dealing with unresolved issues and emotional pain is essential to recovery.

Going to rehab as an in-patient allows you to focus on yourself with no work, family, kids or other responsibilities to distract you from addressing your insecurities and traumas. If you take it seriously you will gain a whole new insight from other people in similar situations and break down the issues that cause you to drink.

A lot of people make the mistake of thinking they're okay because someone else has got it worse. Attendees have mentioned that in recovery circles there can be a lot of one-upmanship with competitive suffering and that you should take no notice of it and just focus on your situation. Rehab is an amazing opportunity to get your life back on track in a wholly supportive environment.

If you live in the US your health insurance plan might cover some of the cost but it is likely you will pay a significant amount out-of-pocket. If money is an issue, go online and look for low budget or free rehab centers that are paid for by Medicaid.

The Family and Medical Leave Act (FMLA) means you can take unpaid leave for 12 weeks for medical reasons and still have a job at the end of it. Because alcohol use disorder is classified as a disease, you can't be fired for seeking treatment

In the UK the residential rehab clinics are highly rated with attentive staff and often resemble five-star hotels. The NHS provides free in-patient detox treatment and outpatient support for those who can't afford to go to private.

Going all-in on recovery support and self-education

Part of the reason rehab works is because you are surrounded by people who are like you. To experience a similar level of connectedness and individual support you might consider joining SMART © Recovery (doesn't mention God) or Alcoholics Anonymous (mentions God). The Buddhist Recovery Network, Refuge Recovery and Dharma Recovery are both based on Buddhist principles.

You can find links to a wide range of support groups at: www.reddit.com/r/stopdrinking/wiki/links.

All these meetings are free and there are lots of them thanks to platforms like Zoom. You do not have to talk. Just go and listen until you feel comfortable participating.

Essential to recovery is learning everything you can. Saturate yourself in knowledge. Immerse yourself in everything sober-related. Read quit lit books, listen to ex-drinker's podcasts, watch YouTube videos and join the online forum r/stopdrinking. As the saying goes, "A smart person learns from their mistakes. A wise person learns from other people's mistakes."

For that extra rehab experience this is a good time to start a daily exercise routine, start eating better by adding more vegetables to your diet and getting at least 7 hours' sleep. You could also try things like meditation and yoga as well as acupuncture, massages, facials and saunas.

If you can afford it, or have insurance that will cover it, find a licensed mental health professional who knows about addiction. Figuring out why you drink is a major part of long-term recovery in addition to getting help for chronic anxiety and/or depression and trauma. A lot of people have found cognitive behavioral therapy especially helpful.

If you can't afford therapy or need more than the hour or so a week of help you get from your counselor, there's a book called "How to Do the Work" by Dr. Nicole LePera which explains how you can be your own best healer. It asks the kind of questions you'd have to think about in therapy and forces you to look more deeply into the reasons why you feel and act the way you do.

75% of people who recover from alcohol dependence do so without specialist treatment. Support groups, books, videos and apps can really help as well as making the effort to improve your health in general.

Doing proper exercise

Daily – or almost daily – physical exercise is a proven way to help you dry out, improve your health and rid yourself of anxiety. The trick is to find something you will commit to doing on set days throughout the week.

It's worth paying for a personal trainer if you can't motivate yourself to go to the gym. Many former drinkers say they were inspired by the "Couch to 5K" running program. Other popular choices are cycling, hiking, swimming and climbing. A lot of people just do a few squats and sit-ups and lift weights at home.

Walk. Get a smart watch or wearable device to track your activity and some audiobooks to make the time pass. There's no need to be extreme about it, just do it every day you for as long as you can.

Alternatively, you can use your energy to improve your surroundings. Sweating it out in the yard pulling weeds, cleaning or painting the house will redirect your focus and dampen your urge to drink. All you need to do is establish one good habit and other positive habits will start building around it. It's shitty at first, but so is just about everything else when you're sobering up.

Joining a sober living community

Sober living houses or apartment complexes are for people who have already been through treatment in rehab or some other type of recovery program. These places accommodate people separately by gender or by their circumstances (e.g., single men and women, women with kids, lesbians, gays etc.).

Support is mostly structured around the Alcoholics Anonymous 12-Step program with regular group meetings. The main rule is to stay sober. If you don't, you will probably be asked to leave as one rogue occupant can set everyone else off.

The residents support each other in staying off drugs and alcohol and pay a share of the rent and utilities. Provided you follow the rules you can stay as long as you like.

Rents are dependent on the location and range of services that are included. Basic shared accommodation like an Oxford House for example might cost less than $1,000 a month.

If money's no object there are single sex luxury sober living properties that offer a personal chef, gym, pool and individual counseling. Expect to pay upwards of $10,000 a month for a private room.

Employing a sober companion

If there's nobody at home to make sure you eat right and stay on track, a sober companion might be the answer. This person does not live with you but is on call 24/7 to support you while you get used to your new alcohol-free life.

They can also be your plus one at places and events where you know everyone will be drinking. Their services are not cheap and can cost anywhere from $900 to $4,000 a day.

24/7 breathalyzer monitoring

Voluntary or court-mandated breathalyzer tests that you take three or four times a day have helped many people stay sober by providing them with a sense of accountability as well as evidence to show they really are not drinking, which is important for things like child visitation or staying employed.

These devices are the size of a cell phone and use facial recognition technology to make sure nobody else is using the device on your behalf. The results are then sent via cell phone to you and your support person, who could be a therapist, sponsor or family member.

These monitoring systems are great for proving you are staying on track and for re-establishing trust with friends and family members. You can allow them to receive regular reports as part of your plan, or send them a screenshot of your results. Plans range from $100 to $360 a month depending on features of the service and how quickly the results are provided.

Some alcohol monitoring devices include Soberlink, BACtrack and SCRAM Remote Breath Pro. Other systems that use the latest transdermal testing technologies include skin patches which change color, electronic patches, ankle bracelets (SCRAM) and watch bands (BACtrack Skyn).

Getting out of a bad relationship

Many people have found that their compulsion to drink to excess evaporates when they leave someone who is argumentative, angry, controlling, abusive or cheats.

An incompatible, stressful relationship is a huge factor that drives binge drinking and relapses. Alcohol is an anesthetic that numbs out the unhappiness in dysfunctional relationships and makes the other person tolerable.

Getting drunk also allows the unhappy party to sleep in a different room, watch TV on their own or otherwise escape for a while.

Conversely, alcohol can act as the glue that holds mismatched people together. If one or both parties stops drinking, they may discover they were only able to have sex or bond with their partner when they are drunk. Without the fake intimacy created by booze, they realize they have nothing in common and the relationship fizzles out.

This kind of disconnection can happen even after decades of being together. (The same thing can happen with friend groups, where you have almost nothing in common apart from drinking.)

It is possible to work through the readjustment – usually with the help of counseling – to forge a more authentic partnership, provided both parties genuinely care about each other and neither is pathologically abusive. AA recommends not making any major decisions about breaking up a relationship or marriage until after a year of mental clarity, especially when children are involved.

Temporarily becoming a recluse

This is a kind of self-imposed house arrest and a lifestyle reset in the same way as a stint in rehab, only here you are in charge of everything and accountable only to yourself. The key to success is to make sure you are always busy.

List as many projects as you can. This includes everything from re-decorating your house or apartment to learning a new craft to sorting through your possessions and selling or giving away stuff you don't need.

Obviously, clubs, bars and restaurants are out and sexual relationships are also best avoided until drinking is off your list of coping mechanisms. Read as much as you can, listen to audiobooks on getting sober and attend online recovery meetings.

Being a recluse does not mean being antisocial. You should correspond with as many people as you like. Contact a sponsor friend when you feel the signals that trigger a drinking session. Alternatively, go for a walk, take a bike ride or clean the windows: anything to get the cravings out of your system.

Gradually add people, places and relationships back into your life when you feel comfortable and unfazed in social situations where others are drinking. People who have done this say the process can take between one and three months.

Doing a stint as a farm laborer

Okay I know this is off at a tangent, but instead of rehab some people have been successful in getting off booze by hurling themselves into a foreign environment. One such choice is taking a labor-intensive farm job where there is nothing to do but work, exercise and eat.

Jobs like this can be found at a horse stable, cattle ranch, pig, fruit or dairy farm; basically, any type of farming operation that provides accommodation. According to those who've tried it you will work hard, put on muscle and come out a different person after six months.

Working on the North Slope of Alaska

Another dramatic change of pace and location is working in Alaska's North Slope oilfields. Oil drilling companies provide their employees with free housing and restaurant-quality food. "Slopers" work 12-hour days often doing hard physical labor in subzero temperatures. Because the money's so good, workers fly in from states as far away as Hawaii.

Jobs in this remote wilderness of untamed tundra include college internships, engineering, construction and service industry-related positions. According to reports it's an alcohol-free workplace that offers decent living standards and pays well.

In Alaska a lot of remote places are dry because of how badly alcohol has torn their communities apart. Natives like the Inupiat and Yupik people would pass out on the street drunk and be found dead, frozen rigid days later. These villages are only accessible by plane, boat or an ice road in the winter and the few hundred residents that live there have no access to alcohol most of the year.

Working offshore

Like all the options here, something about having less choices gives many people a sense of freedom. If you are capable of taking a job on an offshore vessel or oil rig, this would be a good place to stay sober as it will usually be a totally drug and alcohol-free workplace. Oil rig employees have the same amount of time off as they do working e.g. one month on and one month off. The challenge here is not to relapse as soon as you are back on dry land.

Doing jail time

Incarceration is the ultimate wake-up call. The distress and discomfort you go through after being arrested (most likely for an alcohol-related charge) is harsh mentally and physically. Some people say it's the best thing that ever happened to them and credit time in prison for helping them straighten out, while others say it made their addiction worse. Overall, it's a brutal experience and not recommended as a substitute for proper treatment.

Over half the people who go to jail have a substance use disorder. So, as well as a health screening at intake, staff are trained to check on an inmate's condition. If they are showing signs of withdrawals a medical worker should send them to hospital if they are a seize risk.

If their symptoms are manageable, they are usually put on a Valium or benzo taper and given drugs to take home with them on release. Without follow-up meds they will inevitably start drinking again to avoid withdrawals.

There is also a risk that you will get sent to a jail where medically supervised withdrawals are not provided and there is no choice but to go cold turkey. This can cause unnecessary suffering and possibly death (for which the facility can be sued by your nearest relative).

Because it's a bit of a crap shoot as to whether you'll be properly helped or not and because breaking the law can ruin your life, this option is best avoided.

Getting a DUI

Anyone who has been arrested and jailed overnight for DUI will attest that it is a devastating, publicly humiliating, shameful and extremely costly experience with lasting repercussions. For most this is enough to scare them straight never drink again.

For obvious reasons driving your car while intoxicated is a terrible idea and will result in extended jail time if you cause another person's death.

Involuntary hospitalization

Around a third of suicide attempts and self-injury are alcohol-induced and usually result in involuntary psychiatric hospitalization. When a person is suicidal, they can be detained for up to 72 hours according to "The Baker Act" in Florida or "5150 Hold" as it's known throughout the rest of the country.

If you are considered a suicide risk after three days you will be asked to sign a form to say you agree to being held until you are considered stable enough to be released. The alternative is having a judge decide the length of your stay based on a psychiatrist's report.

You can also be admitted to the hospital's psych ward if you are having symptoms of severe alcohol withdrawal and will be sedated and given benzos for a few days. Patients may then be given naltrexone to help them break their dependence on alcohol after they leave.

For many, this whole experience is official recognition they have reached "rock bottom" and the point in their life when they realize drinking is no longer an option for them.

Converting to a religion that doesn't allow alcohol

The Muslim holy book the Quran calls intoxicants "the work of Satan." In Buddhism, alcohol is discouraged because it is not conducive to achieving peace of mind. Some Christian religions also believe drinking causes mental and physical illness and leads to sin.

Religions that do not allow its followers to consume alcohol include Islam, Buddhism, Hinduism, Protestant Christian (Baptists, Methodists, Evangelicals and Pentecostals), Jainism, Mormonism, Seventh-day Adventism and The Baha'i Faith.

Moving to a dry county in the USA or Canada

Many states in the United States allow the counties within them to vote against the sale and consumption of liquor. The majority of these dry counties can be found in Arkansas and Utah. In the Northwest Territories of Canada, alcohol cannot be consumed without prior permission in Nunavut and Yukon.

Living and working in Saudi Arabia

In Saudi Arabia alcohol is illegal. There is no drinking or clubbing and the consumption, sale, and purchase of alcohol is forbidden due to the country's strict interpretation of Islamic law, which also applies to non-Muslims except diplomats.

If you are determined to drink it will be expensive. For example, a standard bottle of Grey Goose vodka sold on the black market can cost up to $500. Drinking on compounds does take place and there's usually a local who can procure booze or has some homebrew for sale.

In fact, some people who have gone there to dry out end up a worse alcoholic than they started by drinking risky local brews or paying extortionate prices for Western labels.

Even in Middle Eastern countries where alcohol is allowed such as Jordan, the large Muslim population means most people won't touch alcohol. You can go out anywhere and find a lot of non-alcoholic clubs and bars because drinking is not culturally normalized like it is in the West.

Alcohol is also banned in Brunei, Kuwait, Mauritania and Somalia.

Getting a degree in addiction

Going back to school as an adult and getting masters' degrees in Addiction Studies and Psychology can keep you focused on the business of staying sober as well as teaching you how to help others going through the same experience. Afterwards you can get a job in the counseling or the rehab sector or start your own private practice.

Moving back in with your parents

Moving back in with either or both of your parents is a common last resort for adults who want to curb their out-of-control drinking. This option is only workable if your parents are not alcoholics themselves and you have a good relationship with them.

It is generally advisable to be up front with them about your alcohol problem because they will likely be supportive and appreciate the fact you confided in them.

You will probably need to stay for a couple of years until you find a job and save up enough money to get back on your feet again. Before you move out it would definitely be worth seeking some sort of counseling and joining a support group so you don't fall back into your old ways.

Starting again

Moving to a new city, state or country where nobody knows you or your history as well as starting a new job and finding a new circle of friends can be the fresh start you need to get and stay sober.

However, sometimes it's better to take time to adjust to life without alcohol before making any drastic life decisions. You will also need therapy to address any mental health issues you have or you'll just take them with you. As the saying goes, "Beware of the allure of the geographical cure."

Relocating won't fix everything. Your habits, flaws, insecurities and everything else that's bothering you will need to be dealt with before you can truly enjoy the benefits of a whole new pace of life and change of scenery.

That said, if you are suffering in an environment where there are abusive relationships, a toxic friend group or health concerns why prolong the agony if leaving is an option? Running away can't solve all your problems, but sometimes it really is for the best.

Having a baby and being a parent

Quitting alcohol – and any other drugs – is probably the first thing most men and women should do when they are planning to have a baby. Pregnancy and alcohol do not go together for both parties involved in its production.[107]

Alcohol damages the sperm's DNA which can increase the chances of having a child with special needs. In the earliest weeks, drinking can also prevent the fetus from implanting into the uterus wall properly, increasing the risk of a miscarriage.

So partying should be out for at least three months before trying to conceive. After that, the risk of fetal alcohol syndrome (FAS) and fetal alcohol spectrum disorder is enough to dissuade most women from hitting the bottle.

After the baby's born a lot of people find being a parent is their wakeup call and a reason to quit completely. As well as losing the desire to drink, waking up in the middle of the night or at 5:00 a.m. to feed the baby with a hangover is horrible.

Plus, you cannot even think about it if you are exclusively breast feeding. Then as the baby gets older, you need a huge amount of energy and patience and the ability to drive should your child need medical help.

Quitting booze is the number one habit new parents give up, above riding motorcycles, recreational drugs, driving fast, not wearing a seatbelt, vaping, cigarettes and junk food.

---

[107] Alcohol's Impact on the Fetus
https://pmc.ncbi.nlm.nih.gov/articles/PMC8541151/#B52-nutrients-13-03452

Taking a CBD product

These products have improved greatly over recent years as well as becoming more affordable. CBD, short for cannabidiol, has proven to reduce generalized anxiety disorder, ease symptoms of stress, pain and inflammation while providing a calming effect. Users report they sleep far better. It can also reduce the urge to drink.[108]

CBD comes in many forms from drinks, capsules and gummies to vapes, tinctures and even face creams. Just be aware that CBD has trace amounts of THC in it which can register as positive on a drug test.

Taking a GLP-1 (glucagon-like peptide-1) probiotic supplement

Drinking alcohol reduces the body's natural GLP-1 activity by around a third, which increases cravings for more alcohol (and food). GLP-1 is a gut hormone that reduces these cravings by triggering the production of semaglutide.[109] In animal studies semaglutide has been found to reduce alcohol consumption and binge drinking by dampening the dopamine response. Probiotic strains of Akkermansia and Clostridium are particularly effective.

Taking naltrexone (or Suboxone)

Naltrexone and Suboxone are relatively inexpensive, patent-expired drugs that kill the desire for alcohol by blocking the receptors in the brain that respond to dopamine and serotonin. Eventually your brain learns not to crave alcohol, typically within three months.

---

[108] Therapeutic Prospects of Cannabidiol for Alcohol Use Disorder and Alcohol-Related Damages on the Liver and the Brain
https://pmc.ncbi.nlm.nih.gov/articles/PMC6554654/
[109] The glucagon-like peptide-1 (GLP-1) analogue semaglutide reduces alcohol drinking and modulates central GABA neurotransmission
https://insight.jci.org/articles/view/170671

As well as dampening down the brain's reward pathway, studies have shown that a person's reaction to naltrexone is proportional to the degree of adversity they experienced in childhood: i.e., the more abuse experienced, the greater the drug's beneficial effect.

If you don't have a bad reaction (naltrexone can cause nausea, fatigue and a general lack of pleasure) it also comes in a monthly injectable version called Vivitrol. This is commonly used in rehab facilities and removes the hit and miss element of having to take meds every day.

Another way of taking naltrexone is The Sinclair Method. You take the drug an hour before you plan to drink so you won't get a buzz. This is a good option for those who are determined to quit as self-discipline and commitment is involved, plus it largely gets around the problem of the drug's emotionally numbing effect.

Taking Antabuse (Disulfiram)

This is the pharmaceutical big guns when it comes to quitting alcohol and essentially scares you out of drinking. When you get to this stage you've usually tried everything: psychologists, psychiatrists, AA, naltrexone, detox and in-patient treatment, most likely more than once.

The first month is hard because you are thrown into instant sobriety. After this adjustment period most people have no difficulties not drinking because things can get bad if they do. You could end up choking on your vomit, getting pneumonia or having seizures or heart problems.

Antabuse is usually taken in pill form at a dose of 500mg once a day for one or two weeks, which is usually reduced to 250mg daily after that. It can also be delivered as via an implant that dissolves in your body over the course of a year.

The side effects of the medication itself include rashes, severe fatigue and in rare cases, liver failure. So you will need to have frequent blood tests to check your liver function. It's not a magic fix, but it has enabled many people stop drinking long enough to break their addiction cycle.

Taking Baclofen

Antabuse does nothing for cravings which are the real problem with addiction, but Baclofen reduces them significantly. You can find out more about this medication at reddit.com/r/BaclofenForAlcoholism/

Taking Gabapentin

Dr Barbara Mason has studied this drug for alcohol dependence and reports that patients on gabapentin saw an improvement in sleep after one week and were four times more likely to abstain from alcohol or dramatically cut their consumption down. [110]

IV ketamine therapy

Studies have shown ketamine can lower cravings for alcohol and relieve depression. This non-narcotic drug has been around for more than sixty years and is usually used as a twilight anesthetic for surgery. In a 2023 review of studies ketamine was found to lower the probability of alcohol use and reduce heavy drinking days.[111] Numerous private ketamine clinics have opened in recent years and they are easy to find online.

Drinking ayahuasca tea

Some people have found they have no desire for alcohol even after decades of drinking after taking a psychedelic drug called ayahuasca. Its effects are so drastic, it has been likened to having three months of psychotherapy in a few days.

Ayahuasca tea is a foul tasting thick, dark substance made from two plants which are boiled and mashed up: the ayahuasca vine and the

---

[110] Gabapentin Treatment for Alcohol Dependence https://jamanetwork.com/journals/jamainternalmedicine/fullarticle/1764009
[111] Ketamine Treatment for Alcohol Use Disorder: A Systematic Reviewhttps://pmc.ncbi.nlm.nih.gov/articles/PMC10237681/

leaves of the chacruna. The practice originates from South American countries like Peru, Brazil, Columbia and Ecuador. The "cleansing ritual" is performed by a shaman lasts around two hours. By the end of the ceremony the participant is relieved of their deepest psychological pains and entrenched addictions.

It is not a fun trip like some other psychedelic drugs and can be an emotionally and physically harsh experience. People report having vivid visions and hallucinations as well as violent vomiting and diarrhea. (Recipients are given buckets to use).

The hallucinogenic effects of the drink are due to dimethyltryptamine (DMT) which produces effects a near-death experience and distorts a person's brain waves to create a vivid "waking-dream" state.

The movie "The Medicine" describes the rituals involved and how this drug has helped participants recover from chronic depression and break self-destructive behaviors and thought patterns.

Despite the results of psychedelic therapy having been largely positive, there are warnings that taking ayahuasca is like playing Russian roulette and the more emotionally and physically unwell someone is, the more their long-term mental stability is at risk. It is also dangerous for those with heart problems.

For these reasons ayahuasca remains illegal in the US. However, psilocybin therapy (with magic mushrooms) combined with psychotherapy has started to become available.

Ayahuasca retreats are organized in multiple countries all over the world. For more information go to "Ayahuasca FAQ" on the Reddit forum r/Ayahuasca or www.tripaneer.com.

PART 13

Books and other resources that have helped people eliminate or drastically reduce their alcohol consumption

Quit Drinking Without Willpower is a highly acclaimed book that presents the idea that alcohol is an illusion and a confidence trick. This groundbreaking text, which includes the famous pitcher plant analogy, has transformed the lives of many. Its author Alan Carr, was a former heavy smoker who read a medical textbook and "saw the light" about addictive substances.

In the Realm of Hungry Ghosts: Close Encounters with Addiction is written by trauma expert Dr Gabor Maté who has over 20 years' experience as a medical doctor. In this highly rated book, he says understanding your inner discontent is the first step towards healing and wellness. He believes " addiction is neither a choice nor primarily a disease. It originates in a human being's desperate attempt to solve a problem: the problem of pain... So, the first question is not 'Why the addiction,' but why the emotional pain?"

Rational Recovery: The New Cure for Substance Addiction and **The Art of AVRT (Addictive Voice Recognition Technique)** are two books written by ex-drinker and clinical social worker Jack Trimpey. He does not regard alcoholism as a disease where you are forever in recovery, but as a behavior that can be modified and controlled. His self-help program has helped many people break addictions to alcohol, drugs and food.

Alcohol Explained is written William Porter, a former British army volunteer and London-based lawyer, started drinking and smoking at

14. Porter describes the chemical, physical and psychological effects of alcohol and the futility of trying to cut down and provides some basic instructions on how to reprogram your mind to be alcohol-averse.

This Naked Mind by Annie Grace, a former international marketing expert and ex-heavy drinker, challenges subconscious beliefs and explains the neurological components of alcohol use in a way readers have found highly influential in losing their desire to drink.

Atomic Habits makes big life changes a manageable concept by breaking them down into tiny, incremental stages. James Clear describes these habits as being "the atoms of our lives," hence the title. The author explains how can people break their attachment to alcohol by making small adjustments to their behavior and environment.

Alcohol Lied to Me: The Intelligent Way to Escape Alcohol Addiction is written by former heavy drinker Craig Beck, the "Stop Drinking Expert." He exposes the lies we tell ourselves about drinking and why cutting down is not the answer. "It's poison in a pretty bottle," he says, and "If red wine is that good for you, why don't they rush you to hospital when you have a heart attack and put you on a Merlot drip."

Quit Like a Woman is written in a quirky style that's funny and easy to read. Its author Holly Whitaker describes society's cultural use of alcohol to numb out and how it is specifically marketed for women. Her philosophy is about "incorporating a softer, more forgiving, inclusive approach to recovery through harm reduction."

The Cure for Alcoholism: The Medically Proven Way to Eliminate Alcohol Addiction by doctors Roy Eskapa and David Sinclair of The Sinclair Method explains why alcoholism is a learned, repetitive behavior that can get too strong in some people. But if the behavior is not met with reward, the brain connections that drive it get weaker.

The authors recommend the use of the FDA-approved drug naltrexone which blocks the reward response and has a high success rate in breaking the addiction cycle when combined with psychotherapy.

The Sober Diaries: How One Woman Stopped Drinking and Started Living is an engaging memoir by former advertising executive Clare Pooley. She represents the "grey area" wine drinking middle aged mom who has a problem. Clare explains how she was able to tell everyone she had breast cancer but was too ashamed to tell anyone she'd quit drinking because it had got out of control.

Sober On a Drunk Planet is a series of books by Sean Alexander a former alcohol and cocaine addict from London who experienced a month in rehab. He trained as a counselor because he understood "all the car crash stuff" that comes with addiction. His approach to recovery is holistic and involves embracing your true self, finding your purpose and taking gut health and nutrition seriously.

Drink? The New Science of Alcohol and Health by British psychiatrist and neuropharmacologist Professor David Nutt takes a science-based look at drinking, hangovers and tolerance as well as addressing alcohol's effects on hormones, mental health and fertility. Professor Nutt has spent over 40 years studying alcohol and its harmful effects on the human body and society. He is not anti-alcohol because he says it's an amazing drug for making people more sociable which is why he enjoys the occasional glass of wine in company.

How I Cured My Cirrhosis at thatliverdude.com is a step-by-step account of one man who reversed his end-stage liver disease with scientific references for all the supplements he took.

How to Eat to Change How You Drink by Dr Brooke Scheller explains what alcohol does to our body from a nutritionist's point of view. It also includes recipes to heal your gut, balance your hormones, regulate your blood sugar and break the crash/crave cycle of addiction.

Wasted – A Documentary by filmmaker Maureen Palmer is about her husband, a psychotherapist called Mike Pond who was addicted to Gatorade and vodka. Despite helping rebuild lives for others he could not help himself and ended up in the ER 15 times as well as jobless and homeless. When AA did not work for him, he set out on a mission to find evidence-based reasons and treatments for addiction.[112]

Alcohol Use Disorder – A New Approach features clinicians, patients and families talking about life-changing medications that are now available for the treatment of alcohol use disorder, namely naltrexone, gabapentin, baclofen topimarate, acamprosate, disulfiram, and ondansetron. (Note: the main presenter Dr Jeff Harries had ALS which is why his speech is slurred in this video. He died in 2021.)[113]

The American Society of Addiction Medicine has a "find a physician" page for those looking for an addiction medicine specialist in their area.[114]

SMART stands for Self-Management and Recovery Training. This abstinence-based program helps you understand why you react to events irrationally and emotionally and use alcohol and other addictive substances to deal with your feelings. It also operates on the premise that you are not powerless in changing your behaviors and are not an alcoholic for life.[115]

30 Meetings/30 Days is a short, simple movie about one woman's efforts to quit her daily wine habit by attending 30 consecutive Alcoholics Anonymous meetings. As one reviewer says, "Someone did their homework on this one and got the AA experience right."[116]

---

[112] https://www.youtube.com/watch?v=SucThhNPjn8
[113] https://www.youtube.com/watch?v=OpcmPYzMMjw
[114] The American Society of Addiction Medicine
https://www.asam.org/publications-resources/patient-resources/fad
[115] https://www.youtube.com/user/smartrecovery/videos
[116] 30 MEETINGS/30 DAYS | Omeleto
https://www.youtube.com/watch?v=psj-P0ku-PY

A Royal Hangover is movie about the Britain's obsession with alcohol and how it compares to other countries' drinking cultures. Its cast includes AA advocate and former addict Russell Brand, ex-Prime Minister David Cameron and Professor David Nutt.[117]

Want to Stop Drinking? Try This Technique is a hypnotic short by Russel Brand which focuses on the simple concept of "one day at a time" which is one of the simple main messages of AA. "Just for today I won't drink."[118]

Alcohol, The Magic Potion: Science Behind the Most Harmful Drug of All is a 2024 documentary investigates the manufacture and use of alcohol in Europe and beyond. Director Andreas Pichler visits several countries to find out what makes us drink, what alcohol does to us, and to what extent the alcohol industry and its lobbyists influence politics and society.[119]

Quit Drinking Motivation – The Most Eye Opening 60 Minutes of Your Life is a 2024 documentary that features Matthew Perry, Dr. Drew, Jordan Peterson, Ben Affleck, Dr. Andrew Huberman, Rich Roll, Daniel Radcliffe, Davina McCall, Lucy Hale, Brian Rose, Mark Manson and Jack Canfield.[120]

Louis Theroux: Drinking To Oblivion is an hour-long documentary about a severely alcohol dependent group of people who are suffering varying degrees of ill health. Louis spends time with them in Kings College Hospital, London and visits them at home as they struggle to beat their addiction before it's too late.[121]

---

[117] A Royal Hangover | Full Documentary
https://www.youtube.com/watch?v=FiSctWh5TF4
[118] https://www.youtube.com/shorts/xyVZxAGCDSU
[119] https://www.youtube.com/watch?v=tw8-oNu3Du0
[120] https://www.youtube.com/watch?v=tbEsacVad88
[121] https://documentaryheaven.com/louis-theroux-drinking-to-oblivion/#google_vignette

Only 20 And Dying a Drunk is an interview with a young guy called Chris who eloquently describes drinking a handle of vodka every 24 hours and how he only stopped when he couldn't keep it down. Then he talks about the horrendous withdrawals, having pancreatitis and how he was scared straight in hospital. [122]

Tucker Carlson talks about functional drinking, getting shit-faced at home, blacking out, embarrassing public drunken moments and the exact moment he decided to quit. He describes his shock at having withdrawals, going to AA and why he's never felt the desire to drink again. [123]

I Quit Drinking Alcohol... But Did Not Expect This is just one of many well-presented and entertaining videos by Mark Manson, author of "The Subtle Art of Not Giving a F*ck." Check out his other messages for an original, irreverent perspective on dealing with emotional pain, stress and suffering and life's problems in general. [124]

Clark Kegley goes into the deeper emotional and practical realities of quitting drinking in a calming authentic way that really resonates. His presentations will help gently nudge you towards becoming a more resilient version of yourself. As well as talking about modest, achievable goals, one of his main messages is just to be easier on yourself. [125]

Ken Middleton, author of "Bamboozled: How Alcohol Makes Fools of Us All" has been a guest on multiple sober platforms including the sobriety podcast "The Stack'n Days" which highlights voices of color,. His website challenges everyone to stop drinking for 90 days. [127]

---

[122] https://www.youtube.com/watch?v=wjlm3YWxqAk
[123] https://www.youtube.com/watch?v=8wPDur6Pk8w
[124] https://www.youtube.com/watch?v=tOuUgGWLYa0
[125] https://www.youtube.com/watch?v=G5XNRn9qaaA
[127] https://thebamboozledbook.com/

Leon Sylvester – a.k.a. Sober Leon, battled with alcohol and drug addiction his whole adult life. His describes his mission as "helping people get control of their drinking without AA or willpower." He also runs his own coaching program called "Soberclear." [128]

Chris Scott's tips for dominating alcohol is a series of YouTube videos featuring nutritional strategies, reframing techniques, neuro-linguistic programming, recovery habits, and much more to help people eliminate alcohol from their lives.[129]

The Huberman Lab is regularly ranked as the no.1 health podcast in the world. Dr. Huberman is a popular resource that makes the complex concepts surrounding neuroscience and addiction easier to grasp.[130]

---

[128] https://www.youtube.com/@LeonSylvester
[129] https://www.youtube.com/playlist?list=PL2GwGzbeywPQV7WxkOJCSfS5kX2E3ld2f
[130] https://www.hubermanlab.com/episode/what-alcohol-does-to-your-body-brain-health

PART 14

Some thought-provoking one-liners

Some of these quotes may read like bumper sticker clichés, but one or more of them may prompt a "lightbulb moment" or be the message that stays with you.

On alcohol/drinking

Alcohol is not the answer; it just makes you forget the question.

Drinking is life on hard mode.

Drinking today is borrowing happiness from tomorrow.

Dangerous drinking is a state of "yets" – you haven't got a DUI yet, you haven't had a medical event yet, your life isn't ruined yet…

Alcohol says "I see you have anxiety would you like it to be debilitating?"

Trying to cure anxiety with alcohol is like drinking saltwater when you're thirsty.

Drunkenness has all the hallmarks of submitting to a demon.

Drinking because today is hard guarantees tomorrow will be harder.

Alcohol convinces you there is not a single thing in life that's worth experiencing sober.

The liver remembers every drink.

Alcohol is like the abusive ex who says "It'll be different this time."

Alcohol is boomer technology.

Treating depression with alcohol is like fighting fire with gasoline.

Alcohol is your best friend until becomes your worst enemy.

A hangover lasts a hundred times longer than a craving.

The memory of drinking is always sweeter than the reality of drinking.

On addiction

The higher the high, the lower the low.

Your problem isn't the problem; your reaction is the problem.

Alcohol abuse is self-abuse.

Drinking to get drunk is like going to war with yourself.

You cannot heal by going back to what broke you.

Addiction is like a fungus; it grows in the dark and withers in the light.

The opposite of addiction is connection.

Chronic drinking is just assisted suicide on an installment plan.

The first one lights the fuse.

Alcohol is a quick high and a long low.

One drink is too many and a thousand is never enough.

The three Fs of alcohol use disorder: fun, functional and fucked.

That same voice that wants you to have one drink will also want ten.

The alcoholic brain consists of two corporations: one that manufactures bullshit and the other that buys it.

On quitting

The time to start unfucking your life is now.

Sometimes it's a day at a time; sometimes it's an hour at a time.

If you keep doing what you've always done you'll keep getting what you've always got.

Think the drink through.

If you can put your whole life into drinking you can put your whole life into something new.

Recovery is about recognizing your triggers and walking away from them.

Recovery means recovering the person you are meant to be.

Genetics is a tendency, not your destiny.

The pain of regret hurts more than the pain of reform.

Addiction is giving up everything for one thing while recovery is giving up one thing for everything.

Be stronger than your strongest excuse.

Recovery is 5% putting down the drink and 95% changing the way you live.

Removing alcohol won't solve all your problems but it will make all your problems solvable.

Nothing changes if nothing changes.

You don't have to wait for the elevator to go all the way down to get off.

Recovery starts with forgiving yourself for everything.

Success occurs when your goals are bigger than your excuses.

In the end only you can save yourself.

On relapse/failure

A random lapse is better than a relapse.

Failure is not falling down it's staying down.

Failure is just a rehearsal for success.

Failure is an experience not an identity.

Failure is your greatest teacher.

Rock bottom is the foundation on which you can rebuild your life.

Never quit quitting.

Progress isn't linear.

Strive for progress not perfection.

On trauma/therapy

Not everything that weighs you down is yours to carry.

You're not a drunk; you're sick and hurting and need to heal.

You're only as sick as your secrets.

The fears we don't face become our limits.

It's not a drinking problem it's a thinking problem.

In this battle there are no losers or winners; there are just sufferers and students.

You have to heal your mind before you can heal your body.

You've already survived your worst feelings.

The fears we don't face become our limits.

Falling apart is a perfect opportunity to rebuild yourself.

Difficult roads often lead to beautiful destinations.

Address your childhood traumas or your romantic relationships will.

A small amount of light removes a ton of darkness.

On coping/life skills

The quality of your life depends on how you deal with your problems.

If you don't learn from history you are doomed to repeat it.

There's no problem that drinking can't make worse.

You're never too old to make positive changes.

Create the life you want; don't settle for the life you have.

Don't hold on to a mistake because you spent a long time making it.

There's still time to become the person you want to be.

Taking control of your life is the most satisfying thing you can do.

Look inside for happiness not outside.

Life is like monkey bars – you have to let go to move on.

Your biggest fear should not be that you aim too high and miss but that you aim too low and settle.

Instead of what you could have been focus on what you can still be.

Some things have to end for better things to begin.

Knowledge is learning something every day; wisdom is letting go of something every day.

On being sober

Being sober doesn't make life easier but it does make it easier to handle.

Why would you go back to your kidnapper?

Your worst days sober are still better than your best days drunk.

The best apology is changed behavior.

Sobriety delivers what alcohol promises.

You'll never wake up wishing you'd got drunk the night before.

Drinking only gets worse; sober only gets better.

You won't find happiness in the same place you lost it.

Getting sober doesn't open the gates to heaven, it pulls you out from the gates of hell.

There's beauty and peace on the other side of the bottle.

Dear alcohol...

I found out that you were even worse than what they said. Sometimes I try to remember the good times, but you actually made me forget most of those memories instead.

Dax – "Dear Alcohol" (MEGA REMIX) [featuring: Atlus, Kelsie Watts, SkyDxddy, Phix, Kayla Rae & more]

https://www.youtube.com/watch?v=2qQ_0i_ixlM

1001 REASONS TO STOP DRINKING

Finally…

If this book has helped you in any way, please let me know. I tried to make these contents as powerful and relatable as possible to help you reevaluate what alcohol means in your life and for the suffering to stop if it has taken over.

If you have any comments or would like to add your anecdote, story or one-liner to the next edition please contact:

1001reasonsdrinkingbook@gmail.com

Also, please would you be so kind as to leave a review if you liked this book – it would be very much appreciated.

COPYRIGHT

For purposes of copyright and obtaining permissions, the testimonial style contents in this book have been substantially edited/rewritten to be significantly altered from their original form/content and have been combined with other relevant materials and information for the purposes of originality and to provide additional information, interest and clarity on a specific subject. The stories herein contain facts and observations from real-life events but are presented in a reinterpreted and essentially rewritten format. Where permissions have been obtained for partial content or subject matter, the authors have requested that they remain anonymous.

Printed in Dunstable, United Kingdom